Bruiser Brody

BRUISER BRODY

Emerson Murray

Edited by Scott Teal

CROWBAR PRESS

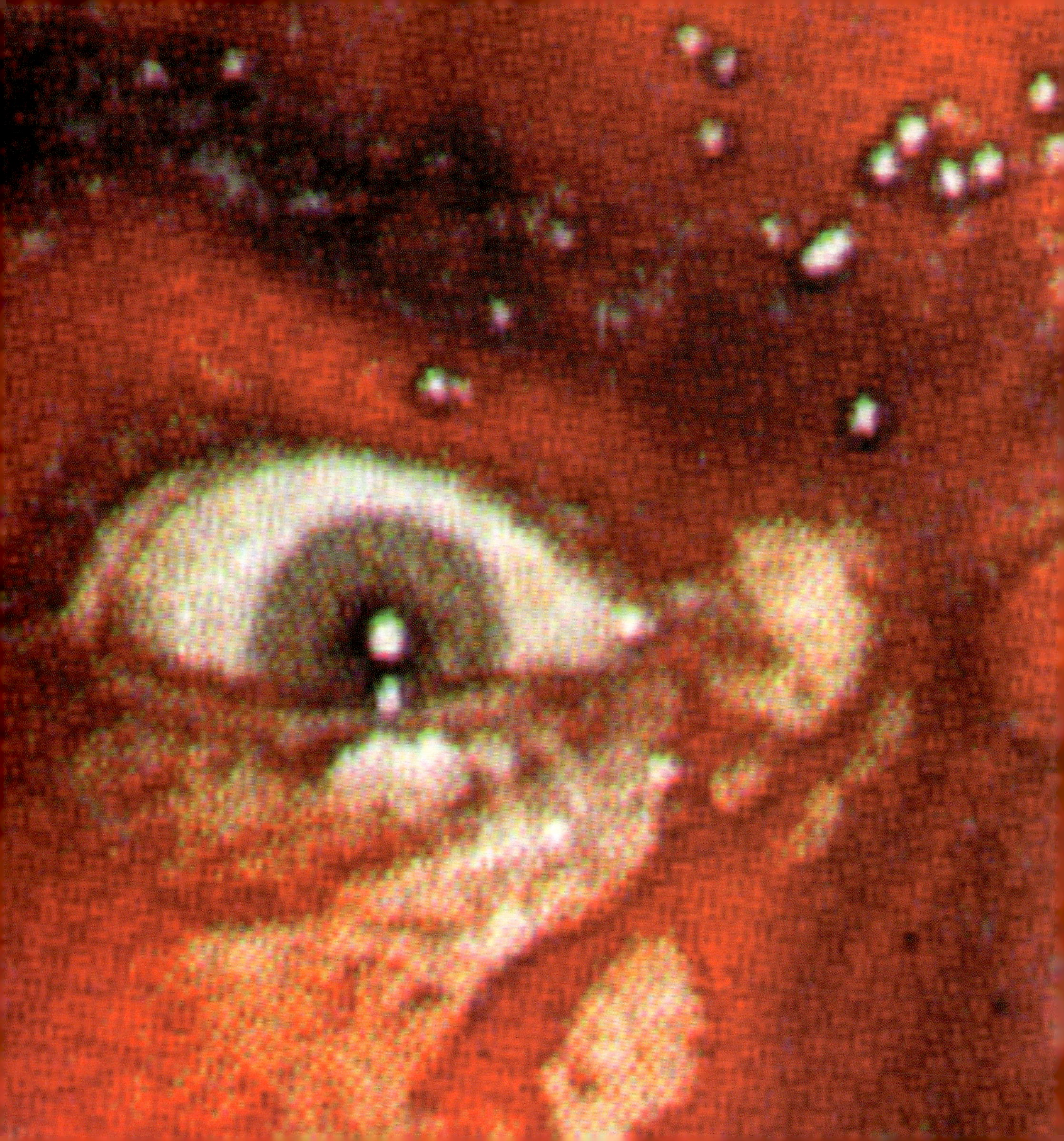

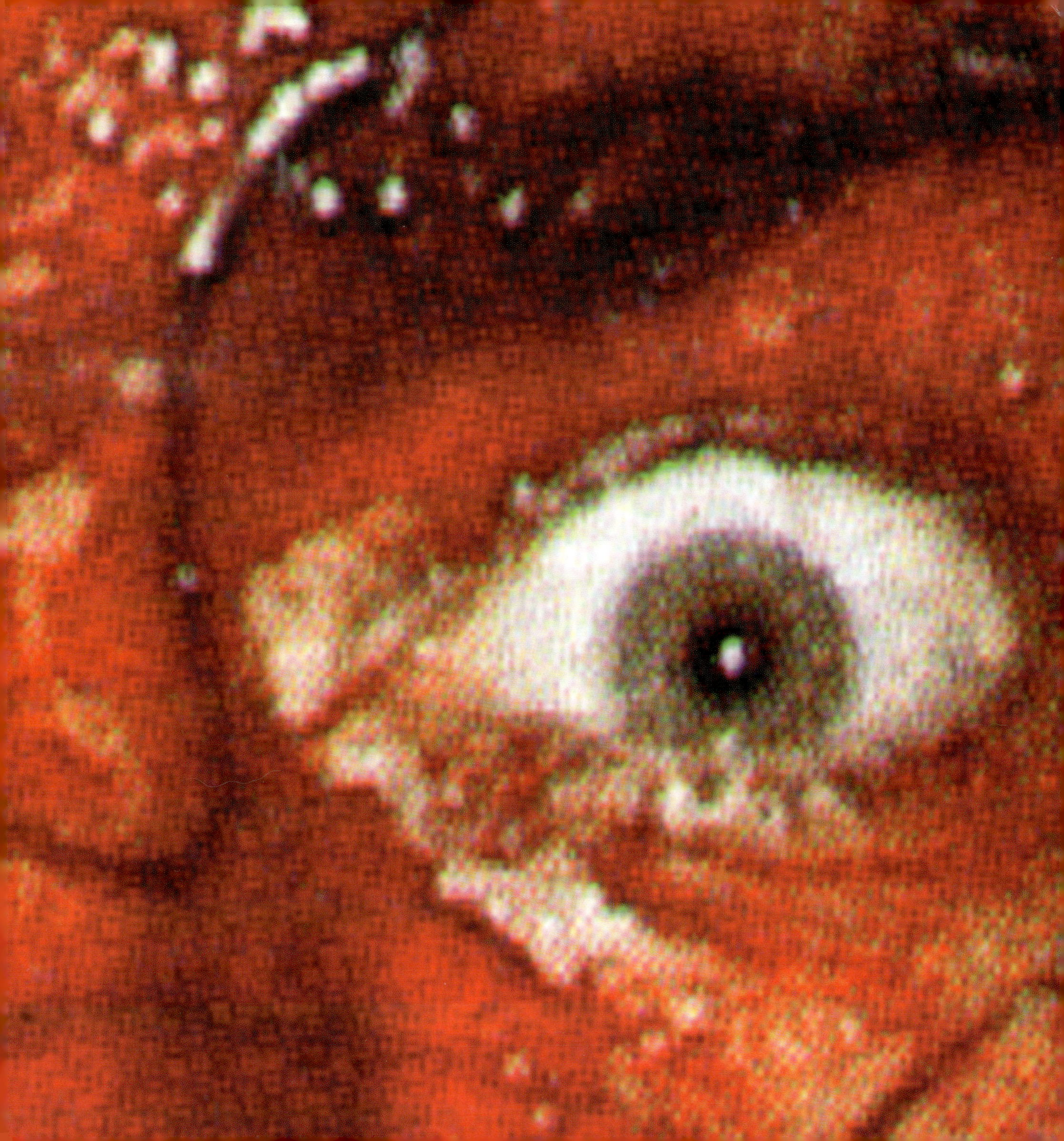

Published by Crowbar Press
P.O. Box 2781
Hendersonville, Tennessee.
www.crowbarpress.com

Library of Congress Cataloging-in-Publication Data

Bruiser Brody/by Emerson Murray
ISBN 978-0-9745545-5-6
1. Murray, Emerson
2. Wrestlers—United States—Biography.

Printed in the
United States of America

First Edition / January 2007
Limited to 1,000 copies.

Cover Photo by Scott Romer
www.scottromerphoto.com

www.bruiserbrody.com

Contents

ABOUT THE AUTHOR

Bruiser Brody was one of my childhood heroes, right there between Bruce Lee and Johnny Rotten. He and Abdullah the Butcher were the only wrestlers that legitimately scared me. They were the real thing.

When I was in junior high school, a teacher let me set up a TV and VCR in his classroom during lunch break and charge a quarter for students to come in and watch wrestling matches from my collection. Bruiser Brody was by far everybody's favorite, and his matches with Abdullah had everyone believing wrestling was quite possibly "real." Even the girls who chimed in with "*Wrestling is fake!*" from the doorway, shut their mouths when they got a glimpse of a Bruiser Brody match.

When Brody was murdered in Puerto Rico in 1988, wrestling pretty much died for me for about ten years.

When I started working on this project in 2000, I was a wide-eyed fan-boy. A mark. Sure, I read the backstage websites, but I had no idea what really went on away from the eyes of wrestling fans.

At the time, I was working in the film/video industry. I was steadily growing tired of working on industrial videos, training videos, commercials, and other, really boring projects. The juicy ones like music videos, short subjects, and feature films, were few and far between. The fact of the matter was that I was tired of working on other people's projects, and other people's dreams. I wanted to do something that I could call my own. I wanted to shoot a documentary. I just needed a subject.

I started watching wrestling again when I was flipping the channels and saw Sean Michaels bloody The Undertaker with a chair on RAW. I watched RAW and Nitro when I happened to catch them, but once I moved into the cult of ECW, I was hooked once again.

I was helping my mom clean out her attic one day and stumbled across my huge box of wrestling magazines. It happened in Hollywood fashion. The first magazine I pulled out was Wrestling Ringside #20. On the cover, Paul Orndorff had Big John Studd down on the mat in a hammerlock. I flipped the magazine over and there was one of my favorite wrestling photographs of all time. Staring up at me was the proverbial crimson mask of Bruiser Brody. The light from above shone down on me, and the angels sang. My documentary would be on the life and death of my childhood hero—
Bruiser Brody!

I had $8,000 in my savings account and was foolish enough to think that could get me somewhere. I talked with a fellow filmmaker and friend, Tim Roper, whose mom once had been Haystack Calhoun's waitress. Tim had no interest in wrestling, but he saw merit in the project and he agreed to help me. Eight grand later, I was in debt and didn't have nearly the material I needed for anything worth a damn, so I started calling around, conducting interviews, and I realized I had the makings of a pretty thorough book on the life of Bruiser Brody.

ACKNOWLEDGEMENTS

So many people helped me out in completing this project.

First and foremost, I have to thank my wife, Maria Belia. I was already deeply involved in this project when I met her and she has stood by me through the entire process.

Thank you to my editor and friend, Scott Teal, who provided interviews, insight, and a countless number of great ideas. In addition to the editing, his contributions to the book include the interviews with Bobby Fulton, Bobby Jaggers, Bobby Simmons, Dick Beyer, Frankie Cain (aka The Great Mephisto), Harley Race, J.J. Dillon, Jerry Grey, Jody Hamilton, Killer Karl Kox, Killer Tim Brooks, Magic Schwarz, Ole Anderson, Paul Christy, Percy Pringle, Roger Kirby, Stan Hansen, and the Missing Link, as well as additions to my own interviews with Tony Atlas and Playboy Gary Hart.

Bruiser Brody's interview excerpts came from The Wrestling Exchange (July, 1980).

Jim Duggan and The Road Warriors were interviewed for me by Danny and Dave from Reality Check TV. <www.realitychecktv.com>

The Steve Williams interview was conducted by Mike Johnson.

The interview with Bruno Sammartino was conducted by Dr. Mike Lano.

Some of Dutch Mantell's quotes were given to me from an audiotape interview he conducted with Dr. Mike Lano on December 16, 1991.

Gordon Grice's, James Beard's, and a couple of Scott Romer's quotes were taken from their articles and posts written for Kayfabe Memories. <www.kayfabememories.com>

Quotes by Bad News Allen, Vader, Dutch Mantell, and some from Stan Hansen were taken from their interviews for RF Video's "Shoot Interviews" series and used with permission. <www.rfvideo.com>

Thanks to everyone who is quoted in the book for sharing their time and great memories.

Thanks to everyone who sent their photographs my way, especially Scott Romer and Eddie Gries.

Thanks to J Michael Kenyon for proofreading the final draft.

My friends and family have also been a great support. My parents each really helped in their own way. Tim Roper spent a lot of hours being the sole member of my film crew when this project first started as a documentary.

Also: Thomas Nores, Chris Psaros, Dr. Mike Lano, Josh Johnson, Lyle Troxell, The 211 Clubhouse, Nate Kruk, John Miele, Matt Farmer, Steve Rizzono, Reality Check TV guys, Don Nagy, Mike Johnson, Vince Fahey, Ricardo Medina, Mike Miller, Michael Hawkins, Manuel O. Gonzalez, Katherine Goodish, Jeanette Cabot, John Stutzka, Jess McGrath, Greg Rufolo, Steve Harms, Roger Deem, Mitch Hartsey, Rick Graham, Jared Schlager, Karin Heymer, the Splatt Family, S.D. Jones, Verne Gagne, and everyone else who helped me along this strange journey.

FOREWORD
by Stan Hansen

I first met Frank Goodish [Bruiser Brody] in the spring of 1966. As a high school senior and a prospective recruit for the West Texas State University football team, I was visiting the campus to look over the school. Brody was already there. He had gone one year to Iowa State, then had moved down to West Texas and was being red-shirted that year.

Frank was a very gifted athlete who had been a first team, All-State athlete in high school in two sports. On the football field, he was strong, fast, and could play both tight end and defensive end. Basically, a red-shirt was just cannon fodder for the starting team, but in my opinion, even though he was a red-shirt, Frank had the ability to be a starter on the team. Unfortunately, he didn't get along too well with the defensive coach and they were constantly butting heads. Athletically, though, he was an outstanding athlete.

I got to know him a little bit more during my freshman year at West Texas. He was still red-shirted because he had just started attending West Texas in the spring of 1966, so the football year of the fall of '67 was my freshman year and Brody was a red-shirt junior. He was three years ahead of me, age-wise.

The next time we met was in 1973. I had just broken into the wrestling business in Amarillo and the Funks sent me to the Dallas territory for a couple of weeks. At that time, Frank was trying to break into the business through Fritz von Erich, the promoter in Dallas.

Fritz owned a piece of the Louisiana territory, so after bringing Frank into the business in 1974, he sent Frank to Grizzly Smith [the booker] in Louisiana. I was already there when Frank arrived. He was only getting about three bookings a week, and I was working no more than five, so we were barely making it. Naturally, since we knew each other, we started to run around together in Louisiana. I didn't know him or hang out with him that much in college, but we had that natural, common bond that came from our shared experiences at West Texas. That was where we first developed a personal relationship with each other.

Our tag team relationship also began in Louisiana. Grizzly Smith was looking for heel talent, and Frank and I must have fit the bill. We were young, dumb, and green to the wrestling business, but we weren't scared. We went into the ring and did everything we could.

People often ask if Frank influenced my style of wrestling when we started teaming up. Actually, Terry Funk and Dick Murdoch were the two wrestlers who influenced me the most, and that was early in my career. Later, when I went to Japan, I watched Tiger Jeet Singh and Abdullah the Butcher, and adapted some of their manner to that of my own.

If anything—and I don't want to be guilty of braggadocio—Frank probably adapted his style to more closely resemble mine. Up to that time, Frank worked for the All Japan promotion, which featured the traditional American, NWA [National Wrestling

Alliance] style of wrestling—chain wrestling and submission holds. He was used to working with people like Dory Funk Jr., Terry Funk, Jumbo Tsuruta, and Giant Baba.

I had established my own style—a more aggressive, faster-paced, non-NWA style—while I was with New Japan. When I went to All Japan (and again, I don't want to sound like I'm saying "I did this" and "I did that"), I probably set the style for All Japan to present a much faster-paced match—less laying in holds and more aggressive moves.

Basically, the major part of my career took place in Japan, and during the three years Frank and I were together with All Japan, the combination of our styles and personalities just seemed to get us over with the fans. Frank and I were probably the most dominant tag team ever, especially in Japan, where wrestling was very physical and exhausting, even bordering on punishing. Very few people could stay with us, and that's basically why we couldn't come to the States.

In Japan, we were together almost every night. In 1979, King Curtis taught Frank about life in Japan outside of wrestling, introducing him to the nightlife, the Japanese culture, and taking him to restaurants that served delicious Japanese food.

When I first started to team with Frank in Japan, we went out almost nightly. We didn't stay out all night or anything like that, but he taught me how to appreciate life in Japan. I really appreciated that because it changed my whole outlook, both personally and professionally. We ate at great restaurants. Until then, I was usually eating at McDonald's, or trying to find the nearest Kentucky Fried Chicken. He introduced me to Japanese customs and traditions. We rubbed up against the Japanese people in local settings. There was just a great time to be found there.

Frank's influence on me changed my whole outlook of Japan. I even remember the time when I suddenly realized that I was no longer counting

the days until I would be able to go home, which is what many of the boys did. From that point on, I really enjoyed the time I spent in Japan, and I looked forward to each tour. I missed the United States, and Mississippi, in particular, but the fact that I fell in love with the country and the culture is what allowed me to stay there as long as I did. I have Frank to thank for that.

Somewhere down the road, I think Frank decided that he wanted to establish himself as a single. In my mind, we were both. We were a tag team first, but we each had a single character that was very unique, especially in Japan. I think the fact that Frank wanted to make a run as a single is what pushed him to make the jump to New Japan. I had already been there, so when he told me what he planned, I told him, "Frank, I've been there. Those people aren't Giant Baba. They're a little bit different."

He chose to make the move, anyway, but things went terrible from the beginning. It didn't work out for him, but it was something that he wanted to do, and I respected him for it.

We got along both in the ring and in real life, and we never had a conflict, even though we were quite a bit different in regards to our personalities and our business aspirations.

I never had a desire to be a booker or promoter. That was one of the reasons why I enjoyed working for Giant Baba and All Japan. Baba was the first promoter that I felt comfortable with, even to the point where I left everything up to him without me questioning his direction. As long as I did my job in the ring, I could leave the arena and enjoy my life outside of the business. Baba took care of everything else, and I trusted his business decisions implicitly.

On the other hand, Frank was an astute student of the wrestling business. He was constantly studying the business—the psychology, the booking, and the manipulations. If things hadn't turned out the way they had, I think he was destined to be a booker, or a partner, in a promotion. In fact, I heard that he had bought into the Puerto Rico promotion just before he was killed. I don't know if that's true because he never mentioned it to me, but I was told that he was getting into the promotion end of the business.

I also had decided that I was going to work in Japan for a certain number of weeks out of the year.

I was going to live on what I made and I was going to budget myself. When I wasn't working in Japan, I was going to spend time with my family. Frank, in-between tours, kept busy wrestling in St. Louis, Dallas, Indianapolis, the Kansas City territory, and other independent shots. We did go to Puerto Rico together a number of times, until I decided that it wasn't worth it to me, but other than Japan, that was the only place we worked together outside of the States.

When Frank and I were apart, we talked occasionally, but he was busy doing his thing. When I was making the movie No Holds Barred with Hulk Hogan, Frank tracked me down out of the blue and asked me for some personal advice. I thought that was nice. We were looking forward to possibly having a good business run as opponents in Japan.

I only worked against Frank one time. When things didn't work out for Frank in New Japan, Baba brought him back to All Japan and teamed him with Jimmy Snuka. Brody and Snuka had been partners in Japan for several years in both All Japan and New Japan.

On November 22, 1987, Terry Gordy and I faced Frank and Snuka in a Real World Tag Team League tournament match. The fact that Brody and I were on opposite sides of the ring led to a lot of talk in the Japanese press and among the fans. Since we had been partners for so many years, to the fans, Brody and I against each other was somewhat of a dream match.

After that match, people in Japan were anticipating Brody and I having a big feud against each other. There was some talk in the office, and I think it was inevitable for us to be against each other, but before any plans could be made, he was gone.

It was probably good that a feud between the two of us didn't happen because, sometimes, your imagination is better than the real thing.

I think Frank had a bad temper in his younger days, but I never saw him allow his temper to get out of hand. He matured a great deal over the years. He was, however, pretty set on what he believed and where he wanted to go. That ambition led to conflict with the promoters.

When he lost his job in Japan, Frank went out and began to promote himself even more heavily than he ever did before. He told me, "I never realized how tough it would be to book myself and find steady work until I lost my job in Japan."

He went from having a secure position with a good promotion, and a lucrative income, to having no guaranteed work or income.

To sum it all up, Frank was my tag team partner and business associate, but more than anything, Frank was my friend. I think he believed and trusted in me, just as I believed and trusted in him. When we were in Japan, we were probably as close as anybody ever was, even though our personalities were quite a bit different.

I wish Brody and I could be sitting at a Yakitoriya in Japan right now, drinking beer and eating Yakatori, and talking about the old times. We would have a lot of stories to share.

Six Blind Men & the Elephant

John Godfrey Saxe (1816-1887)
A Hindu Parable

It was six men of Indostan
To learning much inclined,
Who went to see the Elephant
(Though all of them were blind),
That each by observation
Might satisfy his mind.

The First approached the Elephant,
And happening to fall
Against his broad and sturdy side,
At once began to bawl:
"God bless me! but the Elephant
Is very like a wall!"

The Second, feeling of the tusk
Cried, "Ho! what have we here,
So very round and smooth and sharp?
To me 'tis mighty clear
This wonder of an Elephant
Is very like a spear!"

The Third approached the animal,
And happening to take
The squirming trunk within his hands,
Thus boldly up he spake:
"I see," quoth he, "the Elephant
Is very like a snake!"

The Fourth reached out an eager hand,
And felt about the knee:
"What most this wondrous beast is like
Is mighty plain," quoth he;
"'Tis clear enough the Elephant
Is very like a tree!"

The Fifth, who chanced to touch the ear,
Said: "E'en the blindest man
Can tell what this resembles most;
Deny the fact who can,
This marvel of an Elephant
Is very like a fan!"

The Sixth no sooner had begun
About the beast to grope,
Than, seizing on the swinging tail
That fell within his scope.
"I see," quoth he, "the Elephant
Is very like a rope!"

And so these men of Indostan
Disputed loud and long,
Each in his own opinion
Exceeding stiff and strong,
Though each was partly in the right,
And all were in the wrong!

Moral:
So oft in theologic wars,
The disputants, I ween,
Rail on in utter ignorance
Of what each other mean,
And prate about an Elephant
Not one of them has seen.

Contradictions, Exaggerations, and Downright Lies

Like the enigmatic elephant described by the six blind men, Bruiser Brody was a man of many facets. His was a puzzling personality caught up in the mythic world of professional wrestling, a world where truth and fiction are so intertwined that even the people who knew him best confidently described him in opposite terms. The harder I dug for "the facts," the more I wondered—
Was he a "sweetheart of a guy," or, "an asshole?"
Did he weigh 250 pounds or 350?
Was he 6-foot-4 or 6-foot-8?
Was the person I was interviewing telling me about the man or the myth?

One of the professional hazards for the authors of "wrestling books" is that immediately after publication, the author, (usually someone in the business), is torn apart for their distortion of the "facts." As I interviewed people about Bruiser Brody, I saw why this was the case. Promoters exaggerate! Wrestlers lie! Not out of malice, but more to perpetuate the myth, to spice up the story, to stay with the storyline, to entertain, to make the subject bigger than life.

Wrestlers are accustomed to playing parts and acting out storylines. Stepping back to sort out what is fact and what is fiction is of no importance. What is important is the story! Picture a bunch of guys who travel 250 or more days a year, living wild lives as cultish celebrities, and sitting around the locker room trying to outdo each other's grandiose tall tales, each one more colorful than the last. Through this prism, I began to piece together the life and times of my childhood hero—Bruiser Brody.

Bruiser Brody wasn't the first wrestler to bleed buckets. He wasn't the first to hit his opponents with chairs, or to wrestle in what we now call a "hardcore" style. Wrestlers like Bull Curry and Danny McShain were doing it in the '50s. But if you ask wrestlers today about hardcore wrestling, many of them will tell you they grew up watching Bruiser Brody—the king of hardcore in the '70s and '80s.

Brody was big, and with his black beard, wooly hair, and fur boots, swinging his big chain around in a wide circle as he entered the ring, he was scary. The fans worshipped and feared him. Brody was feared behind the curtain as well. His temperament and hard-line attitude with promoters is legendary. Brody did what he wanted, when he wanted.

The life of Bruiser Brody came to an unexpected end on July 17, 1988. On July 16, he was in a Puerto Rico locker room preparing for a match when he was stabbed by a wrestling booker. He died the next day on the operating table. No one knows why it happened except the man who did it. Over the years, the story of Brody's death has taken on the same mythic proportions as the stories of his life.

In five years of research, I have discovered two things. First, the complete truth is impossibly elusive, and second, the stories themselves are as relevant as the "truth." The history of wrestling is a history of great stories.

Taking that into consideration, I have decided to let the people who were there tell their stories of Bruiser Brody as they remember them. There are contradictions, exaggerations, and more than likely, downright lies. Like the blind men who variously described the elephant as a wall, a tree, a snake, and a spear, Brody was many different things to different people.

What is the truth?

You'll have to decide that for yourself.

MEET BRUISER BRODY

Lou Thesz (wrestler):

Brody was a tough guy. He was a stand-up guy, devoted to his friends and to his family.

Abdullah the Butcher (wrestler):

Bruiser Brody was a professional in the ring, a professional out of the ring, and a good wrestler. We had a lot of tough battles and we drew a lot of money. To me, I was a friend of Brody's.

Tony Atlas (wrestler):

He was one of the biggest draws and one of the most impressive men that has ever been in this business.

Harley Race (wrestler, promoter):

No matter what anybody says about Brody, nobody can deny that he was one hell of an athlete and a good performer. In this business, he had an air about him that got him over almost everywhere he went. On the other hand, he took advantage of that attitude, too. If you were in the ring with him, if you didn't have the guts to cut him off, he'd just eat you alive.

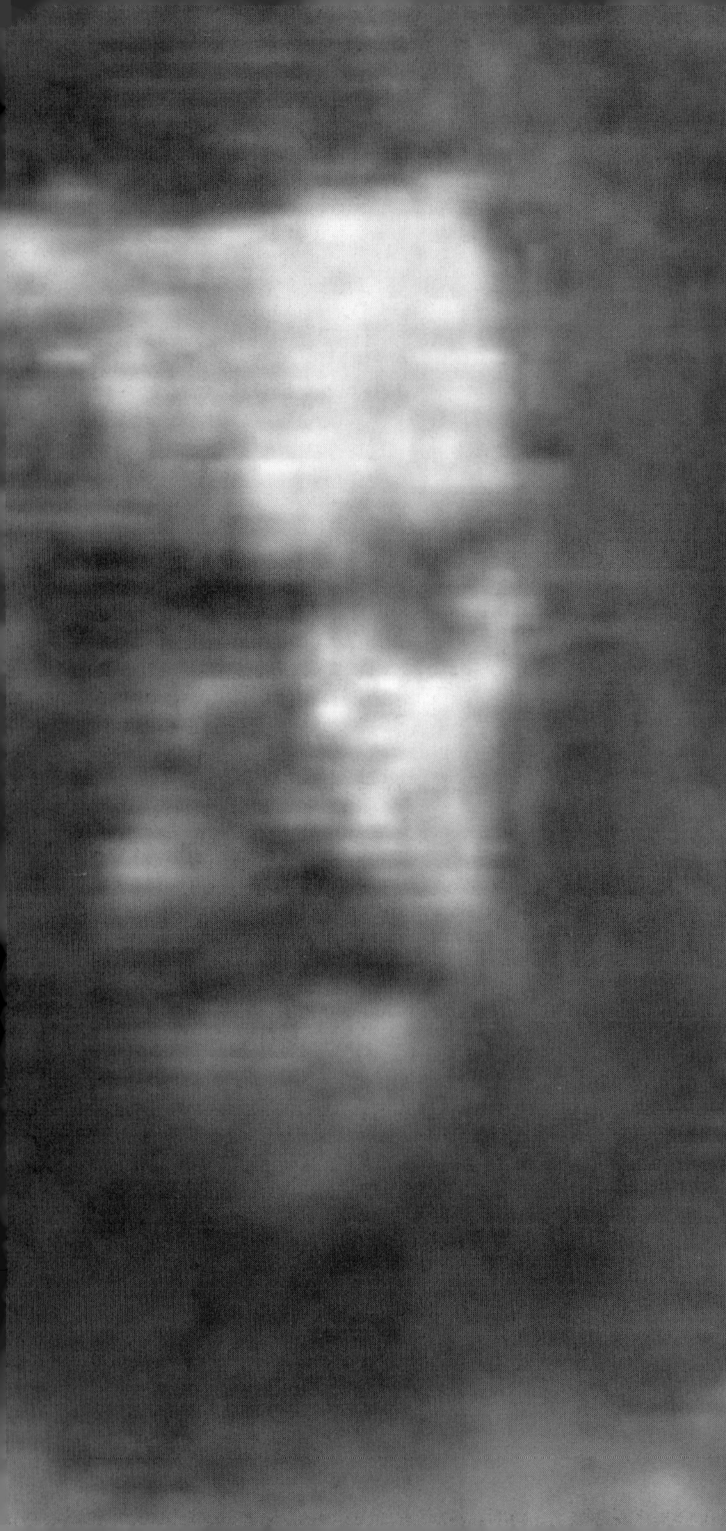

Abdullah the Butcher:

He was different. You got guys like Bruiser Brody, guys like Abdullah the Butcher, guys like Terry Funk, Stan Hansen, Dusty Rhodes. These are the guys that give action. They were professionals. They could go do it. They could give you blood. They could give you guts. They could do anything they wanted to do. That's why Bruiser Brody took off. He was into my style. If he woulda been just another wrestler, he woulda been just another guy grabbing a hold. Brody would throw you in the ring, give you that big kick to the face, take a chair, and hit you as hard as he could. He was a professional.

Gene Lewis (wrestler):

If you didn't pay the price to get into the business and you wrestled Frank, you paid it then.

Abdullah the Butcher:

We were outlaws.

Killer Kowalski (wrestler):

He was a heel, a villain. I told him, "You got to make people notice you. Not your opponent. You! If he turns his back on you, you nail him in the back." These guys nowadays, they turn their back and go to the second rope, and to the fans, and this. Not with me they didn't. They go to the second rope, I'd run across the ring, knock 'em out of the ring, and they'd fall to the floor. Don't ever turn your back on Killer Kowalski. So I taught him that. Stay on them.

Eddie Gries (photographer):

He was a wild man. He couldn't be controlled.

Chavo Guerrero (wrestler):

When Brody was mad about something, he'd let you know. He'd get you back, one way or the other.

Lance Russell (wrestling announcer):

He was feared by all the fans. And I'll tell you what. There were a lot of guys in the locker room who were scared of Bruiser Brody. He was a bad dude.

Larry Nelson (wrestling announcer):

He was relentless. First, the fans would hate him for beating up their favorites, but then, because he says exactly what he's gonna do, and backs it up, sooner or later, they love him.

Road Warrior Hawk (wrestler):

No tag team ever gave us a fearful challenge, but I'll tell you one team that would have. That would have been Bruiser Brody, (God rest his soul), and Stan Hansen. They were working on it in Japan, but money and different factors and tangibles came in, and it didn't happen.

Ed "Moondog" Moretti (wrestler):

He had a head for wrestling. Certain things he did for business, certain things he did for Frank.

Gene Lewis:

He was extremely smart with the stock market. I'd see him reading the Wall Street Journal. Some people might not believe that.

Killer Tim Brooks (wrestler):

Bruiser was very serious, all business. He was a very good friend, and a good family man.

Dave Meltzer (wrestling journalist):

Bruiser Brody was a revolutionary performer inside the ring. He was kind of the classic brawler of his era. Very, very aggressive, big, agile guy. He was one of the guys ... a lot of the time, if you watch tapes of wrestlers from another era, they really don't translate well to the next era, but I think he, because of his aggressiveness, and his size and everything, he would translate well into any era.

Jim Duggan (wrestler):

Probably the greatest big man ever in professional wrestling.

Gary Hart (manager and matchmaker):

There was no arena that he ever wrestled in that he didn't sell out at one time or another. If Brody was booked in a small town with a population of 500 people, the buildings would be full. He was a great attraction in wrestling.

Nick Bockwinkel (wrestler):

Frank Goodish was very private, very to himself. He walked to his own drummer both in and out of the business. Frank was not one of the boys. He went his own way. A private man. He was not one to sit and talk about his kids or everything else.

Gene Lewis:
Frank had the leverage to stand up and he stood up for the guys. He was one of the boys.

Carlos Colon (wrestler and promoter):
He was a very intelligent man. He was an easy man to deal with, but his character was one thing, and the real Frank Goodish was different—easy going and soft spoken. He got along with everybody.

Kamala, the Ugandan Headhunter (wrestler):
Brody was the same outside the ring as he was on the inside. No matter how you look at it, he was just a serious guy. He would crack a smile once in a while, but I respected him. I didn't kid around a lot, but when we were together, I could go kid around, or we could sit there and be serious and not say anything.

Brian Blair (wrestler):
He was definitely a serious guy, but he liked to laugh. He was a straight shooter and kind of a rebel, kind of an anti-establishment type of guy. He always had something bad to say about the promoters, but always had good things to say about the boys.

Larry Nelson:
He was fiercely loyal to his friends.

Sir Oliver Humperdink (wrestling manager):
I thought he was the sweetest guy and a great worker. He was a great person, and that's more important than being a great worker.

Chapter I Childhood

Bruiser Brody was born Franklin Donald Goodish. He was born in Pennsylvania, but his family moved to Michigan when he was still quite young.

Dirty Dan the Barbell Man (Dan Nixon, gym owner):

One time, his wife, Barbara forgot his birthday, but I remembered—June 18, 1946. I'm good with dates. I always remember.

Don Goodish (cousin):

Originally, the Goodish family was German. His parents and my parents grew up in Uniontown, Pennsylvania. We all moved to Warren, Michigan, and we lived about six blocks apart.

Larry Salci (childhood friend):

Frank and I grew up together as kids. Frank and I were both born in '46. When we were five years old, our parents moved into a new housing development. That was after World War II, in the early fifties. Frank's dad and my dad rode together to work for fifteen years. Our families were very close.

Don Goodish:

He and I started playing Little League football when we were nine or ten years old. We played for the East Detroit Jets, Midgets.

Marie Neece (Frank Goodish's first wife):

Frank's mother and daddy, Mildred (Millie) and Frank, were wonderful people. Frank also had an older sister, Gayle, who was married to Gene Allison, and two younger sisters, Gloria and Kathy. Frank was pretty special in that family of girls. I think Millie worked in a Green Stamps store (if you're young, you probably won't know what that is) and I remember she didn't know how to drive. I thought that was really strange, but with the buses in a large city, I guess she just never needed to learn.

Larry Salci:

We lived in Warren, Michigan. Warren was a new and growing suburb of Detroit that became the second or third largest city in Michigan. It was a very large city by physical geography and is still probably the fourth or fifth largest city in Michigan, but it was all suburbs then. What made it grow was that General Motors built a two-square mile automotive development center right in the heart of Warren. It became a magnet for corporate executives, blue collar workers, and tradesman, from all over the world.

Frank and I didn't live on the same street. We were a block apart. We lived in small, identical houses built post-World War II. I think we moved there in 1951 or 1952. They were three bedroom houses with a kitchen, a small living room, and a little dinette; about 1,100 square feet with one bathroom. Our fathers all worked for a living week to week, payday to payday. Neither of us were privileged children, that's for sure, but we had a good childhood. The parents were all close.

The local elementary school was about three blocks

from where I lived, two from Frank. They had an educational summer program there at the elementary school during the summer and we spent literally every day there playing baseball or basketball. During the fall, we turned the outfield into a football field and we played flag football. There were about 25-30 kids from the neighborhood of all ages. At the time, we were just 12 to 13 years old, but we played with high school kids. I think playing with the older kids as we grew up made us tough. They were high school football players and we would get the crap kicked out of us every day. I was a skinny little kid and would come home cut, bloodied, and bruised. Frank was big from day one, and he could hold his own with anybody, even when he was younger.

Frank Goodish as a freshman, junior, and senior at Warren High school.

Leo Sykes (football teammate):

Frank told me one time that he was watching TV with his mom. They were watching the news and a bar was busted for gambling. They showed these guys being led out in handcuffs and there was Frank's dad. He said his mom just started crying. He told me his dad would come home from work, shower, eat, and go to the bar. That was it.

Larry Salci:

His family situation was that his father was a drunk. He was a big man like Frank, and he used to take great joy in slapping Frank's older sister and mother around. As Frank got bigger and stronger, he became the defender of his mother and sister. Frank's dad and my dad both lost their jobs in '59 or '60 during the big steel strike. They both worked for the R.C. Mahone Company, which was a steel fabricating company. My dad went to work for somebody else, while Frank's dad started tending bar in a local bar. Frank kept it from everybody, but as a teenager growing up, Frank and his dad had kind of a love-hate relationship. He loved his dad, but his dad got drunk a lot and very seldom attended Frank's sporting events.

Frank and I were best of friends, very close. We ran around with two other guys named Bob Studer and Terry Hinkle We all lived just a couple of seconds away from each other, hopping some fences and running through neighbors' back yards.

One afternoon, Frank, a guy named

Don Nagy, who was another friend from that neighborhood, and myself, decided to take a walk down the street to the park. Nagy's parents were gone for a couple of weeks and he was staying at Frank's house while they were gone. We get halfway down the street and Frank jumps into a neighbor's back yard, picks up a bicycle of one of the kids, and throws it out in the middle of the street. "*Let's see if a car hits it.*"

I said, "*Frank, what the hell are you doing?*"

After walking about two more blocks, a squad car pulls up and arrests all three of us. We spent the afternoon in Roseville City Jail. The guy who owned the house that the kid's bicycle was in saw us do it and called the police. My parents were just livid. I got quarantined for a month or something like that. Later on, I heard stories, like a time at Iowa State when Frank had stolen a motorcycle and broken into a jewelry store. I don't know if any of that is true, but knowing Frank and how he was, especially during his senior year in high school, none of it surprises me. He wasn't mean and he didn't do anything to hurt anybody, but he was always trying to have fun. But even that got beyond where it was funny and cute. It got to a point where he was destructive to himself. His behavior was beyond the tolerable limits.

Don Goodish:

We hung around a bit in high school. Frank

Hi-Y members Terry Hinkle, President Larry Salci, Don Nagy, Larry Farhat, and Frank Goodish leave school to deliver canned goods to a needy family.

wouldn't take nothing from nobody. I remember going out and his attitude was, "*You want trouble? Bring it.*"

Larry Salci:

He was an All-American high school football player and I was an All-American high school basketball player. Frank was a gifted football player who played tight end in high school. He was also a great basketball player. He was a center on the basketball team. In fact, we won the conference championships in basketball, football, track, and baseball, during our senior year. It was a great athletic class. I played football one year, then I concentrated on basketball. I also played baseball. But Frank and I played a lot of basketball together. I was the leading scorer and he was number two. We made it to the state quarter-finals in basketball and almost won the state championship.

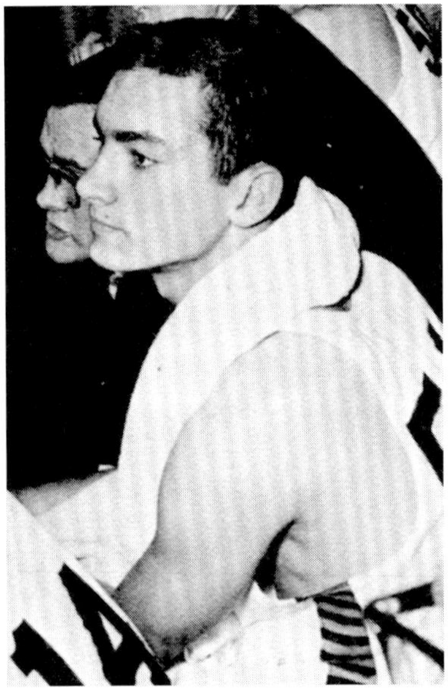

Most people don't know it, but Frank was also an excellent hockey player when we were younger. The elementary school used to bulldoze the outfield and the fire department would come out and flood it. It was so cold in the winter that the field would freeze and stay frozen all winter. Frank was a very, very strong skater and a very good hockey player. We played hockey every winter until we went to high school. He was probably the best hockey player in the neighborhood. He was big and he was mean. He could knock you on your ass in a blink.

Larry Matysik (wrestling announcer and promoter):

He was an all-state basketball and football player in Detroit. He said, "*You wanna know what a good basketball player I was? I just basically beat everybody up, I was a good guard. I just beat everybody up and he'd shoot. We made All-State.*"

Larry Salci:

He was never interested in wrestling as a kid. He didn't wrestle on the team and he never talked about professional wrestling.

Don Goodish:

He didn't even watch wrestling as a kid. His main objective was playing football. He was a football player.

Larry Salci:

Frank had a lot of anger in him. I know that by his senior year in high school, he was so angry at his father that a lot of times, he didn't want to go home. His dad had an alcohol problem and it wasn't commonly known in the neighborhood, except by people who were close with the family. My dad worked with his dad for years and knew that he carried a bottle of whiskey in his lunch basket. We knew that, but we didn't know his dad had gotten kind of nasty with Frank's mother. Frank was just so angry. If somebody on a lark would say, "*Let's go do something stupid,*" and I'll be blunt, Frank would be the first to go do it. It was almost like an escape.

Over the years, I have tried to understand what drove him to behave like that. I just think he was starving for attention. Even though he was a great athlete, he was starving for attention from his father. That's my psychoanalysis, but I'm no psychoanalyst. I have no basis for saying that, but I do know that my parents were very active in my life and never missed a sporting event, and I know what it meant to me when my dad sat in the stands and we won. Frank's dad rarely came to any of his football or basketball games. You could count on one hand the number of sporting events his father and mother attended. I think that really, really ate at Frank.

Above and left: Junior, Frank Goodish on the basketball court.

Dirty Dan the Barbell Man:

His father died shortly after Frank got killed. He took Frank's death real hard.

Brody's father, Franklin Donald Goodish Sr., passed away on December 25, 1988.

Larry Salci:

Frank was a smart kid, but he just academically never applied himself. School became a challenge for him. I kept saying, "*Hey, Frank. If you want a scholarship, you have to get your grades up or nobody's going to take you.*" He barely got into Iowa State. He really struggled with the exams, and it wasn't because he didn't have the native intelligence. It was just a lack of application.

Marie Neece:

He showed me a box full of football scholarship offers that he had received as a senior in high school. He made the All-American high school football team as a senior, so lots of colleges and universities were interested in recruiting him. He picked Iowa State University.

Larry Salci:

Frank wanted to leave. He told me the reason he wanted to go to Iowa State was to get away from his dad. He was going to go to the University of Detroit on a football scholarship and I was going to go there on a basketball scholarship. I thought we could go together, but he said, "*No, I need to get out of town. Get out of the state.*" So, he went to Iowa State.

Chapter II
Outlaws

Frank Goodish was a gifted, natural athlete. He excelled in football, but he didn't have a lot of self-discipline. He first attended Iowa State University, and then the fabled West Texas State University. An inordinate number of professional wrestlers came out of West Texas State. Goodish made lifelong friends and met his first wife there. After being kicked off the football team, he drifted around local junior colleges and did odd jobs until he was accepted into a team in the Continental Football League.

FRANK GOODISH

Frank Goodish attended Iowa State University from the 1964 fall quarter through the summer session of 1965. He majored in Physical Education for Men and played football. He wore #93.

Larry Brazon
(football teammate):

We never met until we became roommates at Iowa State, but we kind of knew about each other from high school sports in Michigan. We both played basketball, but for different high schools, and we both excelled.

There was five of us at Iowa. We were called the Tight Five. Most of the time, if we got into trouble, we got into trouble together. If we drank, we drank together. If we wanted to party, we partied together. And we kind of got kicked off of part of our scholarship. Each time our coach would have a talk with us, we'd always tell him that we'd behave. Frank and I had to go back to summer school one year because we found out that we were both an hour short or something. Frank's dad drove us there and the coach told us to behave. Of course, we promised him that we would. Well, we decided to go out to the bar that very night and we got in trouble our very first night there. We decided to take a couple of barstools.

I'm not making excuses for our behavior, but a lot of it was the rapport with the head coach. It just wasn't good. If you said, "*Hello,*" to the coach, he wouldn't acknowledge you. A lot of good players left because of that coach.

Frank was a caring guy. He decided to join the fraternity and I didn't. He dropped out because he didn't like the way they were treating the recruits. They made one of the guys scrub the floor with a toothbrush. One of the frat brothers came in and knocked the water bucket over, threw paper all over, and told him to start cleaning all over again. When Frank saw that, he picked the frat brother up off the floor and put him against the wall. He said, "*Don't ever let me catch you doing something like that again,*" lowered him down, and walked out the door.

One student at Iowa State had planned to run away and leave his mom and dad. He was just going to take off without telling them. I kind of talked him out of doing that and convinced him to stay and finish school. Frank and I would go to his house to visit now and then. When his parents found out that Frank and I were going to travel to California for part of the summer, they insisted on paying our way. We kept telling them no, but they were so appreciative for what we had done for their son and kept on until we finally accepted their offer. We traveled up the whole California coastline and had a great time together.

Frank had a habit of always checking under the bed, and when we went out west, it paid off. He found money! So, every time we stayed in a hotel, he had to check under the bed.

West Texas head coach, Joe Kerbel.

Larry Salci:

Frank was a tight end at Iowa. When they tried to convert him into a tackle, he called me and said, "*Hey, they want to make me a tackle because I'm putting on weight. They don't think I'm fast enough to play tight end.*"

They told him it was better for the team. He wasn't very happy about that. Then he got kicked out of school.

Marc Allen (football player):

Frank got kicked out of Iowa State for jumping through a plate glass window. They raided a girl's dorm. As they were trying to get away from the security cops, Frank jumped through a plate glass window and got caught. They kicked him out of school.

Larry Salci:

After he left Iowa State, he came back to Detroit for a very brief time, and went to Wayne State University to get his academic situation into a position where he could transfer back to play football. The last time I saw Frank was my sophomore year. I was about 19 years old. I was a starting guard for the University of Detroit and we were playing in a holiday basketball tournament in Detroit. I don't remember who we played, but we had just lost. As I was leaving the field house, going out of the arena area into the locker room, Frank was standing upstairs in a seat yelling at me, "*Great game!*"

That was the last time I saw him. He went from there to West Texas State. I spoke to him on the phone a couple of times, but the last physical time I ever saw him was that night in the field house.

At Wayne State, Frank Goodish enrolled in six classes. He withdrew from American Democracy to 1815 and Freshman Literature. He got an 'A' in Baseball–Track, a 'C' in Individual Sports, Men, an 'A' in Golf, and a 'B' in Individual Hygiene.

Marc Allen:

Then he headed to West Texas State. West Texas State was an outlaw school. I'm talking 1963 to 1967. There was a famous coach there named Joe

Kerbel who picked up outlaws from everywhere.

Leo Sykes:

They recruited guys that had been in prison. Kerbel was an ex-Marine—a real hard-nosed guy. Their scholarship would be semester by semester. If Kerbel could find somebody better, he'd cut them and bring a better guy in. It was just like pro ball. Frank was one of the guys they brought in.

Marc Allen:

In my senior year at West Texas, we had eight guys drafted underneath in the tenth round. That was more than the entire Southwest Conference, which was the Big Twelve. That's eight guys put into the NFL in that one year.

Nick Bockwinkel:

He [Brody], Stan Hansen, Dick Murdoch, Tito Santana, the Funks, Dusty Rhodes, other than Tito Santana, who seemed to be the only sane one, and of course, Dory Funk Jr., they all started in West Texas, and we all swear there was something in the water. I swear to God, when you look at Murdoch and some of those guys, you really got some unique personalities, to put it mildly. Terry Funk being the last of them, and God bless you, Terry, but you still need help.

Dory Funk Jr. (wrestler):

There probably were about twelve wrestlers that have come out of West Texas State University, and I could name about eight of them real fast. There would be Tully Blanchard, Bobby Duncum, Stan Hansen, Dusty Rhodes (I'm not sure if Dusty Rhodes played football or baseball), Terry Funk, myself, Merced Solis (a great tight end at West Texas who later wrestled as Tito Santana). Dick Murdoch played in the alumni football game at West Texas, even though he never attended school there. He loved West Texas and talked about it so much. He grew up in that area, and pretty soon, everybody thought he played for West Texas. He went back and played in the alumni game. The press came down on Dick Murdoch for being unnecessarily rough with the kids. Dick did pretty much what he wanted to do through all of his life, too.

Wrestlers Ted DiBiase, Manny Fernandez, Kelly Kiniski, and Barry Windham also went to West Texas State University. On September 1, 1990, West Texas State joined the Texas A&M University System and changed its name to West Texas A&M in 1993.

Marc Allen:

When Frank came to West Texas in the spring of '66, everybody said, "*He's so big and so pretty.*" I thought he looked like a fucking rat. He looked like a rat before he grew his hair out and before he cut up his forehead. He was a handsome guy—young and innocent—with just a few cuts from running through plate glass windows.

Larry Brazon:

Frank was a caring guy. I decided to leave Iowa and said, "*The heck with this.*" I didn't want to play ball anymore. I was going to join the service. When Frank found out what happened, he gave me a call. He told me to call the coach, so I did, and I talked to him for three hours. A week later, I called the coach

ALO DEFENSE

LES

Frank Goodish, Jr., Tr, Warren, Mich.

Goodish — 77
6-3, 235

One of pleasant surprises in spring drills. . .converted from center to defensive tackle and earned starting job. . .excellent range, speed (4.9). . . needs polish, but has excellent recovery powers. . .good arm-shoulder strength. . .red-shirted last year after transferring from Iowa State. Born 6-1-46 in Uniontown, Pa. . .son of Mr. and Mrs. Frank Goodish of Teela Warren, Mich. . .single. . .has three sisters. . .Major: Education. Hobbies: Weightlifting and tennis. Earned three letters in both football and basketball at Warren, Mich. High School. . .all-state and honorable mention all-America in football. . .coached by Steve Nowak.

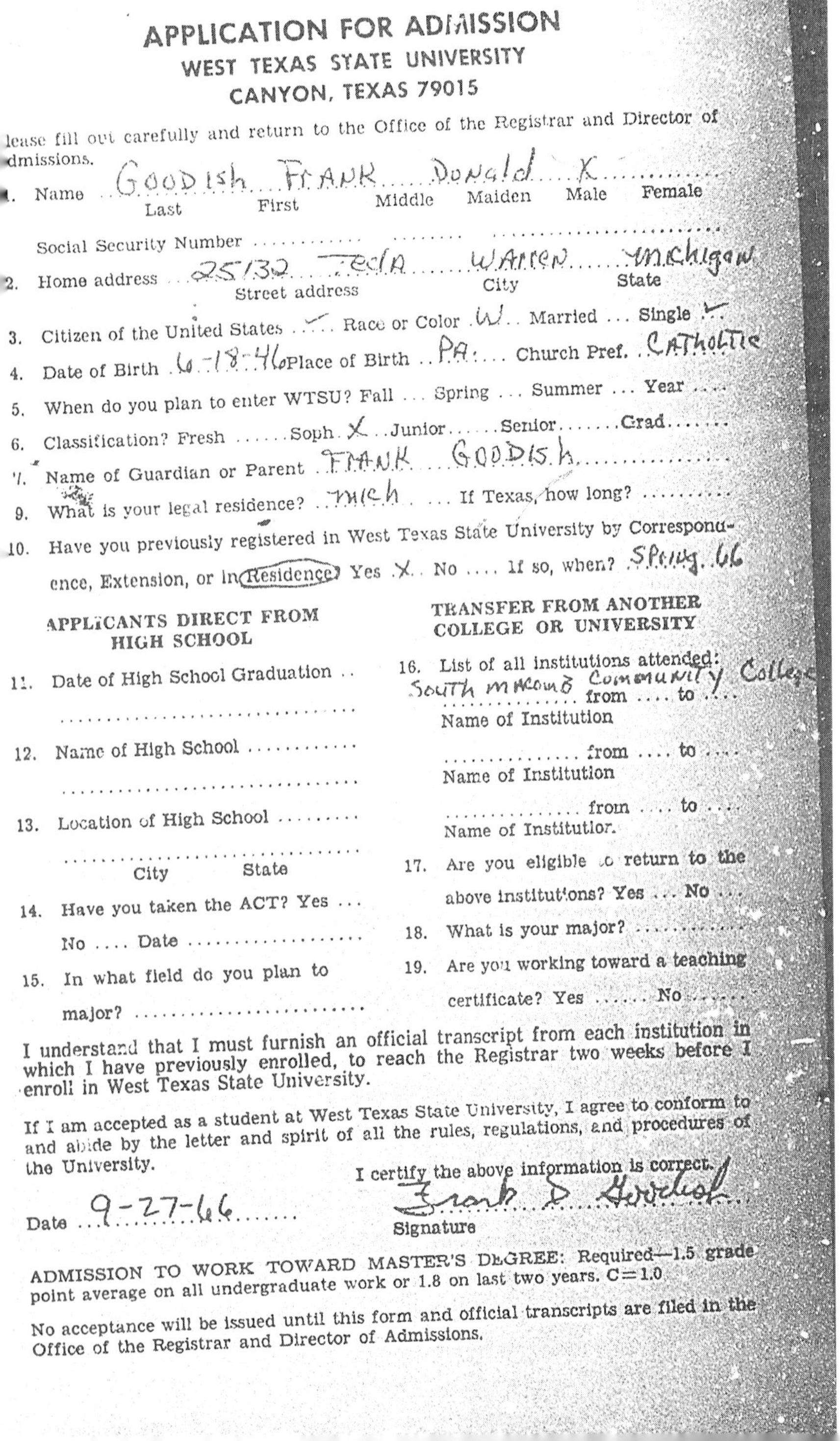

APPLICATION FOR ADMISSION
WEST TEXAS STATE UNIVERSITY
CANYON, TEXAS 79015

lease fill out carefully and return to the Office of the Registrar and Director of dmissions.

1. Name GOODISH FRANK DONALD X
Last First Middle Maiden Male Female

Social Security Number

2. Home address 25132 Tecla Warren Michigan
Street address City State

3. Citizen of the United States ✓ Race or Color W Married ... Single ✓

4. Date of Birth 6-18-46 Place of Birth PA Church Pref. CATHOLIC

5. When do you plan to enter WTSU? Fall ... Spring ... Summer ... Year ...

6. Classification? Fresh ...... Soph X Junior ...... Senior ...... Grad ......

7. Name of Guardian or Parent FRANK GOODISH

9. What is your legal residence? Mich ... If Texas, how long? ...

10. Have you previously registered in West Texas State University by Correspondence, Extension, or in Residence? Yes X No .... If so, when? Spring 66

APPLICANTS DIRECT FROM HIGH SCHOOL

11. Date of High School Graduation ..

12. Name of High School ...

13. Location of High School ...
City State

14. Have you taken the ACT? Yes ... No .... Date ...

15. In what field do you plan to major? ...

TRANSFER FROM ANOTHER COLLEGE OR UNIVERSITY

16. List of all institutions attended:
South Macomb Community College from .... to ....
Name of Institution
.... from .... to ....
Name of Institution
.... from .... to ....
Name of Institution

17. Are you eligible to return to the above institutions? Yes ... No ...

18. What is your major? ...

19. Are you working toward a teaching certificate? Yes ...... No ......

I understand that I must furnish an official transcript from each institution in which I have previously enrolled, to reach the Registrar two weeks before I enroll in West Texas State University.

If I am accepted as a student at West Texas State University, I agree to conform to and abide by the letter and spirit of all the rules, regulations, and procedures of the University.

I certify the above information is correct.

Date 9-27-66 Frank D. Goodish
Signature

ADMISSION TO WORK TOWARD MASTER'S DEGREE: Required—1.5 grade point average on all undergraduate work or 1.8 on last two years. C=1.0

No acceptance will be issued until this form and official transcripts are filed in the Office of the Registrar and Director of Admissions.

back, then I called Frank and said I'd be down. Frank was at the train station waiting for me. That's when I started at West Texas State.

Marc Allen:

Frank was real quiet. His roommate, Larry Brazon … well, both those guys were a little different.

Terry Funk (wrestler):

He'd get that third team fired up when he was out there. He was redshirted in because he had been in Iowa State and he couldn't just step in there and start playing. He had to sit out a semester, so he was redshirted in. He'd trump up all the redshirts, and the goofballs who were on the underneath teams, and get them all fired up, and he'd keep us out there an extra thirty minutes because the coach would get pissed.

Larry Brazon:

In fact, Dusty Rhodes was a redshirt with us. Every Monday, after they finished playing a game on Saturday, we would have what they call the Toilet Bowl. Frank, Dusty, and I would have our scrimmage. We just couldn't wait for the beginning of the next season to play, but things changed. Frank played, but Dusty went his own way.

Marc Allen:

Frank was a big guy. He could run like a deer, but he hit like a mouse. I took him under my wing. He talked funny, like the Yankee from Detroit that he was.

Marie Neece:

In the spring of 1966, I walked into the Student Union Building [SUB] at West Texas State University on my way to the University Post Office and saw this 6-foot-4, 220 lb. hunk that had the best looking legs I'd ever seen. Frank was across the room talking to some other football players, and was wearing a pair of faded, green-jean cut-offs and a t-shirt. At that point, I had no idea who he was, but I was very interested in finding out.

Frank had transferred to WT that semester as a redshirt football player. Every day at the same time that semester, I checked my mail, and every day, Frank was in the SUB surrounded by his friends. Every day, he'd look at me and I'd look at him, but neither one of us ever spoke. In college, I wore big, gold hoops in my ears, and since Frank and his buddies didn't know my name, they started calling me Gypsy (after Gypsy Rose Lee, the stripper). When I'd walk in, they'd all start whistling and yelling at me. "*There's the Gypsy. There goes the Gypsy.*" I would turn beet red and never stop. Of course, I was flattered that he was paying attention to me, but amused that he'd never talk to me. I was as bashful as Frank was, and he was always with a group of guys. That continued all that semester until school was out for the summer.

Terry Funk:

He was crazy. He would run the cars. We would go to bars and we would start at one end of the street. Brody was great at it. We'd all try, but he was great at it. I can't remember the name of the club, but they had parallel parking on the street in front of it. Brody would put one foot on the trunk of a car, take a step to the middle of the roof, then one foot to the hood, and keep on going from car to car. He could run a whole block and never touch the ground.

Stan Hansen (wrestler):

The very first time I ever met Frank Goodish, I was a high school recruit and I was being shown around West Texas State. I had gone to a number of colleges for football and they came, so this guy, Phil Hampton, he was a player on the West Texas team and he was showing me around and showing me the campus, and I said, "*I wanna see your dorm.*" He says, "*Well, we'll go by there later.*"

And he kept putting it off, putting it off, and everything. So finally, I came back around, and finally I said, "*I wanna see the dorm room, where I'm gonna live if I come here.*"

So, he stops at the door and it's about two in the afternoon. He says, "*Now listen. When you come here, you get a roommate. You can't control what the roommate does.*"

I said, "*I understand.*"

He says, "*Well, all right.*"

So he opened up the door and there was a line down the middle of the room. His room was immaculate.

Frank Goodish and Marie Neece, 1968.

Everything was really nice. The bed was made, the books were stacked, and everything. As I walked in, I looked over, and the other bed … there's no sheets on the bed, there's nothing there. There's just clothes everywhere and Bruiser Brody's lying in the bed. And he comes to at two o'clock in the afternoon, going, "*Hey!*"

And [Phil Hampton] goes, "*This is a high school recruit.*"

And [Brody] goes, "*Arrrrr,*" and he turns over, and that's the first time I ever met Frank Brody. So, I'll always remember that, and that had a lot to say about his personality and everything, but we developed a great friendship after that.

Marie Neece:

One night, I had a date with a cowboy—boots, jeans, hat-wearing cowboy—and we went to a club in Amarillo. Back in those days, girls had to be back in the dorm by a certain time, so my date and I were leaving to get me back before the curfew. The club or bar wasn't that big, but I hadn't noticed that Frank and his buddies had come in until we were leaving. Then suddenly, Larry Brazon jumped up a few feet from me as I was passing by and he started yelling, "*There's the Gypsy, Frank. There's the Gypsy.*"

Then they were all yelling and pointing and my date was trying to get me out of there fast. He didn't want any trouble with a bunch of football players. I remember laughing so hard I could hardly walk. Well, I had also had some drinks, I'm sure. Anyway, when I got back to the dorm, I went to bed, and about 2:00 a.m., the phone rang. My roommate got up to answer it and I heard her say, "*I have no idea where Marie went tonight.*" I knew it was Frank, so I took the phone and we talked the night away.

Frank knew my name was Marie, but he didn't know my last name, so he'd been calling every Marie in the WT student directory asking each one if she had been to that bar. After that, I thought the ice had been broken. Was I ever wrong! This became an every weekend occurrence. Every Friday and Saturday night, Frank would call after the bars closed and we would talk and talk, but he would never speak to me in the SUB.

Then one day, my roommate, another friend, and I walked to the post office accompanied by the now normal whistles and yelling. On our way back, Larry came over, stopped me, and said, "*Marie, let me formally introduce you to Frank Goodish. Frank, this is Marie Neece. Now you two have been properly introduced, so get on with it.*"

Frank smiled at me, and I smiled at him and walked out. A couple of days later, I was in the SUB with some friends. They all either had class or wanted to go back to the dorm, but I decided to stay and wait to see if Frank would approach me alone. I nearly gave up, but finally he and a buddy came over and sat down. Eventually, the buddy left, so after nearly a year, I was alone with him in the SUB. He asked me for a date, took me to a football game, and that was about it for that semester.

Then February rolled around and I was going home for the weekend of February 14th. Before I left for the weekend, I checked my mail and found a homemade valentine signed, "Guess Who," printed in red Crayola on Big Chief tablet paper. It was made of a large red heart cut out of construction paper, with little white cut-out hearts on it, and a white arrow glued to the red heart. The paper was folded into two or three sections and a story from a magazine (Playboy, I think) had been glued to it. The story was about a little boy, who was very shy, but he loved a little red-haired girl who didn't know he was even alive, and he wanted to give her a valentine. So, using his Big Chief tablet, he made one for her. Throughout this story, the little boy would say, "And she's the girl for me." At the end of the story, the little boy didn't have the nerve to sign the card, so he signed it "Guess Who."

I remember wondering who in the world would go to so much trouble to make a valentine for me, and do it exactly as the little boy had made his valentine in the story. I suspected that it was Frank, but I had a hard time imagining this big, strong, cocky football player doing that, so I drove home not knowing for sure. About 2:00 that night [Valentine's night], the phone rang at my parents' home. I jumped up to answer it, knowing that it was Frank. When I answered, he said, "*And she's the girl for me,*" and he hung up. That was February 14, 1967.

After that, we started dating a lot.

When that semester ended, Frank had to go home. That was when the Detroit Riots of 1967 broke out. Frank's father owned a party store. I was never there, but I guess that was like a liquor store. I remember Frank telling me he had to go home to help his dad guard the store. It must have been really bad up there.

The living legend, Terry Funk.

I graduated in January 1968, and since Frank was still in school, I tried to find a teaching job in the area. I finally found one in Brownfield, Texas, a small town south of Lubbock. Frank drove down with me when I went for the interview and then helped me find an apartment. I can't remember exactly when he was kicked off the football team and lost his scholarship, but it was either shortly before I graduated or right after I left. Then he moved to Amarillo with some friends, continued to go to school, and worked at night as a bouncer in a popular bar in Amarillo.

Dusty Rhodes (wrestler):

We were roommates in college at West Texas State and bouncers at the Reveler Nightclub, the only nightclub in Amarillo, Texas. [Amarillo] was an Air Force town. Nothing else was there except cowboys and us. Later, me and Frank were at the Batcave, a new club that opened in Amarillo. That was the very first time they had a topless club in Amarillo. When it opened, the place was packed. They had a girl in a little two-piece sitting on a swing, threatening to take it off. A big fight broke out and they almost had a riot. Everybody had to go out the back door.

We also worked at the Airspeed Gas station together to get enough money to go see wrestling on Thursday nights. Yeah, I knew Frank Goodish well.

[Frank] was like a giant Bobby Heenan, or Don Rickles. He always had something really smart alec to say. He had digs on everything. I remember when Frank and I were in a garage one winter. I was under my car changing the oil, I was telling him about my ex-wife. While I was talking, she had walked into the garage. Frank saw her walk in … and he never said a word. She stood there listening to me give her all this shit.

Larry Brazon:

Frank, Dusty, myself, and a guy named Eddie Golecky, would go to the Air Force base. They had one of those rings that would just bounce you all over the place. The Funks were Amarillo's homeboys. We had seen them and imagined that some day we might be wrestlers. Dusty and Frank did it.

Terry Funk:

Wrestling was a different thing back then. We talked to very few people about wrestling. We always felt like if you wanted to get into the business, you would find a way. Frank was really not interested in the business when he left West Texas.

He was kicked off the football team at West Texas for chopping down a cherry tree. He thought he was George Washington. There were these apartments that were owned by a Mr. Graham. He owned Graham's Grocery and he had some apartments there that he rented to college kids. They had some cherry trees out front. One night, Frank took a hatchet to one of the cherry trees. It was a good-sized cherry tree. When they asked him who did it, Frank said, "*I did.*" Of course, there was also some drinking involved.

Larry Brazon, 1967

Marie Neece:

His goal had always been to play pro football, but after he got kicked off the West Texas team, he knew his chances were pretty slim. From what I understand (this is what he told me, anyway), he and a couple of his buddies had been drinking and they knocked down or pulled up a tree in the coach's yard (I think it was the coach's yard because he hated that head coach, however, I could be wrong about whose yard it was.). That spring semester, he found out about the San Antonio Toros.

Larry Matysik:

We talked about the sports part, how when Brody played college football, he could still get by on his natural athleticism, and the fact that he was mean and that he'd beat people up. Tim Van Galder was the quarterback for Iowa State at the time. Later, he became a TV announcer in St. Louis. He was older than Frank.

Anyhow, he ended up in West Texas and he still did good, and then he said, "*When I got drafted by the Redskins, I got up there and found out all these other guys were just as good of athletes as I was, just as tough as I was. The difference was, they'd learned the fundamentals, while I never took the time.*"

We talked about a lot of things, like politics. We talked a lot about money, of course, and he was investing and everything. He was an independent. His politics were exactly the same as the rest of his life. He could love one politician, but a different guy from the same party, "*What an asshole!*"

Totally independent, which is the reason we got along so well. I'm the same way. That's how he was, totally wide open.

Chapter III Footballs and Wedding Bells

Football was what Goodish knew and loved. He put all of his eggs into that basket and ran with it. All of a sudden, Frank was about to start a family and new responsibilities were beginning to press in on him. The NFL wasn't calling and he needed work.

The Continental Football League wasn't just another way for a football player to make a buck. It was also a farm league for the NFL, so when the San Antonio Toros called, Frank went.

When his football teammates reflect upon Frank, they remember a man that no wrestling fan and few wrestlers ever knew. In those days, he was a fun-loving prankster, a sly devil, always out for a good time with the boys.

Marie Neece:

The date of our wedding was June 4, 1968. When I showed up late, Frank thought I wasn't coming. After I arrived, we realized that Frank had left the marriage license in my car. We had each come to the church with friends, so we all had to wait while my friend went to wherever Frank left my car to get the license. The preacher was getting antsy about the whole thing. The marriage ceremony took about ten minutes. We had no cake, no party, and no reception … nothing. Frank had called his coach (I think his name was Coach McCauley) in San Antonio and was told to report to training camp on June 5 … the next day.

When we went to the Toros business office, Frank met some of the players and ran into his old friends, Marc Allen and Dave Whitmire, who were also playing for the Toros. For some reason, Dave and his wife had invited Marc and his wife, Barbara, to move in with them. When they heard that Frank and I had no place to live, they invited us to stay with them until we could find an apartment. Now that

Above: Frank and Marie tie the knot on June 4, 1968.

was interesting. We had been married for one day, and now we were staying with two other couples that I'd never met. But they turned out to be great friends during the time I lived in San Antonio.

Marc Allen:

Frank and his wife lived with me for a while. Can you imagine what it was like having three couples living together? It was wild.

Leo Sykes:

When he came here [San Antonio] to play, he was married to a school teacher named Marie. They lived in some dumpy little apartments just off of Fort Sam Houston. She ended up divorcing him.

Frank and I went to Mexico one time and he didn't tell his wife he was going. Oh, my God! She was throwing all his stuff out the front door. I always thought Marie had a pretty good head on her shoulders.

Marie Neece:

I knew Leo would tell the story of me chucking Frank's things out the door. Leo and Frank came home one morning after staying out all night (much later, he did tell me they went to Mexico). When he started telling me some lie, I did get furious ... mostly because he seemed to think I was so stupid that I'd believe it. I threw underwear, shirts, socks, pants, and even rolled some barbells out the door. And I was yelling. Some poor guy was outside waxing his car, and every time I went to the door and threw something out, he'd look up and then back down real fast. I remember thinking at the time how funny that was. Then the barbells started rolling down the street. When I went back in and pulled out a new suit (that was about the only thing left in the closet), and started out with it, Frank grabbed me by the neck and lifted me up into the air by my head. He wasn't choking me, but it was a little uncomfortable dangling up in the air. Finally, I told him I'd hang up his suit if he'd put me down, so he threw me on the bed. Leo was sitting at the kitchen table with his head down (probably laughing) but he wouldn't look up when I'd walk by and toss. I was almost as mad at him as I was with Frank.

Marc Allen:

Marie was a West Texas girl—real tall, thin, dark hair, and the greatest gal in the world. I wish I knew where she was.

Jerry Jones (football player):

She [Marie] was loads of fun. They were great for each other, but he messed up too many times and she divorced him. He was married when he was around her, but he wasn't married when he wasn't around her.

Bill Lehman (teammate, wrestler):

Frank Goodish came to San Antonio when I was with the San Antonio Toros, a professional football team in the Continental Football League [CFL]. The CFL was pretty close to becoming the OTHER football league. There were a lot of places to play football at that time.

Bill Lehman also wrestled professionally as Siegfried Stanke and Spoiler #2.

Leo Sykes:

He wasn't that tough of a guy. I always told him he looked like Tarzan and played like Jane.

Bill Lehman:

Frank, when he got to the Toros, was a little bit withdrawn, but then he got going with that group of guys. Fun-loving guys.

Marie Neece:

Marc, who grew up in San Antonio, helped us find a cheap apartment near Fort Sam Houston, and I think Frank and I finally felt married. Most, if not all, of the football players worked during the day and practiced in the evenings. Frank got a manual labor job loading and unloading furniture that summer, while I applied to various school districts for a teaching job in the fall.

That fall [1968], Frank enrolled in St. Mary's University in San Antonio as a full-time student and played football on the weekends. I taught school, so between my small teaching salary and the little amount he received from the Toros, we continued to survive, even though it was very little money. Frank had flunked freshmen English five times at five different universities, until he finally had an English teacher at St. Mary's who didn't assume all freshmen already knew how to write, and she taught Frank enough to pass. He was so happy with that C in English. Frank was very creative and had a wonderful way with words, but he didn't have a clue about comma splices and couldn't have cared less.

Bill Lehman:

I was an older guy, a player/coach, and he was wild and wooly. He went out with that group of guys afterwards and messed around at different spots. He was a fun-loving guy, but to be honest, I didn't run with Frank. If you ran with those guys … well, they were something else.

There was Jerry "Ox" Oliver. He was 6-foot-8 and weighed about 315 pounds, but he could run. He had talent that guys in the NFL don't have. He was down from Port Arthur, Texas, and money wasn't his big thing. He just wanted to play football. Marc Allen, who played over on defense, also played at West Texas State. Billy Bob … I'm trying to think of his name. He played at SMU. He was a character. He used to mess around with those guys. There was Bill Grindle who—he's still around here—was a heck of a player, but he was also rowdy at that particular time. He got a master's degree and, eventually, he ended up being the principal of a high school. He's now on the board of San Antonio College. Leo Sykes. That guy used to go into bars and challenge guys to a head-butt contest. Those were the type of guys that Frank was running around with.

Marc Allen:

Nobody really ran with Frank, but we were always around Frank. Frank was dancing to a different beat than everybody else.

Marie Neece:

I had to make Frank a brown bag lunch every day that summer, so I always tried to give him something different each day. He usually took at least three to four sandwiches. One day, I fixed him a peanut butter and mashed banana sandwich, one of my favorites. When he came home that evening, I asked him if he liked it. He said he took one bite, threw it down, and stomped on it.

Frank knew he needed to be bigger and stronger to play in the pros, so he started working out every night at the gym. As a football player, he had always lifted weights, but now he did it religiously. If the gym was closed, he lifted weights at home. He also started eating four meals a day and drinking a protein supplement to gain weight. As soon as I got home from work, I'd cook dinner, we'd eat, and he'd head to the gym. I felt very neglected as a new wife. When I'd say something about it, he'd tell me he was doing it for us, so I accepted it, but I didn't like it. When he finished working out, he and his buddies would go to the "ice house" to cool off and he'd get home late every night. We only had one car, so I had no choice but to stay home.

Magic Schwarz (wrestler, stuntman):

Brody kind of hung around San Antonio at a place called San Antonio Health Club. It was a bodybuilding gym in San Antonio, Texas. He was sort of an icon at that gym because back then, then weren't really a lot of guys his size. Everybody called him "The Big Man." That was his nickname. All the wrestlers that blew through town worked out at that gym, so he rubbed noses with a lot of them. Eventually, they talked him into becoming a professional wrestler. That's kind of where it all kicked off.

Dirty Dan the Barbell Man:

I met Frank through Leo Sykes. When Leo came to town to play football for the Toros, he joined my gym. That was right about 1968. So he brought all these Toros football players to work out, and Frank Goodish was one of them, you know. We became friends and went out and drank a little beer together, and that type of thing.

Leo Sykes:

Dirty Dan the Barbell Man was a World War II vet. He owns a gym here in San Antonio where we all lifted weights. Dan's 81 years old now and he still works out three days a week.

Magic Schwarz:

Dan Nixon was the owner of that gym. His nickname was "The Old Man," but he was dirty, so some people called him "Dirty Dan." When Nixon got old, he sold the gym to somebody else. Everybody had a lot of respect for him and he knew the operation of the gym, so the buyer hired him to work there. He still works there today. They have a reunion every year at that gym.

Ivan Putski (Joe Bednarski, wrestler):

The name of the gym? I really don't know. We just called it Dirty Dan's gym. He was a great guy. He would bend over backwards for us.

The first time I met Brody, it was at the gym. I wasn't in wrestling yet. I was living in San Antonio. I was a high school teacher and I think I was playing football in Canada at that time.

Dirty Dan the Barbell Man:

I was so much older than Frank. I was sort of like a father figure to him, and I thought the world of him. He stayed at my house a few times, you know. He didn't have any money. He used to buy tuna fish because it was cheap. He borrowed one of my two forks and never gave it back. I only had one fork left to eat my tuna with.

I'd let Frank go down to the gym on Sundays, when it was closed, and let him work out. I believe I actually suggested he get into wrestling. We were out one night and he was so bad. I knew he'd do real well. Joe [Bednarski, aka Ivan Putski] worked out at the gym and he helped him get in. Joe was already in the wrestling business, so he helped Frank. I sort of put the two of them together. He was a great guy and I really miss him a lot, you know.

Magic Schwarz:

Frank was probably the strongest guy in the gym. There was another guy named Terry Gilbert. They used to have big contests to see who could lift the most weight. Frank always won. Frank was the hero of that gym for a long time.

There was a guy named Bobby in San Antonio who was a motorcycle racer that I used to race with. He was real cocky and he had a real strong grip. He was in the hospital for almost a year after a can of nitro blew up in his face. While he was laid up, all he did was squeeze those hand exercisers.

He had an antique machine that you put a quarter in. When you squeezed a grip on the machine, a needle would go over and it would tell you how strong you were. He used to go around to the bars and make money doing it because nobody could ever beat him.

One day, he walked into the gym. He was kind of fooling around, showing everybody what it did. Frank was the biggest guy in there, so he told Frank that he would challenge him to the machine. So Bobby goes first and he pegged the machine, which he always did. He knew exactly how to squeeze it to get maximum force on it. Goodish went over and squeezed it, and didn't quite make it over to where Bobby did. When Frank couldn't peg it, he got real pissed off. Bobby was wearing a straw hat looking thing. Frank took it off his head, threw it on the floor, and jumped up and down on it. He grabbed the machine out of Bobby's hand, walked out the front door, and threw it in the middle of the street.

Leo Sykes:

In San Antonio, they have a big, week-long party called Night in Old San Antonio, or NIOSA. Frank and I and Dirty Dan the Barbell Man were there. The Toros owner, Henry Hight, walked up to Frank and said, "*When are you gonna sign your contract?*"

Frank said, "*I'm not gonna sign for what your offering.*"

Henry said something or other about, "*Well, you're not worth that much anyway.*"

Frank took a sip of beer and spit it in Henry's face. Henry slapped Frank.

Dirty Dan the Barbell Man:

Frank had a cup of beer in his hand. When Henry hit Frank, his beer flew and hit the guy behind him.

Left: Dirty Dan the Barbell Man tries to keep it cool as Frank plants one on him.

When the guy turned around, he looked like he wanted to fight Frank, but when he realized how big he was, he didn't do nothing. I shouldn't have done what I did. I hit Henry and split his lip open real wide, like he had two mouths.

Leo Sykes:

Henry's teeth went through his bottom lip. When he took a sip of beer, the beer was coming out the hole in his lip. Everybody had too much to drink.

Dirty Dan the Barbell Man:

Later on, we ran into Henry and he hadn't been to the doctor yet. The cut was about an inch wide and right below his lip. Leo walked over to Henry and said, "*You better get to the doctor, Henry, and get that sewed up.*" We were all crazy. Later, I apologized to Henry.

Leo Sykes:

Henry—the owner of the Toros—he used to love to drink beer with the players, right? We were all just football bums. We would take him out and drink, and hit him up for money that we would pay back out of next year's paychecks. That way, if we owed him money, he probably wouldn't let them cut us. He was this big auto parts business man … rich, but he never figured that out.

Marie Neece:

In the spring, Frank decided St. Mary's was too expensive, so he enrolled at Southwest Texas State University [now Texas State University] in San Marcos. Every morning, he would take me to work and then go to school. About half way through that semester, he quit and applied for, and was hired as, a sports writer for the San Antonio Express.

Marc Allen:

Frank ended up writing a sports column for the San Antonio Express-News. Dan Cook, the sports editor, will tell you the other side of Frank. Dan sort of took Frank under his wing and made a friendship with him.

Dan Cook is a San Antonio institution. He was a sports reporter and columnist for the San Antonio Express-News, and a sportscaster on KENS since the early 1950s. Cook is acknowledged as the originator of the phrase, "*It ain't over till the fat lady sings.*"

Dan Cook (sports journalist):

It was another friend of Frank's who, during the off season, told me that Frank was loading concrete or some such job in about 98 or more degrees of heat. As I recall, he had some sort of degree from a college, which was more than I had, so I offered him a low-paying job on the newspaper here. He answered the Sports Department's phone and, in a short time, he began to write. And, by golly, Frank did have a fair degree of talent for writing. Eventually, he moved to a smaller paper for more pay.

Leo Sykes:

Frank also bought a home north of San Antonio, and he built a house for his parents so they could move down here from Detroit. His dad worked in the auto plant and was used to the city. The quiet of the country just drove him crazy, so they moved back up north.

Leo Sykes:

The Toros traded Frank. Red McCombs, who owns a big auto dealership here, also owned the San Antonio Spurs, Denver Nuggets, and for about seven years, the Minnesota Vikings. He established a team in Monterrey, Mexico; an expansion team for the Continental League. They were the Monterrey Golden Aztecs. Henry was looking to get rid of Frank and sent him to Monterrey. They put the players in a hotel down there and I guess they just raped, pillaged, and plundered those poor Mexican housekeepers. All those guys, living in a hotel, practicing once a day, with nothing else to do but lift weights and drink beer. The Aztecs were only in operation for a short time before Red McCombs folded up the team and the players were dispersed throughout the league again.

Marie Neece:

I told Frank I would not quit my job in San Antonio to move to Mexico. I would go with him for the summer, and I would come to the games on the weekends, but I didn't believe football in Mexico would work. I needed a little more security in my life.

Jerry Jones:

I met him in Monterrey, Mexico.

Fred Ekmark (football teammate):

Frank came on board a little after the team started up in 1969, or thereabouts. He and I had an apartment together in Monterrey. There was about five of us. One morning, Frank woke up me and Jerry Jones. He said, "*You guys got any beer?*"

We said, "*Beer? It's ten o'clock in the morning, Frank.*"

Fred Ekmark

Jerry Jones

That's when I knew I needed to get a real job. We were just kidding ourselves.

Marie Neece:

Big football players were an unusual sight in Monterrey. Frank had gained weight and more muscle by that time, and he had large muscular arms. I remember walking down the street with Frank. Little boys would come up, grab his arms, and he'd swing them around. They thought it was great fun.

Jerry Jones:

We were staying in apartments that were on top of a bank building, probably ten to eleven stories tall. One morning, I woke up and heard somebody laughing in Frank and Fred's apartment. I mean, whoever it was, was just going nuts. It sounded like Frank, so finally I got up and went

FRANK GOODISH

Muy buen tackle ofensivo, jugó su primer año con West Texas State, pesa 123 kilos y mide 1.93 Mts. de estatura, golpea y bloquea con una habilidad y experiencia que lo colocará con cualquier equipo profesional que él quiera.

A newspaper article on the Monterrey Golden Aztecs notes newcomer, Frank Goodish.

over. "*What the hell you doing, Frank! God dangit! Get out of here. I'm trying to sleep!*"

He said, "*Come here. Try this.*"

I said, "*What are you doing?*"

He said, "*Look down there.*"

Looking down out of their window, I saw a manhole in the street with the cover off. Around the hole were these potatoes. We had a sack of potatoes in the apartment and Frank was throwing them out the window down into that manhole. He says, "*Watch this,*" and he threw a potato into the manhole. A second later, here comes this Mexican guy out of that hole, just madder than hell, looking around and trying to figure out who's been throwing the potatoes. He looked everywhere but up.

Marie Neece:

All the wives of the players and friends would sit together, and the Mexicans would watch us for reactions to the game. When we clapped and hollered, they'd clap. If we stood up, they'd stand up. Football was too new to Mexico and they didn't understand the game.

Fred Ekmark:

One night, I went down to Del Rio with Frank, Leo Sykes, and some old gal. I was there when Frank got that tattoo. [Goodish had "Frank" tattooed on his right shoulder.] Leo and Frank were sitting in a bar doing shots of tequila at a nickel a shot. They'd drink a shot, then they'd throw the glass and break it. The owner just said, "*That's okay. I'm keeping track and you owe me.*"

After they got finished drinking, they just got up and left. There wasn't anything [the owner] could do about it. In San Antonio, Frank had restaurants where the gay waiters liked him. When we went to eat at one of them, Frank would pick up the check and say, "*I got the check.*"

And he'd take the check and eat it. Those gay guys would go, "*Oh Frank.*"

He never had to pay for food there.

Fred Ekmark:

We were down there in Mexico at a restaurant and he was singing. This guy says, "*Hey, shut up!*"

Frank just keeps on singing. The guy goes, "*Hey, I told you to shut up!*"

Frank's still singing. When the guy pulls out a .22 [caliber pistol], Frank jumps up and grabs a chair. He's gonna hit the guy with the chair. Here's a guy with a gun and the guy takes off running, with Frank chasing him down the street with the chair.

Marie Neece:

The Golden Aztecs folded sometime in October [1969], I believe, and the league divided up the team among the other Texas semi-pro teams. Frank was sent to Odessa to play for the Rufneks. I couldn't leave my teaching job until the semester ended; so once again, we had a long distance marriage of sorts.

Fred Ekmark:

After we left Monterrey, we went and played for Midland-Odessa. Frank was there for that. That was the Midland-Odessa Rufneks.

We were playing a game in Texarkana. We'd gotten into trouble in Dallas, so there we were. The coaches had picked up some girls in a country-western club and they were bringing them back to the motel. So, Frank's sitting there, and he said, "*Look, here comes the coaches, and man, they got dates, too.*"

Most of the coaches were married, so Frank goes, "*Watch this.*"

He takes off all his clothes. Now this isn't like an inside motel. It's got an outside walkway. So he takes off walking with no clothes on. Here's Frank, six-five, and he walks up to the coach and their girls with no clothes on. The girls go, "*Oh, my gosh.*"

They're all just kind of looking at him. Frank goes, "*Hi, coach!*" And he just kept on walking. Well, the girls turned around and split.

Marie Neece:

In January 1970, I quit my job in San Antonio and moved to Midland with Frank. For some reason (which shouldn't be too hard to figure out), he didn't want us to live in Odessa. Frank started working for the Midland Reporter-Telegram as a sports writer, while I did substitute teaching until I could get a full-time teaching position. Frank continued to go to the gym in Odessa (Odessa is 20 miles from

Midland) every night.

That summer [1970], he finally got the big break he had wanted for so long. One of his coaches—I don't remember which one—sent a tape of Frank to the Washington Redskins, and they invited Frank to their training camp, so I packed his clothes and took him to the airport.

Dan Cook:

He tried out at summer camp at a bad time. It was too close to the regular season when most squads were pretty well set.

Leo Sykes:

He got into some kind of trouble out there. This is all hearsay, but the story goes that he was arrested out there on the practice field because there was a girl that was found dead. I think Frank was the last one she was seen with. I don't think anything ever stuck with that, but Bill Austin was the coach there and he didn't put up with any of that.

Marie Neece:

All the girls loved Frank. He was handsome, charming, witty, and he had a great body, so I couldn't blame them, but they chased and called him at home all the time. That was hard on me and on our marriage.

Unfortunately for Frank, or maybe for both of us, after he left [for Washington], I found out a lot more about the "other" life he had in Odessa and Midland. I decided it wasn't going to bother him at all if I filed for a divorce, so I did.

When he called me from training camp and I told him what I was going to do, he said he'd never give me a divorce. That wasn't the reaction I expected, but by then, it was way too late, and I was way too mad to reconsider. A few days after that, he was either cut from the team or he quit. I was never sure which.

Marc Allen:

After his chance to play for the Redskins, he played for the Fort Worth team, back in the Continental League.

Marie Neece:

I convinced him to go by my lawyer's office to sign the papers. Eventually, he did, and I went to court on October 12, 1970. Frank didn't show up, but I hadn't expected him to be there. Looking back, even our divorce was funny. My lawyer kept telling the judge funny things about Frank. He had even charmed my lawyer! Anyway, the divorce was quick because we had no children, no community property, and nothing of importance. So after nearly five years of having Frank in my life, he was gone.

Fred Ekmark:

Frank worked as a bouncer in a Mexican nightclub there in San Antonio for a short time. He worked on the freight docks in Dallas for a time, too.

Jerry [Jones] and I were at the pool at our apartment complex in San Antonio. Frank was throwing all the poolside furniture into the swimming pool. This was really early in the morning, like two a.m. or something. A manager came out. She was an old gal, probably about forty or so, and she goes, "*You think that's funny?*"

And Frank says, "*Yep.*"

Jerry Jones said something to him and then just pushed her right into the swimming pool. That was another time when I said to myself, "*Time to go.*"

Bill Lehman:

After Frank got out of football, he dissipated, shall we say, for a while. He kind of let himself go, physically, and then he met a guy by the name of Ivan Putski—Joe Bednarski. Joe Bed had also played for the Toros, but then the Toros let him go. Man, that guy was so strong. His arms were so big he could hardly pick 'em up to catch a pass. Joe got Frank working out again. Frank was working for a newspaper, writing sports articles and so forth. Anyway, Ivan really got him working out. He also got him on steroids. Frank had a big frame. He was about 6-foot-6 and he got going on steroids. Of course, if you got working out with Joe Bed, you were usually serious about what you were doing, because he was serious about it. Frank got to be about 310 to 315 pounds.

Marie Neece:

Joe [Bednarski] and Frank were good friends, and both of them loved fried liver. I was a lousy cook (and still am), but once a week, Joe would come over and I'd cook liver and onions for them. The reason I mentioned this is because Joe was probably the one most responsible for getting Frank into wrestling.

Ivan Putski:

Yeah, that's right. She [Marie] used to make us liver. We'd work out and I'd go over to his house, and she'd fix us a bite to eat. What a sweet lady.

I was just getting into the business, and I was always telling Frank he could make some money in professional wrestling. I think he was working unloading trucks or something like that. The Toros had folded and he was just working some old job.

Bill Lehman:

Frank got that killer instinct later on. You know, when you take steroids, it changes your personality. A lot of guys aren't even the same guy. I don't think Frank was exactly the same guy later. I liked the guy. I put him over in Louisiana and I thought he was a great guy. He could have worked a little harder at football. I don't think he worked as hard as he could have worked. He did have a couple of neck injuries and I think the neck injuries are probably one of the reasons he decided to go into wrestling.

Bruiser Brody
Wrestling Exchange magazine, July 1980:

A friend of mine who also played football was wrestling—Walter Johnson. Still wrestles, in Detroit and all up there. I got to visiting with him about it, and he got me interested. Through him I met some other people, and got started wrestling.

Not one of Frank Goodish's football friends and associates had heard of Walter Johnson, but Johnson did play football. In fact, he was an All-Pro defensive lineman for the Cleveland Browns from 1965-1971. Johnson was also a wrestler, based primarily in Detroit. He passed away on June 29, 1999, at the age of 56.

Chapter IV Jimmy Hoffa

Frank Goodish had gone to wrestling shows on Thursday nights in Amarillo while he was attending West Texas State. He knew Terry Funk, who was both a football player and a wrestler. While Frank may have had an opportunity in the wrestling world, football was his love. It wasn't until he realized that he just couldn't make it on the gridiron that he traded in his football helmet and shoulder pads for a pair of wrestling boots and trunks.

Texas promoter Joe Blanchard and former NWA World Heavyweight Champion Dory Funk Jr. in 2005.

Frank's start in the business was rough and controversial. His first "trainer," Joe Blanchard, didn't like him and didn't want him. He soon found a mentor and lifelong friend in Dallas, Texas—Fritz von Erich. Fritz not only gave Goodish a chance in his promotion, but he sent Goodish all over the world to learn and perfect his craft.

Dory Funk Jr.:

Back in those days, the professional wrestler's income levels were right on a level with the pro football players. So, if a kid came out of [college] and signed a contract for $15,000 to play pro football … well, that wasn't uncommon at all in the wrestling business. In fact, there were bigger matches worth more than that. Much more than that. So, at that time, the wrestling business was a very good business to be in, and Brody chose wrestling.

Marie Neece:

One weekend in 1972, I drove down to San Antonio to see old friends from my Frank days. Bill Grindle called Frank and told him I was there and he came over. He had moved back to San Antonio. At that time, I believe Frank was doing some manual labor again, unloading trucks full of frozen meat or something and trying to get into wrestling. I remember asking him what he was doing and he said he was retired. He said he wanted to retire while he was young and then work when he got older. It sounded just like the Frank I had always known. Anyway, Joe Bednarski had gotten into wrestling after he found out how little money teachers made in Texas. Joe had been an elementary P.E. teacher, but with a wife and four or five daughters, he needed something that paid better. So he was helping Frank get into the "sport." Marc [Allen] and a couple of others knew some wrestlers and promoters, too, but I think Joe was the main one who gave Frank the most help.

Dirty Dan the Barbell Man:

I taught Frank his first wrestling holds. I taught him how to bodyslam. When I was a kid, I wrestled amateur in the Navy, but I was always interested in that professional wrestling. I'd go watch it. I knew how to bodyslam and apply armlocks, and I passed that on to Frank.

In the early '70s, the National Wrestling Alliance [NWA] was the strongest wrestling organization in the world. The NWA was a collective of wrestling promotions operating in the United States, Japan, South Korea, the Dominican Republic, Australia, New Zealand, and Mexico. They promoted a single champion, the NWA World heavyweight champion, who traveled from territory to territory defending his title.

Joe Blanchard, who promoted professional wrestling in San Antonio, Austin, Corpus Christi, and Victoria, Texas, worked with Dallas promoter Fritz von Erich from the early '70s until 1985. Sometime during the beginning of his tenure, he met Frank Goodish.

Joe Blanchard (wrestling promoter):

I hung around with the Toros players, but I don't really remember how I met Frank. I think it was through Bednarski.

Ivan Putski.

Leo Sykes:

Joe [Blanchard] started a wrestling promotion here in Texas and started us all. He's a great man. He's a tough man, a real man. We would spend one hour at the gym and three hours practicing our ring work. People thought what we were doing was show business, but they were never quite sure. Blanchard worked the shit out of me for about a year before anybody told me it was show business.

Bill Lehman:

Joe Blanchard had broke in myself and Ivan Putski. He trained us.

Ivan Putski:

I was sent to work for Leroy McGuirk and Bill Watts in Oklahoma by Joe Blanchard. Joe broke me in. Anyway, when I got back, I was working in Dallas one night and there he was. Frank showed up at one of the matches. I had tried to get him into the business, and then he just showed up. I introduced him around the dressing room and that's how he started.

Stan Hansen:

Later on, when I was in wrestling, I went down to Dallas. Amarillo had sent me down there for a couple of weeks to go around. Red Bastien was the booker, and Bronco Lubich was there, and he says, "*You know, there's another kid here that's trying to break in. He went to West Texas, too.*"

I was going, "*Who's that?*" and he says, "*Frank Goodish.*"

And I said, "*Frank? You mean that wild, crazy guy?*"

And he's going, "*No, this guy's the nicest, quietest guy.*"

And I said, "*No, no. Frank Goodish, man. He's the one.*"

I started going off a little about what he did at West Texas, a bunch of these stories, and Bronco goes, "*No, this guy's different. He's the most polite ...*" How he's calm and everything. "*He's over in the other dressing room. Let's go over there.*"

I said, "*All right.*"

I went over there and we go in, and Brody was like 6-foot-4, but when he played at West Texas, he was about 220. Now he's like 300. He's really bulked up. This is maybe four or five years later. So, here's this big guy and he's got this big curly hair, and the big beard and everything, and I went, "*Hey! gollee!*" and all this other stuff. I went to shake hands and I say, "*I was telling them how crazy you are,*" but he just doesn't say anything except, "*Yeah, good to see you.*"

Finally Bronco leaves and he says, "*Hey, man. Be quiet. I'm trying to get into the business and I don't want them to know about all this stuff.*"

He was just trying to get into the business with Fritz [von Erich] and them.

Bill Lehman:

Joe Blanchard didn't want to train Frank because he and Frank didn't hit it off. He didn't care for Frank a whole lot.

Joe Blanchard:

Frank and I weren't friends or anything, but he worked for me some. He started with me for a while, had a couple of matches, and Fritz finished it off.

Frtiz Von Erich.

Bill Lehman:

Joe Blanchard really wanted you to have a lot of intensity as far as the wrestling business. Before he brought anybody into the business, he wanted to make sure they were serious, that they were dedicated. He just didn't think Frank was in that realm. Fritz felt differently and really broke him in.

John Dananay (wrestling author):

Brody came into the Dallas area in 1974 when World Class Championship Wrestling was still known as Big Time Wrestling. He was introduced to fans in the area as "the fan in the seats."

Red Bastien (wrestler, booker):

I was doing the matchmaking in Dallas, Texas, and I matched Frank up in a match there at the [Dallas] Sportatorium. When we get new guys coming into the business, we all check them out, you know. I looked at him and I said, "*This guy is going to be somebody to reckon with. No doubt about it.*"

Bob Roop issued an open challenge to everybody in the audience. If anybody could stay with him for ten minutes, they would win $5,000. A large man in the audience stepped up and accepted the challenge. The following week in Fort Worth, Texas, April 29, 1974, Frank Goodish and Bob Roop wrestled in a special Lights Out Match. Goodish lost.

Fort Worth, Texas: April 29, 1974
Blackjack Mulligan beat Black Angus
Red Bastien and Ken Patera beat Blackjack Lanza and Roger Kirby
The Great Mephisto (Frankie Cain) drew with Jose Lothario
Bob Orton Jr. beat Pierre Martin
Bob Roop beat Doug Somers
Special Challenge, Lights Out Match: Bob Roop beat Frank Goodish
Referees: Danny Plechas, Bronco Lubich

Bob Roop (wrestler):

Frank had his first match with me and it was in Fritz von Erich's territory. He was being trained by "Bulldog" Danny Plechas and Bronco Lubich. I don't know who they had to take bumps because Plechas and Lubich were both older guys, but they were the trainers. A week before that first match, I went down to where he was being trained. I never got into the ring. We just talked over the match. That night, we did a simple thing where he was heckling me from ringside as a fan. He was very noticeable, so I got on him. I don't remember if he challenged me or if I challenged him. I think I challenged him and he accepted. We made a match right there. They didn't overdo it. They must have videotaped it, showed it on their TV show, and made the match. I did an interview about, "*This punk from the audience,*" and all that.

Bob Roop.

Bob Orton Jr. (wrestler):

I helped break him in. Ivan Putski had got him into weights and they got me down to work out with Frank in the Sportatorium. They asked me to teach him a little about the ring, and how to take bumps.

Bob Roop:

It's interesting that it was a Lights Out Match, being it was his first match. A Lights Out Match is a match that takes place after the regular card. After the last match ends, they turn the arena lights off for a few seconds, which signifies the fact that the regular card is over. That means the match that takes place when the lights are turned back on is not sanctioned by any governing body, so anything goes. In essence, there are no rules. If somebody is dismembered and put through a meat grinder, there won't be any charges filed, and the so-called commission won't have anything to say about it. What's interesting about the fact that they used a Lights Out Match for us is the fact that a Lights Out Match was normally used to end a long feud between two wrestlers.

My first match was the first match on the card, working with an experienced pro who led me through it. But Frank was different. He had a great body, he was very impressive looking, and he was much bigger when he started than when he died. He was thicker and his legs were enormous.

Frank Goodish wrestles Fritz von Erich.

The Von Erich Family. From left, Kerry, David, Fritz, Mike, Chris, Kevin.

I really don't remember much about the match itself. You know what? The fact that I don't remember the match means that he was very, very good. I remember the bad matches. I was also young and in shape, and I knew he wasn't going to try and hurt me.

Ivan Putski:

Fritz von Erich saw the potential in Frank. And really, he saw dollar signs in Frank. Fritz was the main guy you wanted to talk to in this area. That's why I took him to Fritz. There was Paul Boesch in Houston, while Joe Blanchard had San Antonio and Corpus Christi, but Fritz was really the main man down here. He had Dallas and Fort Worth.

The Dallas territory was run by Fritz von Erich (or Jack Adkisson if you must), a former Nazi villain, who "crushed" his opponents foreheads with his dreaded Iron Claw hold. Fritz had six sons, five of which wrestled for the promotion. The Von Erich family was at one time one of the most beloved families in Dallas, and possibly one of the most tragic.

John Dananay:

They [Von Erichs] were a family who portrayed themselves as heroes, God fearing, athletic jocks, who stood for all the right causes and fought those who did not. Outside the ring, they were a tight-knit group of country boys who at times had a hard time dealing with all of their successes at an early age. As a fan of theirs, I am a little biased, but I feel people try to create stories about the family because, to be brutally honest, other than Kevin, no one is left to defend themselves.

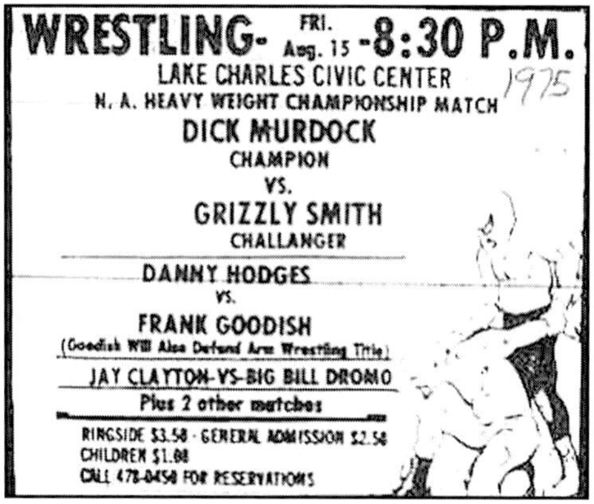

Fritz's sons, Kerry, Mike, and Chris, eventually committed suicide. David, the best wrestler of the bunch, died under mysterious circumstances while touring Japan with Brody in 1984.

John Dananay:

Brody had stated that Fritz was one of the few promoters that he trusted, and he would always return to the Dallas area whenever Fritz needed him. Brody was also very close to the Adkisson boys, especially David. Brody cried openly during the news footage shown of David's funeral.

Kevin von Erich (wrestler):

He [Frank] was like family. He was always there. I miss him a lot.

Marie Neece:

After Frank and I met at Bill's house, we started our relationship all over again, but once again, we lived in different cities and had another long distance romance. He wrote to me nearly every day. Frank came to see me in Dallas and took me to meet some of his friends (he had friends everywhere), and introduced me as his wife, just as though the divorce had never happened. Frank and I talked about what kind of name he should use in wrestling, and we came up with all sorts of good ones. I thought he'd be a really good "bad guy," so I suggested he grow a beard and let his hair grow out … get it good and bushy. I think by then, he had already started to let it grow out.

Frank and Joe [Bednarski] came by my apartment one day to visit before they both wrestled that night, but I never went to any of the wrestling matches they had in Dallas. It was too new to Frank, and I don't think he wanted me to be there to see him, so I didn't go. Besides, I had never been to a wrestling match, and he thought I'd feel uncomfortable or something. Joe and Frank would go to a cafeteria and both of them would get two trays full of food.

Those boys could eat! Our relationship continued in Dallas until I took another job and moved back to West Texas.

Ivan Putski:

Frank used to drive from his house in San Antonio to my house in Austin, and he'd leave his car there and go with me to Dallas, and we'd do the rounds for Fritz. Shortly after Frank started, I left to work for Verne Gagne in Minneapolis for a year, and then got the call from McMahon in New York. The next time I saw Frank was in the WWWF [World Wide Wrestling Federation].

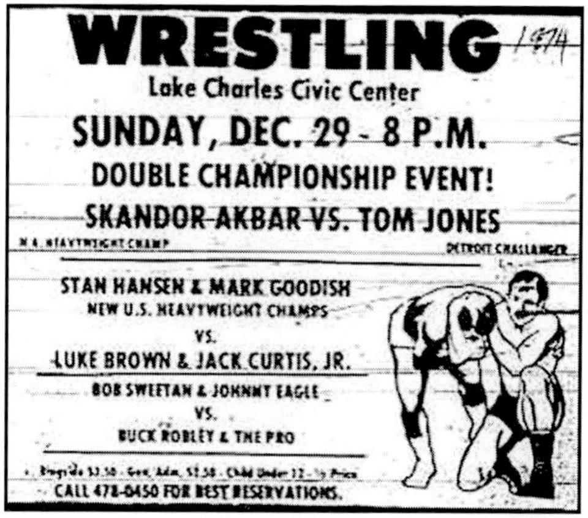

Even with the United States Tag Team title around his waist, the promotion still messed up his first name.

Dory Funk Jr.:

I know about World Class Wrestling. I know about Fritz's Dallas territory. There wasn't a lot of control by the office over the wrestlers. It was a huge territory when it was doing business. If they had a strong piece of talent, the whole territory did well and they drew money, but it had to be a piece of talent that could get over in Houston, Dallas, and San Antonio. If they didn't have strong talent that could get over in all three places, their business would go down. Wahoo McDaniel, Johnny Valentine, Bruiser Brody—during the times those people were there, they drew money and the territory did well.

Frank was quickly becoming a strong piece of talent. Fritz von Erich promoted good wrestling, and at that time, really left the storylines up to his wrestlers. Frank seemed to have a flair for it and flourished, and really came into his own under Fritz. Within a year, Fritz was booking him with promoters all over the country.

General Scandor Akbar (wrestler, manager):

He broke into the business himself. He just started having matches and working out with the boys. He was still green when he came to Louisiana, but he started learning rapidly.

Leroy McGuirk controlled Oklahoma, Louisiana, and Arkansas for the NWA. He also had power over the NWA's Junior heavyweight belt. McGuirk was the NCAA amateur wrestling champion for Oklahoma State in 1931 and wrestled professionally until he lost his eyesight and turned to promoting in the 1950s.

McGuirk's longtime booker for many years was Bill Watts. Watts was an incredible booker who could create storylines that brought the audience to a fever pitch. Even when the match was over, the audience was oftentimes so involved in the story that they would attack the heel wrestlers, and even carried their feelings into the parking lot.

General Scandor Akbar:

Before Frank started with us, he was working at Doug's Gym in downtown Dallas. That's where I first met him. The local promotion in Dallas gave him a shot. Red Bastien was the booker at that time for the Dallas office. We broke Frank in here [Louisiana] after Bill [Watts] had gone to Florida in late 1974 for a short time. Grizzly Smith was the booker for McGuirk until Bill got back.

When I asked Frank, he said, "*Oh, man, I'm all right. I've already got $3,000 saved.*"

I told Grizz, "*He's okay.*"

Frank knew how to pinch those pennies. He could leave home with a hundred dollars in his pocket and come back a week later with a hundred and ten.

Bill Lehman:

Frank went down to Louisiana, which is the territory where he really started out. I was over pretty well already, and they did the thing where he was sitting in the audience, watching the matches. After that, I had a match with him and I put him over.

Above and Right: Frank Goodish and Stan Hansen began teaming in the Mid-South territory. In the photograph on the right, the team has the NWA United States Tag Team belts.

General Scandor Akbar:

In 1974, when he first came down to Louisiana, Frank was living in the Baton Rouge, New Orleans area. We were running three and four towns a night. It was the biggest territory in the nation. There were towns down south, but Frank was only working three or four days a week. One day, when Grizzly Smith and I were on a trip, Griz says, "*You know Ak. I just wonder if Frank is doing all right. He's not making that much money right now.*"

I said, "*Well, I'll ask him.*"

Joyce Grable (lady wrestler):

We was in Louisiana in a mixed tag team match. It was Frank and myself. Donna Christantello was the other girl, but I can't remember who the guy was. Can you imagine someone that tall being teamed up with someone as short as I am, and he had absolutely no idea what to do? It was so weird. It was one of the worst mixed tags I ever had, but I had fun. Until the day he died, every time he saw me, he talked about it. He turned out to be a great wrestler.

Sir Oliver Humperdink:

I first met him in the Mid-South area. Frank had just started, and then later, when I was a manager in Florida … I was sort of the territorial manager there, and when any big name came in from outside the territory, like Brody always did, they'd put him with me. I'd be his manager.

Bruno Sammartino (wrestler):

Bill Watts was always high on the huge college football guys getting into the business.

Stan Hansen:

I went to Louisiana, and after I was there … not too long, a couple of months maybe, then they … or maybe Brody was already there. I can't remember, but Fritz had sent him over to work for Leroy McGuirk, and we knew each other, and that's how we slowly got together.

Dave Meltzer:

They were a tag team as Stan Hansen and Frank Goodish at that time. U.S. tag team champions in the Oklahoma circuit for Leroy McGuirk, the Louisiana and Oklahoma territory. Their paths didn't cross after they left that territory for years and years, and then they were in Japan together.

In October 1974, Frank Goodish and Stan Hansen beat Johnny Eagles and Terry Latham to win the NWA United States tag team title. They held the title for a little more than eight months before dropping the belts to Danny Hodge and Jay Clayton on July 9, 1975 in Fort Smith, Arkansas.

Goodish, Hansen, and their manager, Buck Robeley.

Killer Karl Kox (wrestler):

Bruiser Brody went through a spell where he was eating a lot of tuna fish. When Jimmy Hoffa went missing, Brody, Stan Hansen, and I were at the TV station in Shreveport, Louisiana. I walked up to Brody and said, "*They found Jimmy Hoffa today.*"

He said, "*Where?*"

I said, "*In cans of tuna fish.*"

Hansen went crazy, but Brody didn't think it was too funny.

Larry Matysik:

When those three [Brody, Stan Hansen, and John Studd] broke in together, they called them the Blue Jays. John Studd, who was John Minton, Stan Hansen, and Frank Goodish. Someone explained why they had that nickname, but it didn't stick in my head.

"Cowboy" Bill Watts.

Bill Watts (wrestler, promoter):

Most wrestlers don't have a clue. About six or seven months after I started promoting, a dear friend of mine, who was a star, came to me and said, "*Oh, my gosh, Bill. I'm really worried about you. You've just been a promoter for a short time and you've become like them.*"

And I said, "*No, it's not that.*"

He said, "*Then what is it?*"

I said, "*I found out what assholes all you wrestlers are.*"

I was just dying laughing. I thought, "*You dumb son of a bitch. I haven't changed any. I'm in the business, but if I don't have a bottom line, I'm not here, and if I'm not here, where are you going to work?*"

I worked with Brody, but I never worked with him again after he left me and he developed this … what I call, aberration in attitude. I used Stan Hansen all the time because Hansen was reliable. You had to have a trust and reliability, or else you couldn't promote. Brody was a whore.

Tony Atlas:

That's what he said about Brody? Brody stepped on a lot of toes. What Bill [Watts] means by a whore is that Brody had no loyalty to anybody. For instance, if you work for a company, you're married to that company. It's like a marriage. So, when you cheat on that company, you're whoring around. Like Brody would get himself booked for Inoki in Japan. Then a week before his tour was up, he would switch up at the end of the tour and go work for Baba. That's kind of like me working for Vince McMahon, and the next night, I'm working on the WCW show. People put Brody over strong, and in return, they were looking for loyalty from Brody, but all the sudden, Brody is working for the guys that are trying to put them out of business. He was so big and strong nobody would challenge him.

Bill Watts:

A wrestler doesn't understand everything that goes into being a promoter. The wrestler doesn't have the investment. He doesn't have to do the television production. He doesn't have to hire the venue. They haven't got a clue. All they do is look at the crowd and say, "I oughta get this, this, this, and this." They don't have a clue what it takes to break even. Like Dusty [Rhodes], every territory he was in that he had very much control, he bankrupted. He had no fiscal responsibility. It's hard to have that if you're not on both sides of it. Fortunately, for me, I was on both sides. Yes, I think there were promoters that would screw you, but they're going to try and pay you as little as they can and try to keep you happy. That's just called business. The bottom line is that they're the ones who had to stay in business. Without them, we had no place to go show our wares.

Brody became a folk hero to certain folks who admired this attitude in him, but these folks don't have any concept of business, either. It's just bullshit how people get caught up in stuff like this. A lot of people looked at Brody like a folk hero. It's a lot like the little guy mad at his boss. Well, then Brody was his hero.

The funny thing is, Frank thought he was a big tough guy. I was so tickled. He'd flex and all that stuff. He and Stan were against Danny Hodge and me in a tag team match in … I think it was Fort Smith, Arkansas. Hodge only weighed 220 to 225, but when Brody did something in the ring that displeased Hodge, Hodge just stretched the shit out of him. Hodge just ate his ass alive. He had Brody screaming. After the match, I said, "*Gosh, Frank. Why didn't you just jump up and flex and show him your muscles.*"

He said, "*Shit! He was killing me.*"

I said, "*See, Frank. You can't wrestle, so you gotta be careful when you're in there with someone who can. You're not impressive. You're a big blowhard as long as you're on your feet, but once you're off your feet, you're helpless.*"

Of course, Hansen saw it real quick. He got it. But Frank was kind of amazed. "*Look at him, and then look at me,*" he said.

"*Yeah, but you're the one on the mat getting your ass whipped.*"

But Frank took it well. Still, at that age, you had the chance to form some things with him that made some sense.

Splitting up Frank and Hansen was the best thing that ever happened to them, and they both told me that later. Hansen became a big star before Brody did, but eventually, Brody became a star, too. They were just at a point where they were entertaining each other in their tag matches and there was no growth. They were intimidating to the average guy out there; and they were both big and tough. I don't mean Brody wasn't tough. Hodge took a lot of guys apart that were tough. They just weren't tough when it came to Hodge. Everything is relative. So, it was a dramatic turning point in their careers when I split them up.

In 1975, Fritz von Erich sent Frank Goodish to Amarillo, Texas. Amarillo, and West Texas in general,

Frank "The Hammer" Goodish arrives in Amarillo, Texas.

was Funk country. Dory Funk Sr. began promoting in Amarillo in the 1950s. He had two sons: Dory Jr., who held the NWA World heavyweight title from February 11, 1969 to May 24, 1973, and Terry, who would win that title on December 10, 1975.

Dory Funk Jr.:

He was beginning as a professional wrestler at that time. Still very big, still very strong, still quite green—to use a wrestling term—as all wrestlers are who are in their first year or so. He matured fast and learned the business fast.

Bobby Jaggers (wrestler):

When I got in the ring with Frank, I knew he wasn't going to hurt me. I was going to hit him as hard as he hit me. That was the way it was with the Funks. If you weren't a man, you didn't deserve the check. If you didn't expect to get hurt, you didn't belong in the ring. If I had a dollar for every time I got my eye or my lip busted open, man, I'd be rich. It's called wrestling, not dancing!

Tony Atlas:

I remember when I first met him in Amarillo, Texas, when I was working for Dory Funk. I was sitting at a table and the guys saw me. A wrestler named Sputnik Monroe says, "*Oh, just wait until Brody sees this one.*"

He was talkin' about blacks. Sputnik says, "*I bet you he'll want to slap this one around.*"

When Brody walked into the dressing room, I remember he stopped right at the door. I caught his eye. He caught my eye. I started eating, but we didn't take our eyes off each other. The guys were saying things to him, teasing him, until he finally just got up and left. His face was bright red. Brody knew, even if he had whooped me, it was going to be a headache for him. He used to stare at me in the gym. I used to bench press 550 in the ring. Brody seen it many times. I did 550 in the ring, and I'd do it three times. That's the only reason … if it wasn't for my strength, yes, me and him woulda hooked up that first day. My strength protected me through the years.

Bobby Jaggers:

We were in Odessa, Texas. This was when Frank and I first got to know each other. Frank and I were sharing a room, staying over in Midland [Texas]. We had just finished wrestling in Odessa at the Hector County Coliseum. Frank really ate big meals at night. He wanted to get up to 300 pounds to better his chances of getting into New York [the WWWF]. That was the big joke. I don't eat before I go to sleep, but I used to drink a lot of beer after the matches. So, we went out that night. I was driving a Corvette at the time. I said, "*Let's go get some beer,*" and he says, "*Well, I got to eat. I got to eat before I go to sleep.*"

We went to a liquor store and I got some beer. While we drove around and drank our beer, he said, "*There's a Waffle House.*"

Well, hell. Frank ordered this great big, humongous dinner—eggs, steak, and waffles. I asked the waitress if she'd mind if I went out to my car and got a beer, so she gave me a plastic cup. While Frank was eating, I drank my beer. Well, there were two guys and two girls in a booth right behind Frank. We're sitting there, minding our own business. I was giving Frank shit. "*Damn, Frank. How can you eat all that food?*"

I'm sitting there drinking beer. I had just done this angle on TV with Dory Funk and it had just aired. This girl behind Frank is telling one of the guys, "*Hey, get me his autograph.*"

I had blonde hair and Frank had straight, black hair. He hadn't even curled it yet. I was trying to ignore the girl. All of a sudden, the guy gets real loud, saying, "*You want this fake son-of-a-bitch's autograph!*"

About that time, I made a second trip outside to fill my plastic cup with beer. When I came back and sat down, one of the guys walks over and throws a piece of paper and pencil down. The pencil lands in my lap and the paper lands in Frank's food. The guy goes, "*My girlfriend wants your fucking autograph. She thinks your fake shit is real.*"

I look over at Frank and I see that he's burning. I said to the guy, "*Let me tell you something. You take this pencil and jam it up your ass.*"

I take both the paper and the pencil and hand it back to him. The son-of-a-bitch gets this angry look on his face, throws down the paper and pencil, and walks out of the Waffle House with his buddy, leaving the two girls in the booth. Me

and Frank are laughing about it. All of the sudden, one of the girls taps Frank on his shoulder and says, "*Sir, I hate to tell you this, but I think he's going out to his car to get a gun.*"

Me and Frank, we took off out of that Waffle House at a hundred miles an hour. When we get outside, they had the key in the trunk of an old Ford Torino and were getting ready to open it. Just before they opened the trunk, Frank and I hit those sons-of-bitches, like football tackles. We beat the shit out of them. Remember, back in those days, most of the Waffle House restaurants were adjacent to Days Inn motels. We beat these guys so bad that they ran, hopped a fence, and landed in the swimming pool. Well, when they did that, the swimming pool started turning red with the blood from their cuts. When we went back into the Waffle House to pay our bill, those poor girls said, "*We're sorry. We didn't want to be with those guys, but we really need a ride home.*" So, we had to take those girls home.

Gordon Grice (wrestling author):

When Frank "The Hammer" Goodish arrived in Amarillo in 1975, one year into a career that would become legendary, he made an immediate impact. As he crushed prelim wrestlers on TV, he exuded incredible animal intensity. He was immediately booked into a feud with Terry Funk. Behind the scenes, Funk and Goodish were close friends from their days in West Texas State University football. In the storyline, Funk was a beloved local hero, Goodish a maniacal heel out to hurt somebody. Goodish cracked Funk's ribs with a bearhug, but Funk escaped without losing his International title.

And with his push barely begun, Goodish was just as quickly finished as a top-tier player in Amarillo. The Super Destroyer, played by booker Art Nelson, undercut Goodish's image by using the same finisher, the bearhug, and beating Funk with it for the International title. That result immediately cast Goodish in the role of secondary heel.

Nelson had been overshadowed in the Mid-Atlantic territory by an agile, young giant named Don Jardine, often known as the Spoiler, but in that territory, he was known as the Super Destroyer. Nelson's first move as booker in Amarillo was to cast himself as the Super Destroyer, in the process, overshadowing another agile young giant, Frank Goodish. Perhaps Nelson saw Goodish as a threat. Perhaps the inexperienced Goodish wasn't yet good enough to work long matches against the Funks. Or perhaps the unpredictability Goodish became known for in other regions showed up here and caused him to be held back. In any event, Goodish's loss of stature seemed an injustice. He already had the aura of danger that made fans both fear him and want to see more of him.

Though he was no longer working at the very top, Goodish was not yet through with the promotion. He was shunted into a feud with Western States champ Ray Candy. At 300 pounds, Candy matched Goodish for size, but he was the underdog. The question for most fans was not whether Goodish would win, but whether Candy would get hurt in the process. Goodish soon wore the gold. On a TV rematch, Goodish once again bear-hugged Candy into submission.

His next major program paired him with Scott

Casey. Casey was a talented, young babyface who was getting a big push. He had wrestled both Pat O'Connor and Terry Funk to draws. His matches with Goodish were David-and-Goliath affairs.

Casey eventually defeated Goodish with a sunset flip to take the belt. Goodish cut a classic promo complaining about the loss. "*Scott Casey had me by the seat of my pants!*" he bellowed. To illustrate his point, he thrust his backside at the camera and grabbed a fistful of his own sweat pants.

Though he was tremendously over, Goodish was suddenly repackaged. He appeared on TV one week with his hair done up in many braids. It looked as if a tarantula had attacked his head. Instead of "The Hammer," he was suddenly "The King of the American Hippies." Nick Roberts, a former wrestler who was filling in as commentator that day, remarked that Goodish was sporting "*an Afro-American look.*" Perhaps the hippie gimmick was meant to stop the cheers Goodish was beginning to get and firm up his status as a heel. To a substantial number of Amarillo fans, a hippie was not a good thing.

In the course of his feud with Casey, Goodish teamed with Super Destroyer. Both were killer heels, but their team became a slapstick routine. They failed to communicate, collided with each other repeatedly, and ended up losing the match. Destroyer philosophically remarked that it was always a mistake to trust a partner. He said he would not be teaming with anyone henceforth, unless money was involved. Once again, Destroyer had undercut Goodish, making him look like a fool.

The obvious follow-up feud between Destroyer

and Goodish didn't take place. They did meet in a Bearhug vs Bearhug match in Lubbock, which Destroyer won.

Goodish was gone from the territory not long afterward and he rarely appeared in Amarillo after that. When he did, he was billed as Bruiser Brody, a name he had picked up in the WWWF. In one memorable 1978 appearance, he tried to collect the $5000 Adrian Adonis offered to any man who could defeat him in under ten minutes. Brody pummeled Adonis with a chair and tossed him around the ring, but Adonis managed to hold on for a time-limit draw. A few years later, when Amarillo hosted the talent from Fritz von Erich's Dallas office, Brody appeared occasionally as a babyface.

Dennis Stamp (wrestler):

I never wrestled Frank in the Mid-South. I came to Amarillo in May of 1976, but I don't remember ever wrestling against him at all. We were both heels. We had a week run in the territory. Davey O'Hannon and another kid were in from New Jersey and they had a big Cadillac or something, so the four of us rode together for the week. Goodish started on me. He didn't know me. He only knew me by reputation, but he was on me. He was riding me, and riding me. I always feel like, if there's a problem, I'm not putting it on anybody else. I'm trapped with these guys in

Below: Frank "The Hammer" Goodish prepares for a match in Florida, 1976. The belt is the NWA Florida Heavyweight Title.

their car. We were staying at the same motels, eating together. We were together all the time. He kept it up, riding me more and more, calling me names like chicken, and stuff like that. When we got back to Amarillo, I couldn't wait to get back to my own car. As soon as we get out of the car, I get right in his face, which, I have to look up to him. I said, "*Listen, you big son of a bitch. I've taken all the fuckin' shit I'm gonna take. You may kick my ass, but we're gonna find out right now!*"

And the mother fucker bent over laughing. He laughed so hard that I couldn't even be mad at him. I start laughing. He says, "*I wondered what you were made of. I was trying to find out if you had any balls!*"

After that, we were friends.

Dory Funk Jr.:

I knew because of his size and awesome ability, he was going somewhere. He was very much what the wrestling business needed … a big, strong, athlete that could let people know that they better think twice before they step into the ring against him. That's part of the appeal of professional wrestling. Even as we step into the ring, we're standing four feet above everyone else, and they're all looking up, so there's awesomeness about being in the ring to the wrestling fans. And if you're six-feet-six inches tall, and 300 pounds, and in shape, that even adds

Above and Right: Frank Goodish gets the squeeze from Thunderbolt Patterson and Rocky Johnson in Florida, 1976.

to the awesomeness. Frank Goodish, as he was known in the Amarillo territory, had all the things it takes to be a great wrestler and money draw in the wrestling business. When he was in the Amarillo territory, before he became Bruiser Brody, he was like somebody that would find himself, and you were sure he would be a success in the business.

In late 1975, Frank was sent to Florida through an arrangement with Fritz von Erich. He worked for Eddie Graham's Championship Wrestling from Florida promotion.

Dusty Rhodes:
Florida was Eddie Graham's territory at that time. My godfather, Eddie, was the smartest man in our industry. I'm talking about the business since I don't know about the outside, because obviously, he killed himself. He was my mentor.

Kevin Sullivan (wrestler, booker):
Eddie Graham was probably one of the smartest promoters of all times. He was one of the greatest finish-men of all times, and he knew talent, and he saw Brody had talent right from the start. Brody had come in from Amarillo because there was a relationship between the Funks and the Grahams.

J Michael Kenyon (wrestling historian):
Within two or three years, Brody had blossomed into his own.

Almost upon arrival, Goodish was given a shot at the NWA Florida heavyweight title. On December 31, 1975, Frank Goodish beat Rocky Johnson for the belt in Tampa. The match only lasted about five minutes, and Johnson had held the title for only one week. Goodish lost the belt to Thunderbolt Patterson in March 1976.

Frankie Cain (wrestler):
Frank and I made a few trips together when he was just starting in the business. He used to love hearing stories about the old-time wrestlers. I would tell him about us making trips in beat-up jalopies on two-lane highways. He would laugh and laugh. He was so enthralled by those stories, even to the point of writing some of them down.

The first time he rode with me, he was wearing ragged sneakers [tennis shoes] with holes in the top. Those shoes looked like they had been run over several times by a semi. At first, I thought it was a rib. I thought, "Nobody wears shoes like that," but Frank did. I was leaving the territory, so one night, as a rib, I stole one of his sneakers and threw it away. Frank was close with a dollar, but I thought that would force him to buy another pair.

When I dropped him off at his motel room, I asked him if he'd like to eat breakfast in the morning at a

place called Mammy's Shanty. They had one hell of a breakfast. He said, "*I would love to go to breakfast with you.*"

When I stopped by his room the next morning, I had one hell of a time waking him up. He stumbled out of the room with that long, unkempt hair hanging down into his eyes. I didn't pay much attention and we went to the restaurant. After we ordered our breakfast, I stood up to go use the bathroom. As I did, I accidentally stepped on his toe. He hollered, "*Oh, my damn toe!*"

When I looked down, I saw that he had a sweat sock on one foot and a dirty, white sneaker on the other. I couldn't believe what I was seeing. I didn't notice it before. I asked him, "*Why do you only have one shoe on?*"

He said, "*Don't you remember? Somebody stole it last night. I didn't want to come in with no shoes on. This way, it looks like I just left one behind.*"

Frankie Cain wrestled professionally as the Great Mephisto.

Frankie Cain:

I knew a guy named Chippy who owned a nightclub called The Bootleg Club. He would tell people at the arena that the wrestlers were going to be at his club that night because they would come down just to look at us. I was going down there with Tarzan Tyler, Dick Murdoch, and Dusty Rhodes. Goodish said, "*Frankie, I want to go with you.*"

The first thing Murdoch and Dusty did when we got there was order beer. Tarzan said, "*We're not drinkin' that bullshit beer. If you're goin' out with me and Frankie, you're gonna drink whiskey.*"

Murdoch and Rhodes loved their beer, but they weren't whiskey drinkers. After four or five drinks, they called it quits and stumbled out to their car, but Frank stayed with us. A lot of the wrestling fans bought him drinks. He was younger than all of us and drank drink-for-drink with us. When I saw him the next morning at the airport, I said, "*How do you feel, Frank? Do you have a hangover?*"

He said, "*No, I feel good.*"

I asked, "*How long have you been drinkin' whiskey?*"

"*Oh, that was my first time.*"

"*Are you ribbin' me?*"

He said, "*No.*"

I said, "*Why did you drink so many?*"

He said, "*Well, hell! They were free, weren't they?*"

The American Dream, Dusty Rhodes.

Roger Kirby (wrestler):

I knew Bruiser Brody when he was just plain, old, Frank Goodish. He was a super, nice guy, but even then, everybody was scared to death of him. He was so big and impressive. If he got below 300 pounds, he would panic. When he came to Florida, I was dating a girl whose sister was seeing Larry Hennig. I was living by myself, and Brody was single at the time, so I had Brody and the two girls come over on Friday.

The girls kept him in the apartment for three days. He just about killed himself, if you know what I mean. He went to the gym on Monday and was down to 290 pounds. He lost 14 pounds during those three days. He panicked. After that, he wouldn't let me get close to him.

Killer Kowalski, 2001.

Killer Kowalski:

I was in Florida for a short time. I would wrestle for the WWWF for a year, and then go on the road for a year. I got a call from Vince McMahon [Sr.]. "*I want you back.*"

I said, "*It's only been two months.*"

He said, "*We need your talent.*"

I said, "*I got a guy down here, a real good guy.*"

He says, "*We'll give him a trial.*"

Nick Bockwinkel:

Mind you, promotion is always looking for talent, and they're always looking for top talent, and they're always looking for talent they feel is of main event stature, and can draw a crowd. Brody was somebody who, on a minimal effort—by that I mean two, three TV shows—was impressive enough to where the people wanted to see him. Anybody that rises up that quick, everyone asks, "*Well, what can they do against so-and-so? What can they do against so-and-so?*" Needless to say, in that short period of time, he became a draw.

Goodish was tremendously over in Florida. Announcer/commentator Gordon Solie helped him by calling Frank's matches as if he were a giant star. Frank didn't stay in Florida very long, though. He had bigger things heading his way.

Dave Meltzer:

Kowalski said they should bring him up because he fit that WWWF mold.

Killer Kowalski:

First, I brought him up to Montreal, and made him a champion there.

Chapter V
Good Cop, Bad Cop

Bruiser Brody made his Madison Square Garden debut against Kevin Sullivan on August 7, 1976.
Right: Bruiser Brody and his manager, The Grand Wizard.

In 1976, Frank Goodish emerged as Bruiser Brody in the World Wide Wrestling Federation. Vince McMahon Sr. had broken away from the NWA in 1963 and still controlled his region in the North-East. His palace was Madison Square Garden in New York City. Most wrestlers then, as they certainly do now, consider wrestling there the pinnacle of a wrestling career. Only three years into his career, Bruiser Brody arrived there, wrestling in the main event. But, like many heels at the time, Brody was put through the WWWF cycle. He started in preliminary matches where he destroyed his opponents all around the territory. He quickly worked his way up the program to wrestle champion Bruno Sammartino. He lost to Bruno in nearly every match, and then he was expected to quietly disappear, or make his way as a member of the WWWF stable.

Brody went through the cycle, but on his way down, he just couldn't accept being a member of the stable. It was in the WWWF preliminary matches that he first worked with Jose Gonzales. The two would later work together in Puerto Rico with tragic results.

Ivan Putski:

I was already there selling out all the arenas when Frank came up. I talked with the old man … you know, McMahon Sr., about Frank when I was there.

Killer Kowalski:

So, he [Goodish] came to WWWF to do a dark match. They were very impressed with him, so they had him come back again, and from there, they hired him. They gave him the name Bruiser Brody.

Stan Hansen:

Brody came in right after me and the two of us, we kind of watched each other's back, and we were definitely the outsiders. We probably were more paranoid then, so looking back, I think if I would've done things a little different, I'd of had a little better relationship with the office, but I didn't.

Brody appeared in a couple of preliminary matches. He made his Madison Square Garden debut against Kevin Sullivan on August 7, 1976. One month later, on September 4, he wrestled for the title.

Kevin Sullivan:

It is the Mecca of all sports. It's Madison Square Garden. It's pretty amazing. I wrestled Brody when I was a young man and it was great. He had just started and he was going to be pushed with Bruno.

On September 4, 1976, Brody

faced WWWF World heavyweight champion Bruno Sammartino for the first time. Brody dominated the match and pinned Sammartino—one, two, three. It looked like the WWWF had a new champion … until the referee discovered Brody had used the ring ropes for leverage while pinning Sammartino. The decision was reversed, Brody was disqualified, and Sammartino kept his title. Bruno got his revenge the next month in Madison Square Garden, beating Brody to a pulp in a Texas Death Match.

Bruno Sammartino:

Frank Goodish, Bruiser Brody, was one of the biggest and strongest young men I ever faced in the ring. He and Stan Hansen were often nervous because they'd arrived at the big show, Madison Square Garden. What happened with Stan breaking my neck, that was legit, but it was because he was nervous for one of his first appearances in the Garden in front of over 22,000 people. He slipped and screwed up a move, and it cost me, breaking my neck. He apologized profusely in the locker room and didn't mean to do it. I understand it was just nervous jitters.

Dave Meltzer:

When he wrested Bruno, he was huge. He was all steroided up, probably like 330 pounds. He was green, but he was the kind of guy they liked to go against Bruno, the big powerful guys.

J Michael Kenyon:

Once Brody showed he could work Madison Square Garden, there was no problem. It was pretty easy.

Brody and Sammartino wrestled in every major city throughout the Northeast. They even had the first cage match ever held at the Nassau Coliseum.

George Napolitano (photographer):

When he was in the WWWF, I used to pick him up at the hotel and drive him out to the Nassau Coliseum. He'd talk about how he was a sportswriter for newspapers out in Texas.

Kevin Sullivan:

I enjoyed being around him. Frank Goodish was a paradox from Bruiser Brody. Frank was a funny, witty, intelligent guy

Killer Kowalski:

You have to learn to talk, to get yourself over to the people, and to the office, too. The WWWF was where he became very good at talking.

Left: Bruiser Brody and WWWF Champion, Bruno Sammartino.

Dick Steinborn (wrestler):

When Invader [Jose Huertas Gonzales] was here in the States wrestling, he was always kidding around, and he would do anything to get on your good side. He was a fairly decent worker.

Dave Meltzer:

It was in that WWWF run that Brody first met Jose Gonzales. They had a match at the Nassau Coliseum, which was probably the start of the whole thing because Gonzales never forgot how that match went in 1976. Brody was a star and Gonzales was a mid-card guy. Brody just didn't give him any offense.

Jose Huertas Gonzales

Tony Atlas:

Brody busted him up real good. He almost tore his lip off. He was really bleeding. Jose just went crazy. When S.D. Jones and me was leaving the arena, Jose was driving his car in circles around the parking lot, yelling out the window. S.D. stopped him and said, "*Man, you've got to get to the hospital.*" While S.D. was driving him to the hospital, Jose said ,"One day, I'm going to kill that son-of-a-bitch." That was in 1976. Twelve years later, he stabbed Brody in the dressing room.

Dave Meltzer:

Gonzales held the grudge for over a decade.

Killer Kowalski:

I was sitting there and Brody walks over to me and he says, "*See this guy? He's responsible for me becoming famous.*" He points at me. "*Thank you very much.*"

George Napolitano:

We used to go eat chicken fried steak and he loved that Tex-Mex style. We'd go out all the time.

Gary Hart:

In the latter part of 1976 and January 1977, while Bruiser Brody was in New York working for Vince McMahon, he called me and inquired about a position in Dallas. I told him that the territory was full and that I could not use him at that time in the way he would want to be used. I told him to give me a call back after six or seven months, which he did.

I believe he really respected me for my honesty. I wasn't the type of guy who would say, "*Yeah, come on in and we'll see what we can do for you.*" I always meant what I said and said what I meant, and when I leveled with him, I think he realized that. I believe that was the beginning of a bond that Bruiser and I had. He knew that he could always come and talk to me about different things, and that I would tell him my true feelings and true beliefs.

Opposite: Bruiser Brody takes on WWWF Champion, Bruno Sammartino.

Dave Meltzer:

Brody wrestled Bruno for a while, but he, Vince McMahon Sr., and Gorilla Monsoon had some problems, and he left the territory. He had a hard time getting work after that big WWWF run.

John Dananay:

Brody was forced out of the WWWF when he had a verbal, near physical dispute with WWWF mainstay Gorilla Monsoon regarding pay.

Not only was Gorilla Monsoon a mainstay in the WWWF, but he was an owner and worked as a booker. Whenever Brody had a dispute with a paycheck, Monsoon refused to deal with him. Brody went to Vince McMahon to resolve the issue. Monsoon, furious that Brody had ignored the chain of command by going over his head, confronted him and fined him. Brody was smart enough to bite his tongue, but the writing was on the wall.

Killer Kowalski:

Three years isn't really that short of a time. He was doing independent shows.

Gary Hart:

After Brody started working for me in 1977, he never left. Sure, he worked in other places, but I was always his booking agent and matchmaker. Even after I left Texas and was working in the Carolinas with the Great Kabuki, he called and asked if I would represent him, even though I was just talent at the time.

Near the end of his WWWF run, Brody was already booking himself out around the various Texas territories. Brody also beat Fritz von Erich for the NWA American heavyweight title in Dallas on January 3, 1977. Shortly after this win, Brody left the WWWF. His last match was a battle royal at the Boston Gardens on February 7, 1977. The next day, he was back working for Fritz von Erich in Dallas and beat Tank Patton to retain the NWA American title. That same night, he won a 12-Man Bodyslam Battle Royal. The following day, February 9, he was back in San Antonio working for Joe Blanchard, defending the NWA American title against Moondog Mayne.

Brody continued to work around Texas for Blanchard, Von Erich, and doing spot shows for Paul Boesch, the NWA promoter in Houston, Texas.

Joe Blanchard:

I know he had latched onto Buck Robley. Buck was always trying to manipulate, maneuver, and steal your towns. I had Robley as a booker for a while and I had to fire him. It was like having an enemy in the camp. I think Robley was here when Frank came through again. I don't know how Robley got here, though.

On April 12, 1977, in Dallas, Fritz von Erich beat Brody and regained the NWA American heavyweight title, only to drop it back to Brody the following night. During April, Brody also wrestled Michigan superstar, The Sheik, in a couple of bloody matches.

In May 1977, Brody and Mike York beat Jose Lothario and Cien Caras for the NWA Texas tag team title. They lost the belts to Gino Hernandez and Jimmy Snuka three months later. Also in May, Brody wrestled NWA World heavyweight champion Harley Race a few times around Texas. They even went to a 60-minute draw a couple of times.

On July 25, 1977, Brody lost the NWA American heavyweight title to John Studd in Dallas.

Even though Brody worked all over the country, his home base was Texas, and he got his bookings from the Dallas wrestling office.

Above: WWWF mainstay Gorilla Monsoon applies a leglock.
Right: Andre the Giant has Bruiser Brody in a bearhug.

Gary Hart:

I was Bruiser's booking agent from 1977 through the '80s. He worked for me throughout Texas, Oklahoma, and Louisiana. He also worked in Minnesota for Verne Gagne, in Indianapolis for Dick the Bruiser, and in St. Louis for Sam Muchnick.

The way we handled that was that Brody would get the dates from the offices outside of the Texas booking office. He would bring them to me and we would discuss which shots he wanted to make and the ones that he didn't. I would then play the role of the bad guy by calling the promoters and say, "*Brody's not available for this, this, and this, but he is available for this, this, and this.*"

I was his matchmaker, booking agent, and sometime-manager for a little more than ten years. I was the guy he depended on to make sure he was taken care of, which I was glad to do because Brody was one of the guys that I could put in any town, in any position, and know that the people would line up to buy tickets. We had a very good relationship.

At that time, he really didn't have a relationship with Fritz. Fritz did not get involved with the day-to-day wrestling. One thing I will say about Fritz. When he hired me as his booker, he stayed out of the way. He did not put his nose into the business.

In August 1977, Gary Hart sent Brody to wrestle in Australia and New Zealand. Brody was there until early October. During the tour, Brody primarily wrestled in six-man tag team matches with his old partner, King Curtis, and an alternating partner. Several times, they faced Sivi Afi, Mark Lewin, and another alternating wrestler. While staying at King's Cross in Australia, Brody also met his future wife, Barbara.

Gary Hart:

Off and on from 1968 to 1973, I had wrestled and managed in Australia, and I knew a guy there named Larry O'Day, who was an underneath guy for the Australian wrestling office. Jim Barnett had sold the promotion to Buddy Fuller and Eddie Graham, but they didn't last too long. When they pulled out, Larry took over the promotion. He had problems getting talent, so he contacted me and asked if I had anyone who might be able to draw money in Australia. Australia wrestling was a lot like wrestling in Texas. It wasn't looked at as sports entertainment. The wrestlers beat the shit out of each other. I told Larry that I had a guy here, Bruiser Brody, who would be perfect for him, as long as he had good, strong opponents.

The good thing about Australia was that it was a country of immigrants, with a large population of Italians, Greeks, and Lebanese. Australia was a lot like New York was with the ethnic guys. Bruno Sammartino appealed to the Italians and Pedro [Morales] drew the Puerto Ricans. One of the big draws in Australia was a guy named Mario Milano, a big rugged Italian who stood 6-foot-4 and weighed about 270 pounds. They also had a Greek by the name of Spiros Arion and a Lebanese named Sheik Wadi Ayoub.

When Bruiser went to Australia, he wrestled those guys and they did fantastic business. He also went to New Zealand for Steve Rickard.

In those days, a round-trip ticket to Australia was right at $4,000, so you had to be something really special to be brought in. If I remember right, I got Brody $732 Australian for his first tour, which was $1,000 a week American, plus a bonus of anything over their weekly average. I think their weekly average at the time was $40,000 to $50,000, so I'm sure that Bruiser bonused every week after the first four or five weeks that he was there. He went back several times after that.

Bruiser met his wife, Barbara, in Sydney. She's originally from New Zealand, but a lot of people from New Zealand move to Sydney or Melbourne because it's a little more cosmopolitan. They both lived in the King's Cross. I remember the first time he came back to the States, he told me that he had met a girl there that he really liked a lot. I said, "*Are you going to bring her here to this country?*"

He said, "*Well, I don't know yet.*"

The next time he went back, I believe when he went from Australia to New Zealand, she went back to New Zealand with him, and he met her family. When he left New Zealand, he brought her back to this country and they got married here.

J.J. Dillon:

My first appearance in Australia was on March 22, 1978. When I first went in, I managed Brute Bernard. They brought Brute in and shipped Bruiser Brody out (you can draw your own conclusions about their perceptions of talent) a couple of weeks after I came in. He [Brody] met his wife, who worked as a receptionist, in Australia. She went to America with him, they got married, and had a family.

Brody's second tour of Australia and New Zealand was in March 1978. While there, he won and lost the World Brass Knucks title. He also injured Bugsy McGraw so badly that McGraw and Mario Milano had to forfeit their NWA Australian tag team title.

On May 28, 1978, Brody beat Dale Valentine [later known as Buddy Roberts] in Houston, Texas to win the NWA Texas heavyweight title. In August, he and Gino Hernandez beat Kevin and David von Erich in Fort Worth to win the Texas tag team title, only to drop the title back to Kevin and David on September 4.

During late August and early September, Brody began traveling and mixing up his Texas bookings with dates in Kansas City and St. Louis. He had several bloody matches against NWA World heavyweight champion Harley Race in St. Louis, Kansas City, and Texas.

On September 10, Brody lost the Texas heavyweight title to David von Erich in Dallas, but the very next day in Fort Worth, he beat Fritz von Erich for the NWA American heavyweight title. On Christmas Day 1978, Kevin von Erich took the American title away from Brody in Fort Worth.

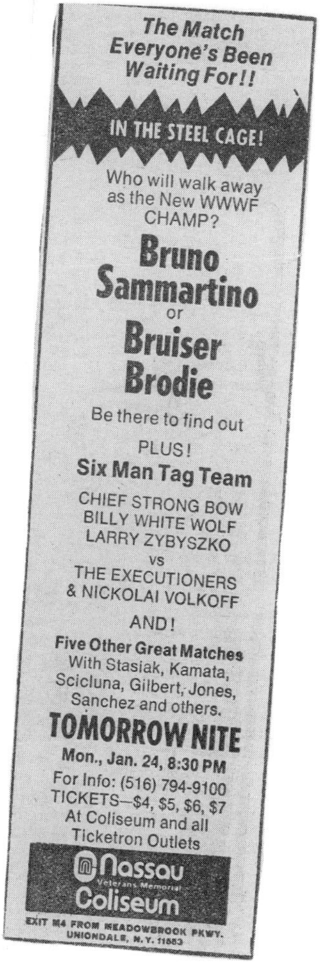

Above: No respect! These promoters just can't get his name right.

Chapter VI The Intelligent Monster

In Japan in the '70s and '80s, two wrestling companies vied for control of the professional wrestling industry—All Japan Pro Wrestling [AJPW] and New Japan Pro Wrestling [NJPW]. All Japan was owned and run by Giant Baba, a 6-foot-10 Japanese behemoth. New Japan was controlled by Antonio Inoki.

Brody became a much bigger star in Japan than he ever would in the United States. Most American wrestlers who toured Japan only did so one or two times a year. Brody went over there several times a year. When he wasn't there, Japanese film crews would come to the U.S. and tape his big matches for broadcast on Japanese television, so Brody was visible to the Japanese public year round. He was both feared and loved in Japan. Photographers followed every move the "Intelligent Monster" made around the country. Merchandise of all types bore his likeness.

Brody started working for All Japan, later unceremoniously jumped to New Japan, and then jumped back. He was such a superstar that almost anything he did in Japan could be forgiven. When he died, the country went into a state of mourning. He was as big as Elvis.

Dave Meltzer:

Brody had worked for Fritz [von Erich] in Dallas and he'd become a real big attraction there. He'd become a big attraction in St. Louis, as well. Fritz and Baba had a good relationship because they had wrestled each other in the '60s and the '70s, and Fritz felt that Brody would be perfect for Japan. When he went to Japan, from day one, they pushed him really hard to be a big star … and he came through. A lot of guys get that opportunity, but it doesn't work out and they fade away. He got over really big.

Brody's first match in Japan was at Korakuen Hall in Tokyo on January 2, 1979. He won a handicap match against Motoshi Okuma and Masao Ito in 5:04.

Dave Meltzer:

Japan had been built forever on the idea that the top big foreigners face the Japanese natives. The Funks in the late '70s became like pseudo-Japanese.

Above: Brody has All-Japan owner and star, Giant Baba, right where he wants him.

They were babyfaces. Mil Mascaras and Destroyer [Dick Beyer] ended up being like that, too, but Brody and Hansen against the Funks [Terry and Dory] became a big money program. It was foreigner versus foreigner and the fans didn't care. It was a great attraction.

In Brody's first televised match in Japan, he and his old Florida tag-team partner, King Curtis Iaukea, wrestled Giant Baba and The Destroyer. Brody was met with silence when he was first tagged in. He wrestled the match in an almost reserved fashion … that is, until the match spilt out of the ring onto the arena floor. From then on, Brody took charge and the thumping and bumping began. He was aggressive and chaotic, and constantly barking, while King Curtis simply watched. Brody really had very little defense in this match. Baba hit him a couple of times, then Brody unleashed an atomic drop, his big knee, and pinned Baba at the 9:50 mark. A new legend was born.

Dick Beyer, the Intelligent, Sensational Destroyer (wrestler):

I don't have anything to say about him. I always thought Frank was an asshole.

Later in the tour, on January 21, 1979, Brody and Baba had a singles match in Osaka.

Gene Lewis:

If you're a success in this business, you're going to spend a lot of time on the road. You're away from home a lot. When you go

to Japan, you're gone for three or four weeks.

Dave Meltzer:

After the first tour, he wouldn't get pinned, and eventually, he was considered an unbeatable monster. That really led to his glory years.

Success was bringing changes. Upon returning to the States from Japan, Brody almost immediately stopped doing jobs for other wrestlers. For Brody to lie down, he had to be sure the storyline eventually put him on top. Sometimes, if he had tremendous respect for his opponent, he would agree to do the job. That was a rare occurrence.

On February 2, 1979, he no-showed a scheduled appearance in St. Louis, something he never would have done in his earlier days.

Another example of his change in attitude was his series in 1979 and 1980, where he won and lost the NWA Texas Brass Knuckles title a number of times. Some of the time, he legitimately dropped the title in a match; but at other times, he simply left the territory.

The first time Brody won the Brass Knuckles title, he took it from Mark Lewin on June 10, 1979, in Dallas. Lewin regained the title on July 22, then dropped it back to Brody a week later. Brody dropped the title to Toru Tanaka the next month, then regained it later in the year. He vacated the title in early December 1979.

Brody returned to Houston to win the title on March 3, 1980, once again from Mark Lewin. He vacated the title once again, then returned on November 14 to beat Stan Stasiak. This time, Brody held onto the title until August 1981, when he left the territory and once again vacated the title without losing it.

Above: Pages from a biography published in Japan.

Brody and Kerry von Erich also won the vacated NWA Texas tag team title in a match against Mark Lewin and Killer Tim Brooks on July 23, 1979. They vacated the title shortly after that when Brody again left the territory.

Gary Hart:

In May 1979, Bruiser had a physical scare. He and

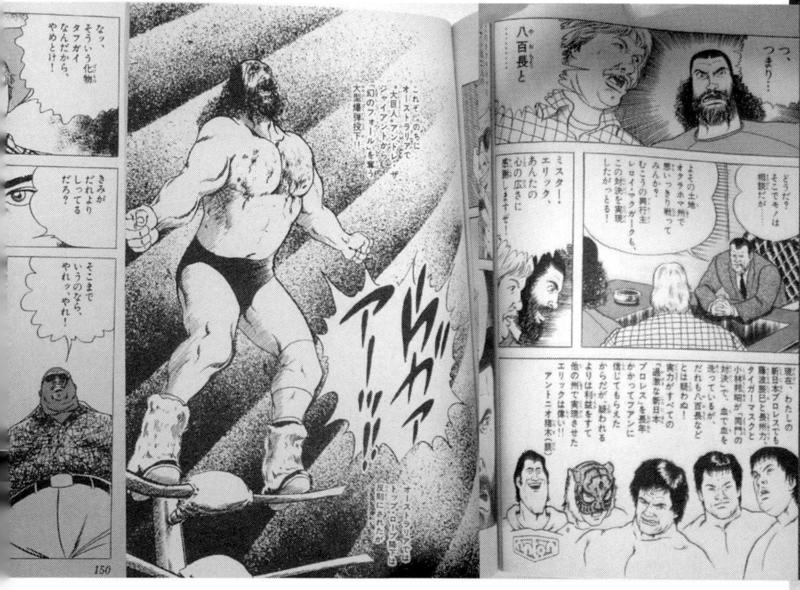

Mark Lewin were training partners. They were really competing heavy on training and they were doing extreme amounts of weight on their legs. Brody went down one day and couldn't get up. He was in the hospital for three or four weeks. He was really hurt, really bad. But, like typical wrestlers, when he got out, we said that Lewin injured him in the gym with a barbell.

Right: A real weight training injury is turned into a storyline. Bruiser Brody vows revenge against Mark Lewin for injuring his knee.

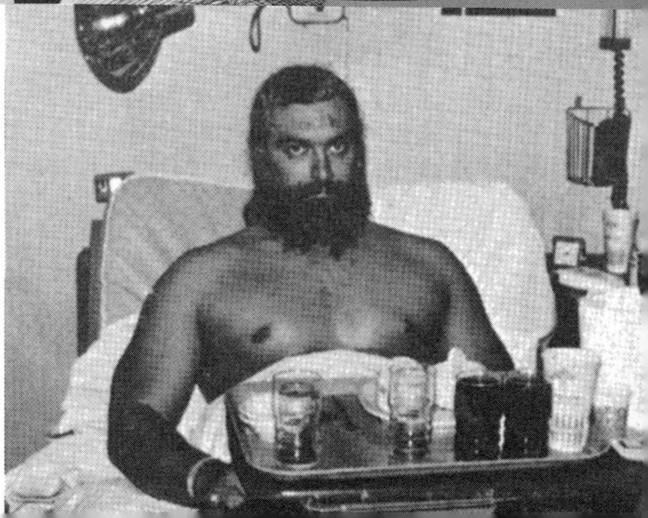

Chapter VII King Kong vs. The Bruiser

Above: King Kong and King Kong pose together for a quick shot, 1976.

Shortly after he returned from his first tour of Japan, "King Kong" Brody made his debut in Indianapolis on March 3, 1979. He had three matches—he won a battle royal and defeated Dutch Savage and Wilbur Snyder.

Indianapolis was run by Dick Afflis—Dick the Bruiser—a cigar-chomping, beer-drinking, gravelly-voiced, fireplug of a man. Afflis was an influential brawler who started his own branch of the Los Angeles' World Wrestling Association [WWA] in Indianapolis in April 1964.

George Napolitano:

He really became known as King Kong Brody later. We were driving past a billboard and he said, "*That should be my gimmick!*"

So I went out and bought the poster of King Kong, and I took the picture of him next to the King Kong poster that he used for his publicity. Then I took some pictures of him with a big gorilla head.

These photographs were taken in 1976. George's story really reflects a very early concept. In fact, WWWF Wrestling program #63, which George Napolitano was the editor of, has a photograph of Brody on the back cover with a caption: "*Bruiser Brody – The man they call "The King Kong of Professional Wrestling" is going all the way to the top in professional wrestling according to his manager, The Grand Wizard.*"

Brody began using the "King Kong" name seriously in St. Louis in July 1978. Dick the Bruiser and Bruiser Bob Sweetan were working in St. Louis and Brody would have just been another Bruiser there. So, when Brody went to work in Dick the Bruiser's own territory, it was pretty clear there would only be one Bruiser in the long run.

Abdullah the Butcher:

See, a lot of promoters try to change you. A lot of promoters say, "*Let me change this guy's name because I made him.*" Sometimes, they try to drag you and change you.

Dory Funk Jr.:

That's not a big deal. I wrestled for Vince McMahon and they changed my name to Hoss Funk. It's not a real change. It's just a nickname. You know I've had more wrestling fans drive me crazy over that, saying, "*Well, why'd you do that?*" It didn't seem to be any big thing at all, but evidently, it was. I don't know why they made him change his name to King Kong Brody.

J Michael Kenyon:

Brody and Dick the Bruiser went back and forth between Indianapolis and St. Louis, fighting over who should be the real Bruiser.

Brody had wrestled Dick the Bruiser before. They had a series of matches in October 1978 in Kansas City.

Dick the Bruiser (wrestler):

(as quoted from a Kansas City program October 1978)

"*I have been the Bruiser for a long time. Once these come-lately bruisers see me, their first thought is to take a powder. All he [Brody] is, is a little bigger than I am, but size means nothing to me.*"

Now, however, Brody was in Dick the Bruiser's territory, and in the end, that would decide who walked away as the real Bruiser.

Dutch Savage (wrestler):

Dick was jealous of Brody and he let Brody know about it from the get-go. He made it known to Brody under no uncertain terms that Dick was the only Bruiser. How childish can you be? Dick always took a delight in seeing how much he could deprive anyone of anything that could only make him money and his territory better. He would cut off his nose to spite his face.

Brody actually beat Dick the Bruiser in a match on April 1, 1979 to win exclusive use of the name "Bruiser." Dick the Bruiser, for a short time, called himself Dick the Loser during interviews, while

Above: King Kong Brody and Dick the Bruiser in a test of strength.

announcer Sam Menacker called him, "*Just plain Dick.*" Later that month, Dick the Bruiser's WWA title was also held up when Brody defeated him via disqualification. On June 9, 1979. Dick the Bruiser got revenge when he defeated Brody by countout to win the vacated WWA title.

Since Dick owned the WWA, he could call himself anything he wanted, so even though Dick never won back the title of "Bruiser," on August 4, 1979, "King Kong" Brody defeated Dick the "Bruiser" for his WWA title in a Texas Death Match. Brody held the belt for over nine months until Dick the Bruiser regained the title on May 31, 1980.

Greg Lake (wrestler):

I worked with Brody twice in Indianapolis for Dick the Bruiser's group, the WWA. The first time I worked with Brody, he just threw me around like a rag doll. When I tried to come back on him, he got really mad. He started stiffing me and kicked me in the chest three or four times in a row. I could hardly move for a week. It was very painful. In a way, it was my own fault. I had been told not to come back on him, but I did, and he kicked me, and he pinned me with that big knee. The second time I worked with him, he was okay. I just let him do his thing and it was fine.

Paul Christy (wrestler):

We were sitting in the Indianapolis dressing room one time and Brody said, "*I don't have any friends.*"

I said, "*Yeah, you do. I like you.*"

He didn't say anything, but he had a strange expression on his face when he looked at me.

One night, I wanted Bunny for something. Brody said, "*I'll get her for you.*"

He walked out and knocked on Bunny's dressing room door. When Bunny opened the door, Brody was kneeling down. In a low, quiet, monotone, he said, "*Christy wants to see you.*"

Brody jumped to his feet and she took a quick step backwards. It scared the heck out of her because she was fairly new in the business at the time. Here was this big, scary-looking guy on his knees, talking in a monotone. Brody rubbed a lot of people the wrong way, but for some reason, he was always nice to me and Bunny.

One night, Bunny and I were talking about a cruise we were getting ready to go on. It was our first cruise. Brody started talking about how he didn't like boats. He told us that he was afraid to get out on the water. He wanted to be able to see land.

There are many stories about Brody's locker room fights. I've researched all of the ones that I heard about and none of them have panned out, except for his fight with Dick the Bruiser. I have a feeling some good folks didn't want to admit to me about tangling with Brody, but this fight with Bruiser was pretty well confirmed.

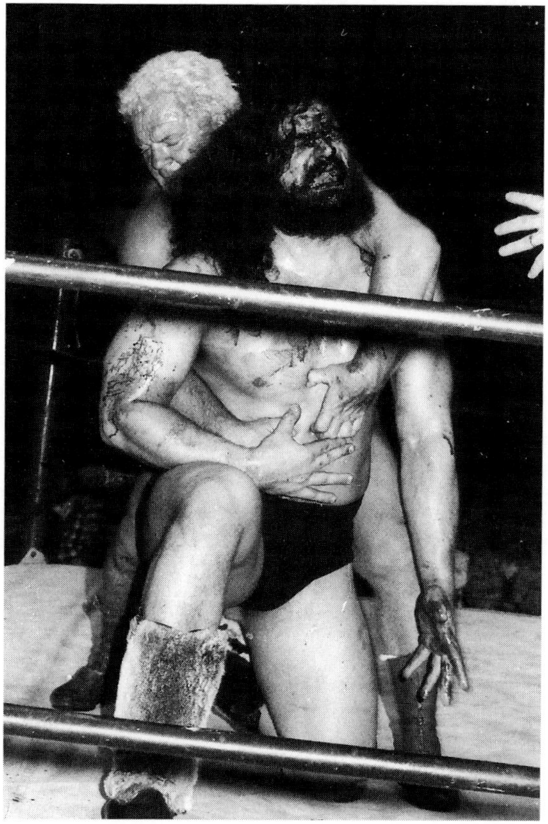

Scott Romer (photographer):

Brody's locker room fight with Dick the Bruiser was over a payoff.

Dutch Savage:

Unfortunately, the last time that I seen Brody before he died was in a locker room in Indianapolis, Indiana. It was at the Expo Center where the main house TV show was done once a month. Dick had been giving Brody quite a lot of crap for about as long as he had been in the territory. Even though it was a packed house, Dick gave Brody a humiliating pay check.

Scott Romer:

Brody said, "*You're saying I came all the way here to wrestle for a lousy $175!*"

[Dick the] Bruiser said something to him. I don't remember to what effect, but Brody shoved him against the wall and cut [Dick's] head open. Bruiser was down and said, "*Why you ... I'm gonna ...*"

Brody just said, "*Look at you, old man. You're lying there bleeding. You're not gonna do anything.*"

Spike Huber (wrestler):

Bruiser went after Brody. He threw a chair down the hall at him. That was about it. I witnessed that.

Dutch Savage:

It was no secret that Dick was an avid gun addict and packed one at all times. I was showered and dressed and just hanging out to drink beer. I told Brody to grab his belongings and we went out the back door to my car on the spot. Brody still had his wrestling boots and trunks on. We drove fifty miles to my house and it was cold weather. It was a long time shivering for Brody until my car got warm. After it was all said and done, we decided that it was better than getting shot. We didn't talk much that night, and when I finally took him back to the Indy airport, I went inside and waited for his plane to arrive. We hugged and said goodbye. He thanked me for everything and I told him that I hoped to see him soon under better circumstances.

J Michael Kenyon:
Dick the Bruiser was not a very big guy. He was only about 5-foot-9, a fireplug, and Brody was 25 years younger.

Spike Huber:
They were too much alike.

Brody's last appearance on one of Dick the Bruiser's WWA cards in Indianapolis was January 24, 1981, when he wrestled Spike Huber.

Brody returned to Texas every couple of months throughout his career. It was where he and his family lived. It was where he got his start in wrestling and he got his bookings out of the Dallas office. He could always count on Gary Hart to put him into a program when he was there, and Hart never interfered with his Japanese tours.

Therefore, it is no surprise that while he was wrestling for Dick the Bruiser's WWA promotion in Indianapolis, he also worked in the Texas territory. On November 11, 1979, he once again won the American heavyweight title. He beat the Spoiler [Don Jardine] in Houston, Texas. The match was a 2-out-of-3 fall match. Like Brody, the Spoiler was also a brawler, and the two looked pretty evenly matched in size. Brody won the first fall after delivering his "King Kong Bodyslam" and his big knee drop. In the second fall, the Spoiler gained the advantage and wore Brody down before putting him down with his claw hold. Brody stomped, kicked, and strangled the Spoiler during the third fall, and finally delivered his big knee from the top rope to pin the masked man to win the title. But this program was short-lived, too, and by Christmas, he had dropped the title and moved on.

Also, in late 1979, Brody had another series of matches with NWA World heavyweight Champion, Harley Race. The two drew huge crowds in Houston, and even in St. Louis, where they had wrestled before, but Brody was just starting to become well known. Race prompted Brody to go to Kansas City and wrestle for his Central States promotion. For a short period, Brody divided his time between Texas and Kansas City.

Harley Race:
He was a good kid then, but he changed.

Harley Race.

Chapter VIII
New Attitude

Bob Geigel (wrestler, wrestling promoter):

Pat O'Connor and I came into Kansas City in 1962. I had talked to Gust Karras a couple of months prior and he said he thought he'd like to have a couple of partners. So, when I saw Pat O'Connor at a match in Winnipeg, I talked to him about it. Pat and I had always been pretty good friends and I said, "*Pat, are you interested in going into a promotion?*"

He was kind of interested, so we met with Gust Karras and we made the deal. Then we took in Harley Race as a partner. He and Pat had been NWA World heavyweight champions and that gave us a lot of prestige.

Bruiser Brody came in here in the late '70s. He was living in San Antonio when we got him. We had bought part of St. Louis. We just owned partials for a while, and then we bought it all out when Sam [Muchnick] retired. Muchnick was our partner for about seven or eight years.

Bobby Fulton (wrestler):

Pat O'Connor walked up to Brody one night and held out his hand. "*How're you doing, Bruiser.*"

Brody said, "*I ain't shakin' your hand. I don't like your kind.*"

Pat just looked at him in astonishment.

Brody won the NWA Central States tag team title with Ernie Ladd in Kansas City on February 2, 1980. They won the title in a tournament where they faced Ted and Jerry Oates in the final round. They lost the titles the next month to Bob Brown and Dick Murdoch on March 20, 1980.

On April 10, 1980, also in Kansas City, Bruiser Brody pinned Bob Brown to become the NWA Central States heavyweight champion. This was a momentous occasion and a real show of faith on the part of the bosses in Kansas City. Brody was a star. He performed well and drew big gates. His relationship with promoters, in general, was still really good at this time. That would all change after he established himself in Japan. His connections there were getting stronger. He went to Toronto, Canada, in late June 1980, and wrestled a couple of matches with Scott Irwin against Giant Baba and Jumbo Tsuruta, who were visiting from Japan.

Brody laid down for fellow Texan, Dick Murdoch, on May 22, 1980, in Kansas City, and lost the Central States heavyweight title.

Brody was also doing his own thing within the squared circle and getting into trouble. In late 1980 in Houston, Brody took liberties with Dick Steinborn and was fired.

Dick Steinborn:

Paul Boesch brought me into Houston, and on Friday night, I was supposed to wrestle Brody. It was supposed to be a disqualification finish and he got hot. So, we were in the ring. I'm doing my thing, he's doing his thing. I thought everything was fine … and then the disqualification happened and I got my hand raised. Brody comes up, grabs a hold of me, and throws me through the ropes. He didn't give me enough time to prepare myself. He bailed out of the ring and grabbed a steel chair. When he came down onto my back with that chair, he didn't hold back or nothing. He stormed off to the dressing room. Paul Boesch was pretty mad. I said to myself, "*There are two things I can do. I can let it slide, or I can walk in there, hit him right across the face with a chair, and bust his teeth out.*"

But I knew my life was involved if I did that. I knew, from all my years, "*This guy is a real bad ass.*"

I didn't have to do anything. As it turned out, Paul Boesch came into the dressing room, chewed his ass out, and fired him right there.

Brody returned to Texas for a brief period of time. On January 4, 1981, in Dallas, Texas, he had a famous match against Andre the Giant where he body-slammed the Giant with one arm!

On January 11, 1981, Brody and Kerry von Erich won the NWA American tag team title in Dallas from Gary Young and Gino Hernandez. They dropped the titles in late April when Brody left to go to Japan. This was the beginning of Brody's rocky road with promoters as he struggled to balance his financial needs and his commitments. When Japan called, Brody followed the money and went.

During Brody's All Japan tour in April 1981, two major events happened. The first was it being the first time he faced Abdullah the Butcher, who many believed would become his arch rival.

Abdullah the Butcher:

The first time I wrestled Bruiser Brody was in Tokyo, Japan. Brody came in there, "*Huss, huss, huss!*", screaming, and I was doing the same thing. We picked it up from King Curtis.

The second major event took place in Matsudo, Japan, on April 30, 1981, when Brody was booked

Above: Brody and Jim Brunzell.

in the finals in All Japan's NWA International heavyweight title 8-man tournament. Brody was scheduled to face Dory Funk in the final match, but he was injured earlier in the tournament and was unable to compete.

Terry Funk:

Brody broke his ankle. That was totally a shoot. We had to come up with something and the only thing we could come up with was for me to wrestle my brother.

Instead of sending the fans home angry with no final round to the tournament, Dory had his first title defense that night. For the first and only time, Funk wrestled his own brother, Terry Funk. Dory won the match and the tournament.

Ed "Moondog" Moretti:

Brody got along great with Baba. When he was on the card, they knew they were going to do big business. His name alone meant big business.

Having established himself as a star in Japan, Brody was getting regular offers to tour with All Japan. His relationship with Baba was mutually beneficial. They were making a lot of money for each other. Brody had another memorable All Japan tour in October 1981.

Ed "Moondog" Moretti:

He smartened me up in Japan. He told me that if the Japanese hit you, you hit 'em back twice as hard.

Harley Race:

Myself and Nick Bockwinkel were in Japan for Baba. At the end of every year, they always had the big tag team tournament. Out of respect for Nick, I'd start the match one night, and he'd start the next. We'd just kind of rotate it. It just happened to fall that when we drew Brody and Hansen, it was Nick's turn to start, so I told Nick, "*You'd better let me start this tonight. I've been around these guys for quite awhile.*"

Nick, of course, who's been around longer than me ... you know how Nick talks. "*Never mind, my boy. I will handle it.*"

They near ate him alive. When he finally got over to tag me, he said, "*My God! What in the hell is going on?*"

If you fired right back at them, they'd stop that crap right away and have a good match, but as long as you let 'em take it, they were gonna take it.

Chavo Guerrero:

Brody was one of my mentors, man. Our time together was in Japan. We were usually on the same tour. Six weeks. We'd been there about four weeks and were doing the bus situation. That's getting up at five or six in the morning and traveling eight to nine hours, then wrestling, then traveling. It's hard. Over there, it was almost like a shoot every night. So Bockwinkel gets there and I have a front seat on the bus. They're not assigned seats. We'd been there for a while. Bockwinkel comes in there and the bus is full, except in the back, and he goes, "*Well, where am I going to sit?*"

And Brody says, "*Hey, you're not the champion here, man. You're like anybody else. Take that belt of yours to the back.*"

I loved it. I loved it.

On October 7, 1981, Brody had a rematch with an old foe. He wrestled former WWWF champion Bruno Sammartino to a double countout in Kanegawa, Japan.

Brody and Dory Funk Jr.

Two days later in Tokyo, Brody faced Dory Funk Jr. for the NWA International heavyweight title. It was the match Japanese fans had been waiting for since Brody had been injured in the tournament in April. The match was short and Brody won in 9 minutes, 36 seconds by disqualification. Funk won the title back later in the year on November 1st in Tokyo.

The All Japan Real World Tag Team Tournament has been one of the annual highlights in Japanese wrestling for the last quarter century. Each November and on into December, All Japan hosts eight teams in a tournament. The tournament in 1981 was from October 27 to December 13. It was Brody's first and he teamed up with Jimmy Snuka.

Jimmy Snuka (wrestler):

Brody was a wonderful guy. I mean, we clicked, brother. We'd known each other for a long time, even before we went there [Japan]. I met him down in Houston, Texas. We just got to liking each other. We said, "*We can create some serious damage.*"

He had just started out, too. It was perfect. We were teaching each other back and forth.

Brody and Snuka made it to the final round of the tournament to face Dory and Terry Funk in Tokyo. As they came down the aisle before the match, they shocked everyone as they were accompanied by Brody's old friend, Stan Hansen.

Dave Meltzer:

Hansen was a big star for New Japan, and Brody was becoming the big foreign star for All Japan. [When] Hansen jumped to All Japan, they became the two big heels.

Stan Hansen:

Brody had become one of All Japan's top gaijin [foreigner] and he had a great partner in Jimmy Snuka, so it wasn't like I was going over there to jump in with Brody. It was against the Funks and

Bruiser Brody and Jimmy Snuka vs. Dory and Terry Funk
All-Japan's Real World Tag Team Tournament
December 13, 1981
Kuramae Kokugikan in Tokyo

The Funks and Bruiser Brody with Jimmy Snuka and later Stan Hansen had a lot of great battles in the beginning half of the eighties. This is my favorite of their matches for a couple of reasons. The Real World Tag Team Tournaments had been an All-Japan staple since 1977. This, and the fact that New-Japan wrestler Stan Hansen secretly jumped to All-Japan that night make this match historically significant. More than anything, I love to see the combination of talent and styles in the ring. Each of these athletes is different in presence and technique. Stan Hansen at ringside is the cherry on the sundae.

The fans reaction to the Funks entrance is extremely positive and unusually loud for a normally reserved Japanese audience. The Funks were mainstays in Japan and had even won the first Real World Tournament in 1977. Brody and Snuka's music plays for a long while before the cameras cut to them backstage and we see that they are followed to the ring by Stan Hansen. When the trio of villains makes their way onto the arena floor the crowd erupts into "Hansen! Hansen! Hansen!" Brody swings his chain around and The Funks clear the ring.

Terry Funk and Jimmy Snuka start the match. Terry Funk has that pissed off drunken old school wrestler style that I have always loved. He moves like rubber and suddenly stiffens and throws some punches and then loosens up again. Snuka has a very muscular physique but he moves like a big cat. He wears boots in this match but it does nothing to hinder his tight acrobatic, old school heel style. Neither wrestler acts like a face, either. When Terry tags Dory Funk in, the crowd lets out a big cheer. Dory move very slowly, very deliberately and there is something so genuine about his style. He attempts the same suplex three times. He can't power Snuka up. He can't power Snuka up. And when every wrestler fan is waiting for Snuka to reverse the move like every other typical wrestling match, Dory surprises us and lifts Snuka up and crashes him down. He's so smooth that when a wrong move is made he can follow up so fast you think the move was intentional.
Brody is tagged in to a respectable cheer from the audience. Brody mixes his big man, bully style with a little pinch of Snuka. He leapfrogs over Dory Funk and cracks off one of his beautiful dropkicks to the face.

Dory tags Terry in and Brody misses a second dropkick. The match is wrestled like a well oiled machine. There is not as much outside the ring brawling as in some of the other matches these men have had. Dory does throw Snuka out of the ring at one point and while Dory takes care of business, Brody and Terry take off fighting through the stands. Dory outwrestles and wears down Snuka in the ring and order is restored as Brody and Terry Funk return to their respective corners. The Funks have full control of Snuka. Terry pushes Snuka into his corner and points at Brody. He wants Brody. The two trade blows until Brody picks him up and pins him into his corner so he and Snuka can double team him.

The Funks again take control of Snuka. They work

on his knee mercilessly and Dory applies the famous Funk Spinning Toe Hold. Brody comes to save his fallen partner and Terry Funk drops him and attempts to apply the hold on Brody. Brody kicks Terry and he goes crashing out of the ring onto the floor. Brody follows. He takes hold of Terry and hurls him into Stan Hansen's charging Lariat. Terry Funk crashes to the floor. His neck is badly hurt and he is down on the ringside floor. His nose is also badly hurt, it bleeds and Dory can do nothing, he must go on alone.

Dory Funk manages to bloody Brody on a ringside post and hold his own for a while. But, a couple of Snuka headbutts almost take Dory out. Dory kicks out at the two count and the crowd goes nuts.

Brody and Snuka tag and re-tag beating Dory badly, but nothing they do keeps him down. He keeps kicking out. The crowd roars with each kick out.

Dory mounts a comeback on Snuka and gets him in the Spinning Toe Hold, but Snuka makes the tag to Brody and Brody comes off the top rope with a big chop, he then delivers his big running knee drop for the three count. Terry Funk still writhes in pain on the floor. Even as the heels hold their trophies aloft Dory Funk comes back for more. He is met with Hansen's elbow and when it looks like Dory Funk is going to suffer a major beating Giant Baba and Jumbo Tsuruta enter the ring. Baba chops Hansen's head until he is bleeding. Tsuruta chases off Brody and Snuka. The heels make a break back to their locker room.

Baba. It was a great moment. It was an exciting match. The people were shocked that I was there. The electricity was flying, man. The thing that happened after the match ... Brody and I just lost it and I think I led the way. Frank was right there. We went down to their dressing room and just established ourselves right there.

'Dr. Death" Steve Williams (wrestler):

Before there was Stan Hansen, there was a man by the name of Bruiser Brody. The man was so popular over in Japan, you could say he ruled it! His popularity was big over here, but in Japan, they really loved him. Then, after his death, they tried to push Stan Hansen into his place, but Brody was the man even after death. Hansen didn't connect with the people like Brody did.

Brody and Hansen would become one of the strongest, most dangerous, and most influential tag teams Japan has ever seen.

Dave Meltzer:

They were put together as a tag team and they had that three or four year run where they were the unbeatable tag team, and that was really like the glory years for him, and probably for Stan in a lot of ways, too.

New Japan was Friday night, All Japan was Saturday night, and these shows were prime time, network television, getting 15-20 rating points.

On April 21, 1982, during another tour of Japan, Brody would once again win the NWA International heavyweight title. He pinned Dory Funk in Osaka, Japan, in 15:15 to win the title. Brody and Hansen also wrestled a group of All Japan wrestlers several times in the United States in Florida and Kansas in early 1982.

In April 1982, Brody had a short stint back in Joe Blanchard's Southwest Championship Wrestling [SWCW]. He won the SWCW Brass Knuckles title and teamed with Dick Slater to win the SWCW World tag team title.

Joe Blanchard:

My promotion, Southwest Championship Wrestling, started because the booking office in Dallas wasn't giving me any talent. It was almost a necessity. Fritz's kids [the von Erich's] were all being billed as main eventers in Dallas, but they weren't look at as main eventers down here. They were killing business.

Fritz and I started about the same time and I had known him for a lot of years. Fritz was not a bad guy. I wasn't uptight with him or particularly angry with him or anything. He just didn't recognize the difference in clientele between Dallas and San Antonio, and when you build a town around Fritz von Erich and his four kids, and they never lose, and you just feed villains to them, it didn't work down here. They weren't that good. We have Mexican people down here, and at that time, we were 50% Mexican. A lot of them were just out of Mexico and they needed more action … smaller guys who could work in a different style, guys who could fly better. Fritz was building the territory around his kids and these villains, big guys who couldn't leave their feet and couldn't do anything. The matches were dull and it was costing me money. I couldn't make it work. Then he [Fritz] had Gary Hart in there as a booker, and that's like having an inmate in charge of the asylum. In our area, it just didn't work. Maybe what I was doing wouldn't have worked in their area. We have a different population down here. The Valley was something like 80% Mexican and you have to cater to those folks. You've got to draw them. You've gotta have guys flying around.

Dusty Wolfe (wrestler):

So, Joe [Blanchard] broke away in late '78 or early '79. I didn't watch for two months and I remember when I started watching again. It was obvious something had happened. It was all being shot out at The Junction and it was obvious that it was real low rent. Everything had changed.

For a short time in 1982, Southwest Championship Wrestling and Joe Blanchard were billing newcomer Jim Duggan as Bruiser Brody Jr. It lasted a very short time, and within two years, Duggan and Goodish would be having a minor feud in San Antonio.

Jim Duggan:

Brody always told me, years ago, he said, "*If you carry something to the ring, carry something you can use. Forget those feathered boas and sequined robes.*"

Big Bruiser used to carry that chain, so I've been carrying a 2x4 ever since, 'cause you never know when one of these young guys might get out of hand. You might have to whack 'em.

Dusty Wolfe:

The TV program that was on here in San Antonio on Channel 4 for all those years was actually in the time slot owned by a guy named Fred Behrend. It was never Joe Blanchard's. It wasn't always on Channel 4, but it was always Fred's time because he was the General Manager of a big car lot down here. The car lot owned the hour.

In December 1982, Southwest Championship Wrestling began airing on the USA Network. It was one of the first nationally-televised wrestling shows. It didn't last long, however, as the cost of putting the program on the air was thousands of dollars per show.

Larry Matysik:

I was also working with the Blanchards, Tully and Joe, who had the USA Network spot. A couple of times they said, "*Why don't you come down and do TV here and give us some ideas?*" They did a horrible spot where they literally dumped horse shit on Bobby Jaggers and Scott Casey on USA cable, and within the next few weeks, USA cancelled them. And who got USA? Vince [McMahon Jr.]. Think if we would have blocked that.

Joe Blanchard had been having a very tough time with the financial end of staying on the USA Network when Vince McMahon came down in August 1983, and paid for a year's worth of TV shows in advance. One Sunday morning, it was SWCW, and the next, it was the WWF.

Joe Blanchard:

Then he [Fred Behrend] teamed up with Dallas and they came in against me. He worked with the sales person who handled his North Central Ford account and took our local wrestling slot and puts the Dallas show on there. We were left with just the Mexican channel, Channel 41. We were left in a tight spot. Man, I hate to bring up all the negatives. I'm through with it and I don't want anything to do with it. I don't really talk about it anymore. I'm sorry I was ever in it, if you really want to know. I liked wrestling in college. I was good at it and I respected it, and I don't know how or why I ever got into professional wrestling. If I had it to do over again, and know what I know now, I sure wouldn't be in it again, I'll tell you that.

Dusty Wolfe:

The end of May '85 is when Joe turned it over, sold it, was swindled, whatever, to Fred. Whatever Joe says, I believe Joe.

Joe Blanchard:

Behrend got the promotion the same way I did … well, I got it legally. (laughs) He swindled me.

Bruiser Brody was now a legitimate international superstar. By mid-1982, he had firmly established himself both in the United States and in Japan. He was making big money touring Japan several times a year. In the States, he was an outlaw, but he was also the top independent wrestler in the U.S. in the '80s. Bookers were willing to pay to have him on shows, knowing their ticket sales would go up, but they also had to be willing to deal with Brody.

Brody had changed. Brody started doing what he wanted, when he wanted. If he thought he wasn't getting paid enough, he walked out. He changed matches in the ring. He would tear up the arena, throwing his opponent around the building, and smashing him with whatever he could get his hands on.

He also controlled his own finishes because the Japanese press kept tabs on his matches. The All Japan office didn't want their stars losing too many matches in the States. Fickle Japanese fans would turn on a wrestler if he lost too often. Brody made enough money for his family to live comfortably in Japan, but he must have had his reasons for leaving Japan and continuing to wrestle and travel all over the world.

J Michael Kenyon:

When you talk about his independence and/or his arrogance, insofar as promoters in this country were concerned, it is because he was over so big in Japan. Once he got over in Japan, then he could do whatever he wanted in America. He didn't even need to be here because he made so much over there.

Dave Meltzer:

He had a lot of enemies in wrestling because he wanted to do things on his terms, and when he became a big star in Japan, he had that fallback. A lot of American promoters hated dealing with him because he knew that no matter what he did, he was going to still be a star in Japan, anyway, and he wasn't under their thumbs like virtually all the other wrestlers were. Promoters weren't used to wrestlers like that.

Bobby Fulton:

The first time I met Bruiser Brody was in San Antonio. He was always nice to me. He used to call me Shorty. He used Tommy (Rogers) and me on a show at the Fox Theater when he was the booker in Dallas. To me, he was a gentle guy, but he was business all the way. If he ever got the idea that he was getting the short end of the stick, he would be gone.

Bill Watts:

I remember later, when he became a big star, his personality changed. His word became no good. He was unreliable. He came to me one time in Dallas and said, "*Hey, boss. How come you never use me anymore?*"

I said, "*Frank, I like you as a person. I'd like to be your friend, but I don't ever intend to book you because you've become a person that your word is no good. You agree to terms and conditions and then, when you get there, you try to hijack the promoter.*"

Then I said, "*I'm not going to put up with that. I just don't deal with people like you.*"

He said, "*Well, I understand.*"

I said, "*Well, what you're doing is wrong.*"

And yet, I liked him enough to say "*Hi,*" and to talk to him when I saw him.

Gary Hart:

As his matchmaker, I realized that Brody needed to work with a strong opponent. If you tried to use Bruiser Brody to make somebody look good, you were just going to make yourself look bad. Bruiser was the type of guy who, if he could make money with you, he would. But if you ever tried to make somebody else look good at his expense, there would be hell to pay.

I was successful as Brody's matchmaker because I would talk with him and ask him for his opinion on business decisions. I would ask him, "*Would you feel comfortable working with this guy?*" or "*Would you feel comfortable doing that angle?*"

If Bruiser said, "*I really don't want to get involved with that,*" then we wouldn't go down that road.

A few people who booked their own towns, like Paul Boesch and Joe Blanchard [Houston and San Antonio], would occasionally book Brody with somebody who he wasn't interested in working with. When that happened, he would just "*Bruiser Brody*" them. When I say, "*He would Bruiser Brody them,*" I mean, he would just go out and kick the shit out of them.

Abdullah the Butcher:

Sir, there's a long story about Bruiser Brody. Brody worked hard. What he done was he went out and produced. With any promoter, the only thing he wanted was money. He wanted what was coming to him.

If you got hurt in Japan or anyplace … today, it's altogether different. You get hurt now, WCW, they take care of you, or whatever, they still pay you. But when we were doing it, you got hurt; you were on your own. If you didn't save your money, you were out. Promoters hated Brody and they hated me, because the one thing I wanted was my money.

If I went out there and drew people, I wanted my money. If you can't get your money, you said, "*Hey, I wasn't paid*."

These guys have big contracts now. We had to go out and draw people.

Gary Hart:

Bruiser was more of an independent agent than anyone else I knew. Even though I was his booking agent, Brody would get out and about. He would go all over the country. So really, he did not have a lot of conversations with Fritz. I'm sure Fritz liked him and respected him because he made Fritz a lot of money.

In those days the booking office got 25% of the gross, so having Bruiser Brody on your card really helped you. Dallas, essentially, was the booking office. Fritz, along with me and Ed Watt, controlled the talent out of that booking office, and I usually kept anywhere from 16 and 20 guys. Bruiser Brody's appearance in a town would raise the gross somewhere between $3,000 to $5,000. When you figure 25% of that, it's a nice chunk of money that wouldn't have been there. I always felt that Brody on the card meant another 20 to 25% of the gross. Not only in Texas, but everywhere. He was one of those guys. You just put his name on the card, put him with a good opponent, and business booms.

Look at Kansas City. No one drew money in Kansas City except Bruiser Brody. An average card in Kansas City, without Harley Race, would have been $1,600 to $1,700. Same thing with Florida. If Dusty Rhodes or Jack Brisco weren't on the card, you didn't draw any money. Same thing with Brody, but he drew wherever he went.

With Bruiser Brody in Dallas, my average house was about $12,500 a show. Brody on the card would add another $2,000 to $3,000. Like Houston was a $10,000 to $12,000 town. With Brody on the card, it would automatically be $15,000 to $16,000.

Brody himself never asked for a guarantee. The only thing Brody wanted was an opportunity, a fair amount of TV time, to be positioned right on the card, and good opponents. Bruiser was not a guy that said, "*Give me money and I will come.*" Bruiser said, "*Give me an opportunity and money will come.*"

In those days, most promoters—not all, but most—paid somewhere between 25% and 35% of the gross to the wrestlers. The way we did it was, 16% went to the main event, 8% apiece. If it was a tag match, it would be 4% apiece. If it would have been two guys and a manager, it would be five-and-a-quarter. But Brody, he went on the percentage.

Nick Bockwinkel:

He was extremely talented, very respected for his talent and his ability. One might admire his independence, but he created it in such a non-productive, negative manner.

Tony Atlas:

It took six months to get a wrestler over, back in them days, to become popular with the people. You stayed in a territory for two years; it took six months to build you. So what Brody used to do is when the six months is up, he would go work for somebody else. Now this promoter got all this money invested in him and he's gone. After they

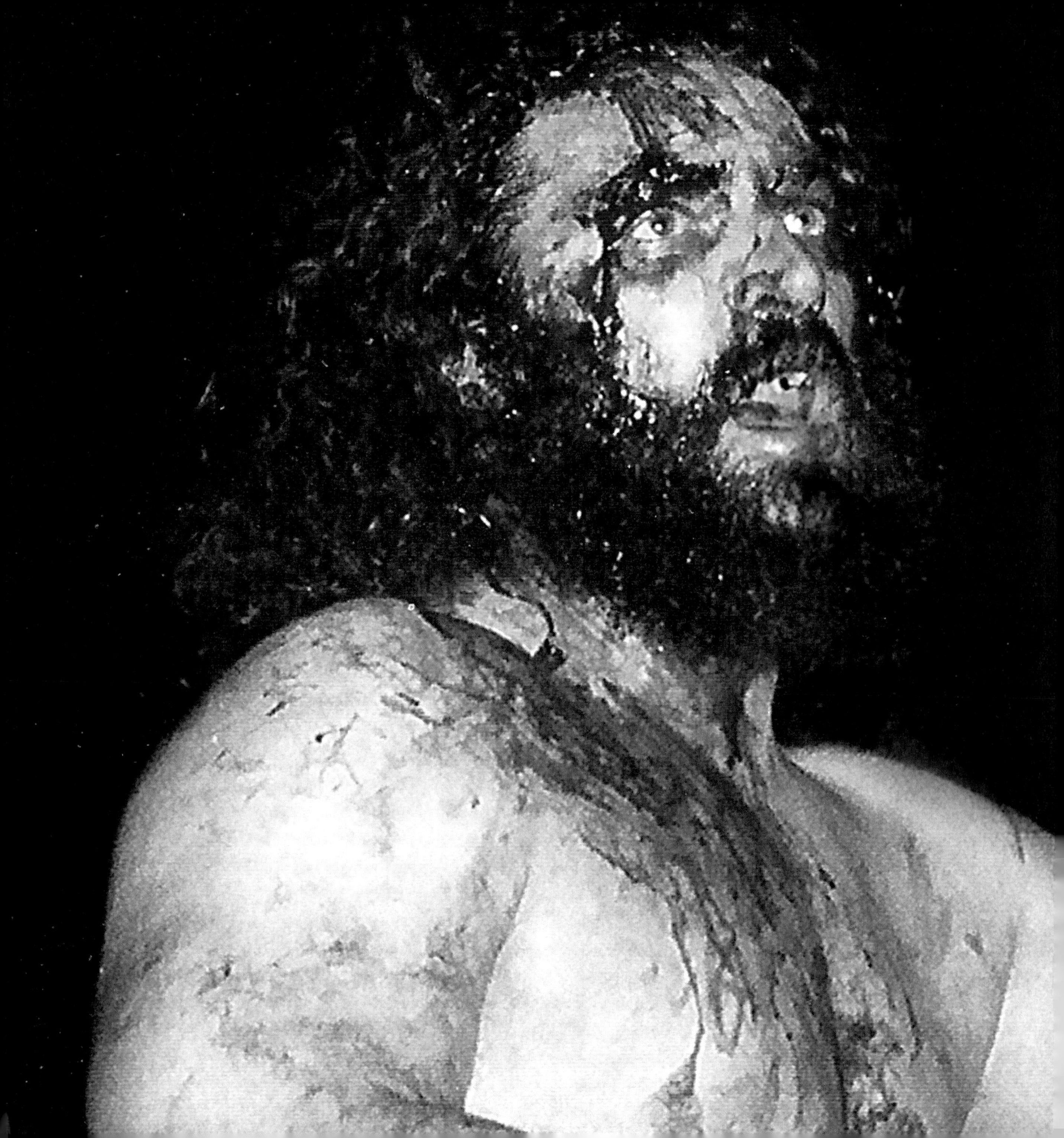

finished the building process, he knew exactly when to leave. He'd take off and go to another promotion, and then they'd have to start building him up. They were always pissed off at him, but he was just so immensely strong and big that they was afraid of him. What are you gonna do. You don't want a fight with Brody.

Bobby Fulton:

Brody was going to work for Angelo Poffo, Randy Savage's dad, in a town in Missouri, but he got a better offer from somebody else, so he didn't show up. A few days later, Brody got a letter from Angelo that said, "Where money lies, honor dies."

Dory Funk Jr.:

Brody was famous for his attitude. He was known as somebody that you don't mess with, and in some ways, that made him a cult hero with the wrestling fans. It's obvious everybody wants what they can't have, and everybody wanted Brody on their cards in the independent promotions. Sometimes, the smaller promotions were in competition with bigger ones. Quite obviously, his success in Japan was huge, and really, he demanded his price over there. He worked for several different companies over there. He was loyal to who would pay.

Nick Bockwinkel:

Brody, I think, thought he was just above certain aspects of the business, and if you wished to be above it, hey, that's fine, but at the same time, regardless of the profession, we can all offend it. Regardless of what we're doing, whether the TV interview business, or working for General Motors, can we offend the profession somehow? Easily done; more easily done than trying to do it right.

Kamala:

I don't know that he would stiff promoters. I never heard that. I can't remember hearing that. No, I can't. I know Brody would speak his mind and speak what he means. I think that's the reason he's dead now. He would just speak his mind in a business way. He'd tell them, "I have to have this," and that was that. They'd have to do it or he wouldn't come in. That's all I know of that. I can't say nothing bad about him. If I knew anything bad about him, I'd say it. Not because he got me my biggest payoff. I just don't know anything about that. I know promoters were hesitant around him more than the way they were around other wrestlers. That's just the way Brody was.

Jim Duggan:

Wrestlers are the labor; the office is the management, of course. He was having trouble with a promoter down in Texas. I was working with him in a main event at the Hemisphere Arena in San Antonio. We had twelve, probably 14,000 people at the arena. The show went real good. I went out there and Brody sat down on his butt. I grabbed him in a headlock, and for 20 minutes, we sat in a headlock.

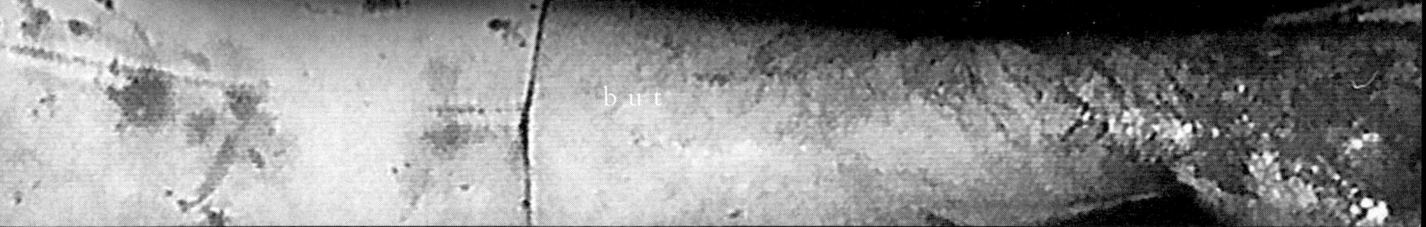

The worst match you'd ever want to see. The crowd was booing, throwing stuff in the ring. But from then on, Brody always got his money, 'cause they could make him go to the ring, but they couldn't make him wrestle.

Larry Matysik:

I learned a lot about the psychology of the ring from him … how he liked to double cross now and then to keep the match lively. He'd double cross to keep the match lively and then say, "*Sorry, man, sorry, man. I heard you wrong.*"

The good ones knew how to work with him. I saw a match in St. Louis. He did a match with Flair that went an hour for Japanese TV. It would hold up today. You know, modern wrestling—bump, bump, bump. It basically was that. He and Flair both told me afterwards that they were sore for a fucking month after that match. That's when we became pretty good friends. He knew I was going to split at that time.

Jim Duggan:

He would take no guff from the promoter. I remember Jim Crockett was saying, "*Everybody that comes to the Omni in Atlanta, Georgia, they better be in a sport coat and tie.*"

We're all a bunch of wrestlers, were on the road all the time, who's got a chance? So, we're all sitting around, all of a sudden you hear the crowd pop and yell. Here comes Brody in the front door. He's got on a teeny, tiny, sport coat he could hardly get on. He threw his bag in the ring, climbed in the ring, climbed out of the ring [on the other side], went into the dressing room that way. Brody would make an entrance wherever he went.

Bobby Simmons (referee):

Bruiser Brody worked Atlanta TV one Saturday morning against one of Lars Anderson's trainees. The poor kid had probably never been in the ring before, and he was scared to death. He was simply fresh meat for Brody to slaughter and all he was supposed to do was listen and do what Brody told him to do. The house lights were still on when they got into the ring and the crowd began to yell as Brody stood in one corner of the ring, stomping and snorting. When the bell rang, they met in the center of the ring and locked up. I don't know if the kid was scared of Brody, or just nervous about being in the ring, but he froze up and would not turn Brody loose. The kid wasn't hurting or punching Brody. He was just hanging on. Brody finally had to get stiff with the kid just to get him off. From there, the match was all Brody as he hammered the kid around the ring and finally pinned him.

After he pinned the kid, Brody threw him out of the ring and started to walk back to the dressing room. As fate would have it, there was a wheelchair sitting off to the side of the studio that was going to be used in a commercial on the following day. Brody picked the kid up off the floor and slammed him butt-first into the wheelchair, then kicked the chair so that it began to roll. And roll it did. It rolled right across the TV set where Gordon Solie was talking. The people at home didn't see Brody slam the kid into the chair. They only saw the chair roll across the screen and Gordon watching it go by.

The beauty of the whole incident was Gordon. Being the professional that he was, Gordon never said a word about it as the chair, with a limp-as-a-biscuit wrestler sitting in it, rolled past. He just gave it one of his patented looks and kept right on talking, as if nothing out of the ordinary had happened.

Bruiser Brody and Gordon Solie.

The TV station was bombarded with telephone calls from every imaginable association having to do with disabilities and handicapped people. They even got a call from the FCC, who wanted to know what we were thinking. It was all pure coincidence that it happened. Brody saw the chair and reacted. I do know that the wheelchair never showed up in the studio again.

Brody was supposed to work a nearby town that night, but he left town and disappeared. I don't know if Jim Barnett asked Brody to leave, or if Brody got scared and took it upon himself to leave, but I do know that he left town that night.

I didn't have many dealings with Brody, but that incident got Jim Barnett and me a face-to-face meeting with Ted Turner.

Gary Hart:

When charitable organizations or other groups ran fundraisers for high schools to purchase band and football uniforms, wrestling equipment, and things like that, the coach, or the PTA, or the principal, would say to me, "*Mr. Hart, if we could have Bruiser Brody, we know we could make enough money to buy new uniforms for our football players,*" or whatever.

He was so remarkable that just his presence at any school he went to would make their goals. A lot of people didn't know that Bruiser did that. I mean, Bruise could have been in St. Louis, or Indianapolis, or wherever. If I would say to him, "*Hey, Bruise, there's a school district in Abilene and they're trying to raise money to go on their class trip,*" or something like that, Bruiser would forgo a bigger payoff just to make the show. He was a great guy like that.

J.R. Obrecht (family friend):

It was my twelfth birthday. My stepdad at the time knew a guy named Larry Irvin. He was somewhat connected in Centralia, Missouri. Larry Matysik and Brody ran around together, and Larry Irvin and Larry Matysik were friends. My stepdad asked Larry, "*Hey, you think you and Brody could swing by this birthday party?*”

Larry Matysik asked Brody and he said, “*Yeah, I'd love to.*”

It was actually on the way to Centralia. We weren't expecting it, and my mom wasn't really expecting him to come by, until they just showed up. We were downstairs just playing games and he came downstairs, and him being so big, it, just took one person to turn around and see this big giant in our basement, and everybody just surrounded him. He said, “*Who's the birthday boy?*”

Shyly, I said it was me, and my mom said, “*Let's get some pictures.*”

He stayed for 15 to 20 minutes. I'm 30 now, so that was March 1988.

Joe Blanchard:

Frank would let himself be booked and then wouldn't make the town, or he would be late. If he'd get there, he'd do something, fight outside the ring or do something silly. So, he was a problem. More of a problem than he was worth as an attraction, as a matter of fact. He hurt my business, and in so doing, hurt the money that the other guys made. He was always trying to manipulate and maneuver and you always had the feeling he was trying to take over the business.

Ivan Putski:

Frank kind of changed after he made a name for himself. He was so big and he got over real fast, but later he would just do anything he wanted. If he didn't like what somebody was saying, he would just leave. I was working with Joe Blanchard one summer and Joe asked him to do something, put somebody over or something, and Frank just left. I don't understand why he did that. He was working main events. What the hell else do you want? He was so humble at first. He would do anything. I remember driving him around and telling him stories. He would just listen and do anything. But once he got over, it seemed like it was just, my way or the highway. Different strokes for different folks.

Gary Hart:

Every year, I used to go to the National Wrestling Alliance meeting in Las Vegas where all the promoters and bookers would congregate for a week, and talk about business and direction, and who's going to be the next world's champion and everything, and

Above: Brody and Larry Matysik show up unannounced at J.R. Obrecht's twelfth birthday party.

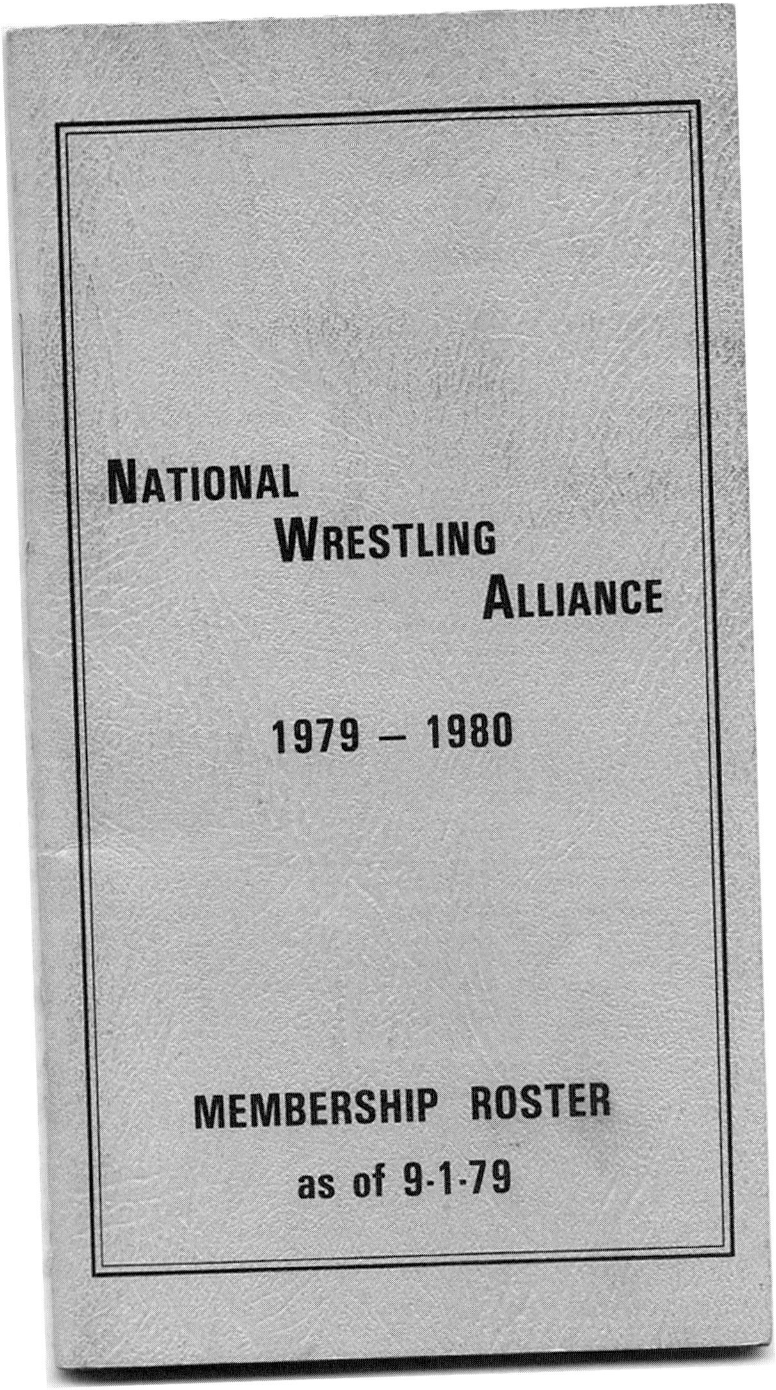

every year, you would get a little green book with every promoter, every matchmaker, their home phone number, their home address, and their office number, and Brody asked me, "*Gary, could I get one of them books?*"

I said, "*Brody, no, man. Nobody can have these books. You cannot have one.*"

So, he told me a couple of months later, "*You know, I really need one of them books. I would do anything in the world for you if you would just get me in touch with one of them books.*"

So I said, "*Okay, Bruise. I have an old one lying at home from last year. I'm going to give you this book, but if you ever tell anyone that it was me who gave you this book, I'm through. No promoter would ever give me another job as a matchmaker or TV producer. This is the kiss of death. If anyone ever knows that I was the one who supplied you with this book, I'm out of business.*"

He never revealed the secret. He used the book like crazy. People are calling me like crazy. People are calling from Australia, New Zealand. Pat O'Connor's calling me. Verne Gagne's calling me. "*Hey! We talked to Bruiser Brody and he says he works for you, but he has some open dates.*"

So I told him, "*Bruise, you sure do use the book, don't you?*"

He says, "*That's why I wanted it!*"

In all of our years together, I must have given him seven or eight books. When I got my new book, I would give him the old one, and if there was anything that had to be changed, home number or anything, I would change it for him before I gave it to him. Brody had the office number, the home number, and address of every promoter that belonged to the NWA. But, he never told on me. I think you're the only one I've ever told that story to. They can't fire me no more!

Marc Allen:

Frank had a way of pissing everybody off. He pissed off every promoter in this country.

Gary Hart:

Bruiser was a man's man. He would never lie, never deceive you. If he said he would be there, he would be there. His word was his bond. In all the years I was with him, he never broke it one time with me ... not once.

Nick Bockwinkel:

Somebody said one time that Brody and Stan Hansen agreed to try and screw over every promoter they could. Whether that's true, I don't know, but it sure seemed like it.

Stan Hansen:

From Frank's point of view, he felt like he had been screwed over by the promoters, so he looked at promoters like they were the enemy.

For All Japan's 1982 Real World tag team tournament, Brody teamed with Stan Hansen. Once again, he met the Funks in the final round. Late in the match, Hansen delivered a Lariat to a bloody, beaten Terry Funk outside the ring. Terry Funk rolled around in

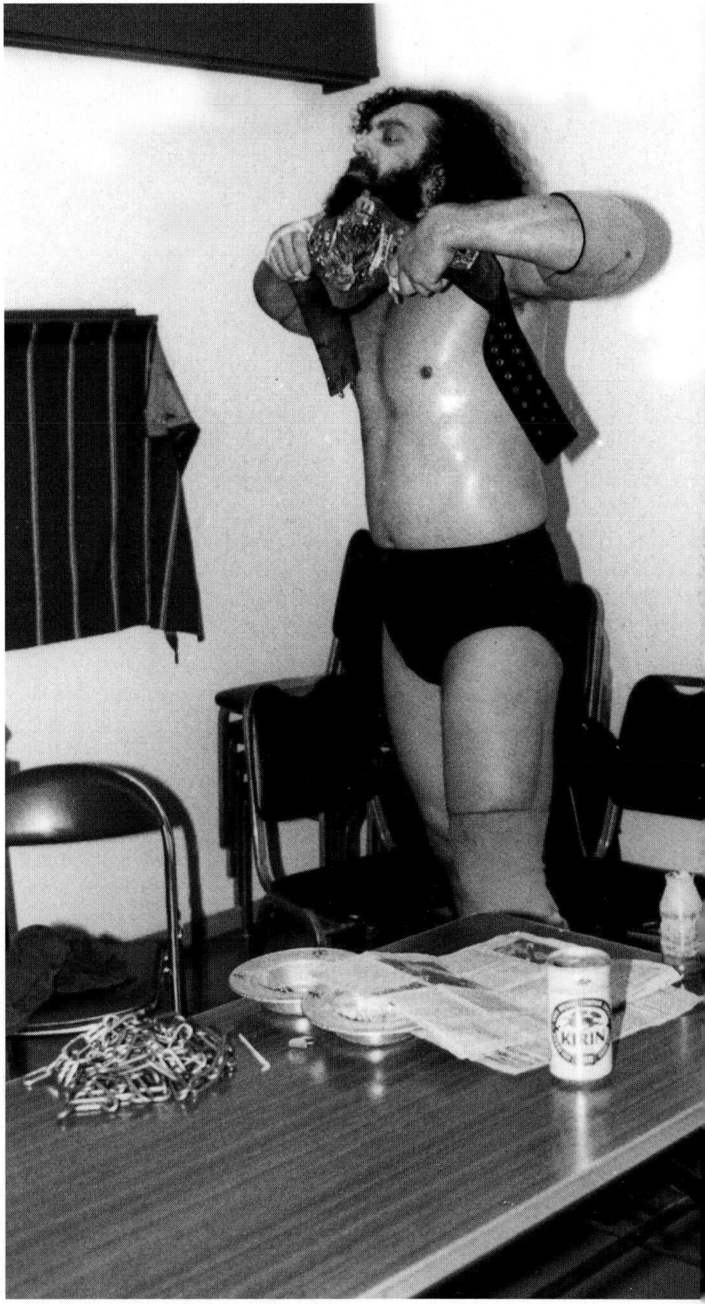

Brody prepares for a match in Japan.

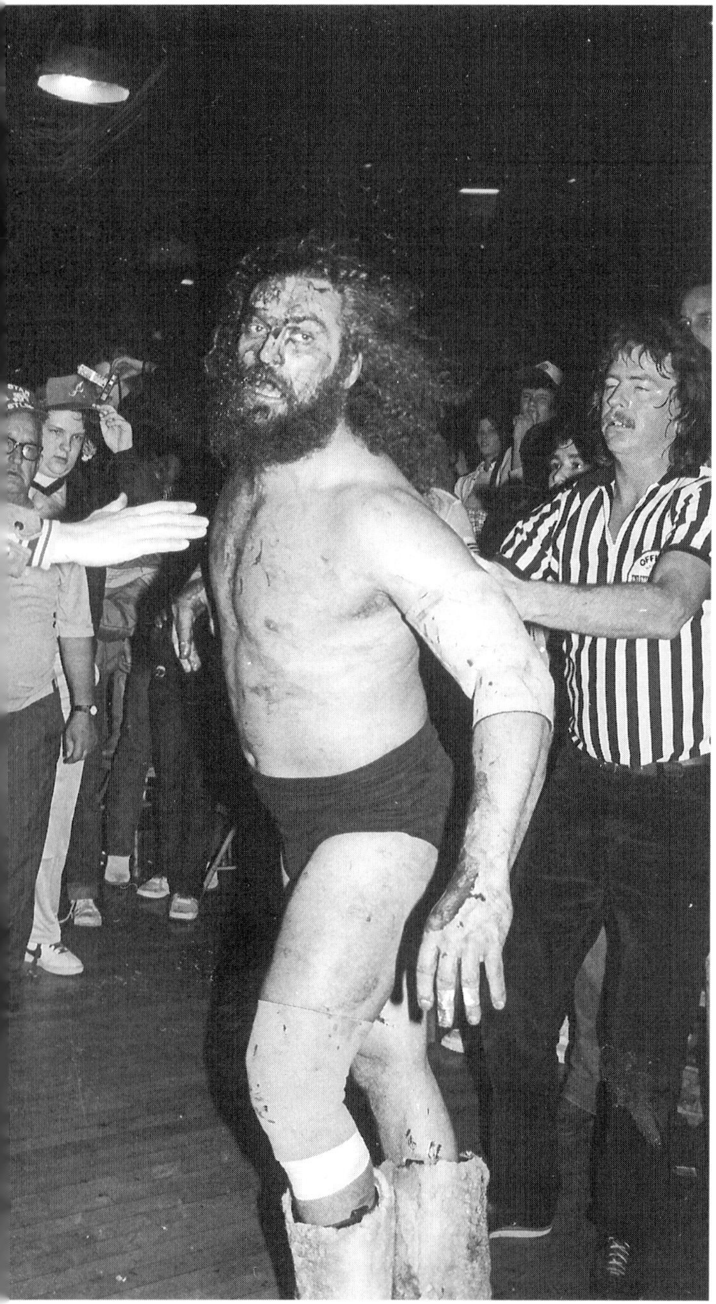

pain while Brody and Hansen beat Dory Funk to a bloody pulp inside the ring. At one point, Brody held Dory Funk and Hansen lined up another Lariat. Hansen came rumbling down, only to hit all three—the referee, Dory Funk, and Brody—with his big Lariat. Secondary referee Lou Thesz tried to restore order, but got thrown out of the ring. The Funks won the tournament by disqualification. Brody and Hansen won the fight, but lost the war.

The incredible matches Brody and Hansen had with the Funks all over Japan became legendary. Their physicality bordered on shoot fighting, and their brutality was something from a horror film. No other wrestler could follow their matches. Belts or no belts, their matches were the main events for Japanese crowds.

Dave Meltzer:

His aggressiveness and his style never stopped. It did change the work rate and how a lot of the wrestlers in Japan worked. He toughened a lot of the Japanese natives up. I think it led to the style in the later '80s and in the '90s where the Japanese guys that worked for All Japan were really tough guys. It was a catalyst for elevation of the product for sure.

Nick Bockwinkel:

He was very respectful in Japan. Both he and Hansen … that was their payday. They spent six months of the year in Japan. Consequently, they walked the real straight professional line in Japan with Baba. They worked very hard, pounding and thumping the guys that were there. Maybe gave a little latitude to Mr. Baba and a couple of the other top hands, but they didn't screw that up because that was their bread and butter.

Chapter IX Killer Heels

St. Louis was the heart of the National Wrestling Alliance. From 1950 to 1960, and from 1963 to 1975, St. Louis promoter Sam Muchnik was the president of the NWA. Muchnick had been involved in wrestling in St. Louis since 1932 and was the most respected wrestling promoter in the world.

Many of the NWA's greatest matches took place in St. Louis. Brody's battles with Harley Race, Kamala, and Ric Flair clearly stand out as some of his best matches. Whether it was Muchnik's presence, the fact that many of the matches were for the NWA title, or that many of the matches were taped for broadcast in Japan, Brody's bread and butter, Brody thumped, bumped, sweat, and bled, and gave his all every time he wrestled in St. Louis.

Larry Matysik:

Well, St. Louis was not a territory. It was one town. Sam Muchnick had made it that way for years because he was the NWA President. He was the Vince McMahon of his era. He had access to anybody he wanted, anytime.

Nick Bockwinkel:

Funny the conversations I've had with people there. Brody never jacked Sam Muchnik around. I don't know if the fact that Sam was President of the NWA and was respected as an icon for so long could have been part of it.

Dave Meltzer:

When Sam Muchnick asked Brody to lose, he did lose. There was never a case of him refusing to do jobs for Sam Muchnick.

Harley Race:

Brody had a reputation as a businessman. He was never a guy who would say, "*Okay, I'll be there on such-and-such date,*" and then no-show you. He would always show up, but what you were never quite sure of was what frame of mind he'd show up in.

No-showing us was a little bit different matter than no-showing other places in the country because at that point in time, Muchnick controlled the NWA title, and Brody really, really wanted to be involved in that. He knew a no-show there would automatically default any hope he had of that. However, there was never any talk of putting the belt on Brody because right at the time that he was there [Kansas City], [Dick] Murdoch was there. Dickie was considered [for the title], but somewhere in every match, he had to do the Fred Sanford shuffle. That was the only thing that stood in Dick's way. Everybody knew that Dickie could have a match with anybody out there. He was that talented. Everybody knew that. But in that era, they didn't want the cartoon stuff, and as long as Muchnick controlled the belt, that wasn't going to happen. Regardless, they were there at that same point in time, and Dick had Brody edged out as far as that was concerned.

Next: Brody and Flair had several classic battles in St. Louis. This match went nearly a half an hour before Jerry Blackwell interfered.

Bruiser Brody vs. Ric Flair

2/3 Falls, Checkerdome, St. Louis, MO, February 11, 1983

This is easily one of my favorite matches of Brody's. It has most of the standard qualities of both a Ric Flair and a Bruiser Brody match; the move sets, the defensive time allotment, and the flawless in ring story telling. This match does not have any blood and Brody is clearly the babyface. The crowd is hot throughout the entire match. The Checkerdome lights stay on throughout the first fall allowing you to see how huge the audience is and to see their genuine intensity.

Announcer, Larry Matysik stands in the ring as Brody enters. Flair follows with several police officers. The crowd boos for the most part but there is a lot of general screaming and excitement.

Matysik introduces Ric Flair first. From my understanding the previous bout, Harley Race vs. Giant Baba, was abysmally slow, but the crowd really wakes up when "King Kong" Brody is introduced. Referee Lee Warren pats both men down and the match starts.

Brody uses a lot of submission holds during the match. I'm sure it is for pacing purposes to go the whole sixty minutes. The match was recorded by American cameramen and shipped to Japan for airing on Japanese television. It is interesting to me that Brody wrestled the match in a mixture of his style with a bit of Japanese submission wrestling style thrown in. At that point his matches in Japan were thump and bump. It wasn't until his later matches with Inoki where Brody slowed down his pace to the Japanese style a bit more.

Of course, Flair sells Brody's shots for maximum effect, but Brody really sells for Flair as well in this match, something he didn't do frequently, even in his other matches with Flair. Brody flops and sells almost like he did in his WWWF days. Brody sticks with his "big man" style as well. He reverses Flair's failed suplex attempts, reverses Flair's bodyslam and piledriver, and generally out muscles Flair.

The first fall comes at the 21:04 mark. Brody pins Flair after his big knee drop. The crowd explodes.
The house lights, disappointingly, are turned off at this point. The crowd doesn't let up. The cheering and excitement hold at an even pace for the entire sixty minutes. When Brody pins Flair for ONE, TWO, and the ref stops the count because Flair's foot is on the ropes, many people in the audience scream THREE, thinking Brody is the new NWA world champion. A "Brody! Brody!" chant goes up.

At the 43:44 mark, Brody and Flair wrestle outside the ring and on the ring apron. At the count of eighteen Flair makes it back into the ring and Brody is counted out. They are even at one fall each.

Both men are dripping with sweat and slowing down. Flair wrestled many sixty minute matches in his career. But Brody, who has only wrestled a few, keeps up with Flair move for move. Not may "big men" in wrestling could go an hour without blowing up.

After Brody suplexes Flair and rolls over to cover him, the bell rings out. Larry Matysik climbs into the ring to announce that the one hour time limit has expired with each man having one fall. Ric Flair would keep the NWA World Title. The crowd "Boos!" furiosly.

In his own autobiography, Ric Flair has cited Brody as one of his top opponents. They wrestled six times in St. Louis alone and all of their matches were incredible. Their one hour draw on February 11, 1983 has to go in the top ten 60-minute matches of the last thirty years. For their hours work each wrestler was paid $5,958.81.

Larry Matysik:

So basically, they [Pat O'Connor, Bob Geigel, and Harley Race] had bought out Sam, but they had many different ideas on how to run the actual business side of it. I'm talking about the money side of it. Where Sam always held money, he would never … the checking account was never below $5,000, which was a lot of money in those days. If a bill came in the ten o'clock mail, we had a check written and out in the mail at noon. But, that's because Sam recognized wrestling had a real shit reputation, and by doing things like that, and by his background in the sports community, and eventually mine, we were able to overcome that. Even though some people may want to look down their nose at wrestling, they really didn't do it at Sam. We just did the whole business differently.

When Sam retired, the next day, Geigel wrote a check for everything in the checking account. The checking account was zero, so I quit. Sam interceded right away and I went back and they put money in the checking account. It just broke their hearts to have to do that. We kind of had bumps like that over the next year, year-and-a-half. Then I split from them in February of '83 and started Greater St. Louis Wrestling Enterprises in June of '83.

Everybody said, "*Oh, you're not going to get talent on your own.*"

Well, I had talent out my ass. Didn't know what to do with it. I had more than I could use. Randy Savage, Adrian Adonis, Bob Orton, Brody, Dick Murdoch, Fritz von Erich behind the scenes, Terry Gordy, the Freebirds, and had it lasted longer, the deal was already set—the [Von Erich] boys, David and Kevin and Kerry—all three of them were coming to me with [Michael] Hayes and Terry Gordy, plus Brody and Murdoch. I wasn't hurting for talent. And Frank was a key guy because that's when he and I … we'd always been good friends from the late '70s when he first came to St. Louis.

And of course, Frank said, "*In a heartbeat, man.*"

Because he had been in a lot of fights with Geigel

Above and Next: Brody wrestles Ric Flair to a 60-minute draw in St. Louis, on February 11, 1983.

and those guys about money, and we just clicked on a business end, too. Right before he was killed, we were going to go into athletic management. Not just wrestling. We wanted to actually get into, like, people that sign contracts for baseball players. In fact, I have a t-shirt here I kept—Brody Athletic Management, which of course was, BAM, with King Kong Brody and Larry Matysik running the deal. Larry does this part and Frank does this part of it. It was more of an idea that was just starting to sink in when he was killed.

So, Brody came along and we became tight, and I was tight with Fritz behind the scenes and cut a separate deal with Fritz. I spent two days down at the ranch with him and the boys in Denton. David wanted to jump right away. David was the one I was closest to. He was the most independent-minded one, and in those days, you gotta remember, those guys were hot as could be.

Harley Race:

He worked for us in Kansas City and St. Louis. For some reason, he always thought I stepped ahead of him in the Kansas City market. He thought he wasn't able to be there more than he was because I was there. That was totally false because I wasn't around here. I was always on the road. The spot was there for him, like it was in St. Louis. He did big business in St. Louis and made big money there. After Sam [Muchnick] died, Brody came into St. Louis a few times when Larry Matysik tried to run shows in the area, but even then, Brody always thought that I was the thing that was in his way in this area.

Gene Lewis:

I remember Brody wrestling up in St. Louis. He was the main event Friday night for Geigel and his promotion, and then Saturday, he wrestled for the opposition and sold out the same arena. Frank was believable, and the people believed in him.

I Was There by Harry White

Brody vs. Flair, 2/11/1983

When the Checkerdome/Arena would be the host of a card instead of the usual Kiel Auditorium home of wrestling, the fans knew something special was coming up. Few, if any, could realize just how special and how memorable that card would be. Over twenty years later I can still only use the same word I used when the 60 minute bell rang an end to Flair/Brody, WOW! A simple word for a complex match, but when one was left almost breathless a longer word description would have been difficult.

The St Louis Blues hockey team had many Checkerdome/Arena sellouts as did the St Louis Steamers indoor soccer team. Neither of those mainsteam attractions packed more rabid fans into the building than Flair/Brody. It would be hard to say that any of those mainsteam fans saw anything more wild or thrilling than what wrestling fans saw on Feb 11, 1983.

What a great pairing for a wrestling match to capture the imagination and build a feud. Not just the usual good vs bad but the pretty (in Flair) vs the non pretty (in Brody). Set the stage with an indecisive Kiel main event and push it until it packs the Checkerdome and bring with it a big contingent of Brody watching Japanese press to push the limits of the building fire code.

St Louis wrestling had a long history of long main events. I had been lucky enough to see some excellent hour draws in Funk/Brisco, Race/Sammartino, Race/Rocky Johnson, and barely recall a Thesz/O' Connor bell to bell. They all seemed to have a part where you could run out and grab a quick hot dog because you knew there would be some two minute long headlocks somewhere during the match. Except for the first few minutes and the one minute rest period between falls, the action of Flair/Brody appeared to be non stop fast and furious. There were two reasons for this. One, the action was actually really fast and furious and two, the Race/Baba match preceeding it was fought to a slug like pace. Few if any wanted to leave their seat as the fans began to realize they were seeing a match unlike most others. The ones who did leave their seat did so involuntarily as participants in fan fight after fan fight were escorted out. I sat right in the middle of the Arena and half way up from the floor. It was a good panorama view of the ring, the floor and a part of the rest of the building and I will never forget the view of the match and the crowd which was as hot and emotion filled as any crowd I have ever seen.

The match can be seen on video. Like a joke that loses something in translation, there is no way a video can capture the speed of movement, emotion and intensity of this epic encounter. I consider myself indeed fortunate to have not only seen this great match but one of the most unique athletes ever to grace a wrestling ring, do an interview and cut a commercial. A match seen over 20 years ago could either be forgotten or the memory diminished among hundreds of other matches but this one never will.

Brody was very close with Larry Matysik, but he worked for Matysik's opposition, too. Brody was truly an outlaw. If a promotion could come up with his fee and transportation, and if the date was clear, Brody would go.

Meanwhile, in North Carolina, Dory and Terry Funk were beginning a short run with Jim Crockett, the NWA promoter. The Funks tried to secure Bruiser Brody and Stan Hansen a spot with Crockett, as a steady place for them to work in the U.S.

Stan Hansen:

Brody and I actually went to the NWA one time, kind of for a try-out one time. Our style ... and it was a choice between getting the Road Warriors job, and that's who they ended up bringing in. They got the job and they had a great run, and they made a lot of money, and they were very successful. Crockett naturally wanted for them [the NWA] to be first and Japan would be second, and we just couldn't do it.

Dory Funk Jr.:

Brody and Hansen were big, awesome, killer heels. Their theory brought money. They created an image that was scary to the fans sitting at ringside. If they really wanted to, they could pin anybody, and that's the kind of image you got with Brody and Stan Hansen. I actually was working in North Carolina and brought Brody and Stan Hansen to Jim Crockett. We put them in the ring for their first match to let Crockett kind of see how good these guys could be. (laughs) They broke one kid's jaw accidentally with a clothesline. They demonstrated what they could do and that they could draw money. They waited and waited for Jim Crockett, and he never did talk about money, so they left.

In July, August, and September of 1982, Brody was wrestling in Florida. He wrestled as a heel against Dusty Rhodes, Butch Reed, and many others.

Dusty Rhodes:

He knew he had Japan to fall back on, and we knew that, too. The business was run differently in those days. It was run territorially and everyone protected their own. In Florida, we used Frank more as an attraction. We brought him in and out. He just came in for short runs.

Brian Blair:

I was getting a push here in Florida about '82 and they brought him in to work with me, but they wanted him to beat me because I think then he was going to work with Dusty after that. They were going to do something where I kind of beat myself, something like that. Well, Frank pulled me aside and said, "*Screw that. I'm not going to beat you this way. Here's what we're going to do.*"

Anyway, he ended up giving me one of the best matches of my career. I think we were at Fort Homer Hesterly Armory that night. He wound up having us both counted out. He gave me most of the match. He made me look like a giant killer.

On June 16, 1983, Brody and Kerry von Erich once again won the NWA American tag team title, taking the belts from Terry Gordy and Michael Hayes at the Reunion Arena in Dallas. They held onto the belts until September 1983, when Brody was injured and the title was stripped.

The Missing Link (wrestler):

When I first went to Dallas as the Missing Link, Brody wasn't finished, but he had had his big run, so they put the two of us against each other. The Missing Link had to get over, and Brody knew how to help me do that, so we had a good thing going. But Brody didn't just give it to me. We went toe-to-toe. After 15 minutes, I asked, "*Should I sell now?*"

He said, "*What the hell's the use?*"

They had individual chairs in the Dallas Sportatorium. When we went out onto the wooden floor, he picked one up and hit me over the head. When he hit me, the funniest thought went through my mind. I thought about how cartoon characters were driven into the floor when they were hit over the head. That's exactly how I felt. He hit me with that chair harder than I had ever been hit by anybody. When Brody hit me, I felt like my feet were being driven into the wooden floor.

Brody and I were okay. We were good friends, and we had good matches, but neither one of us wanted the other one to shine. He was willing to give me something, but he plowed into me like a mad bull that night and made me work for whatever I got.

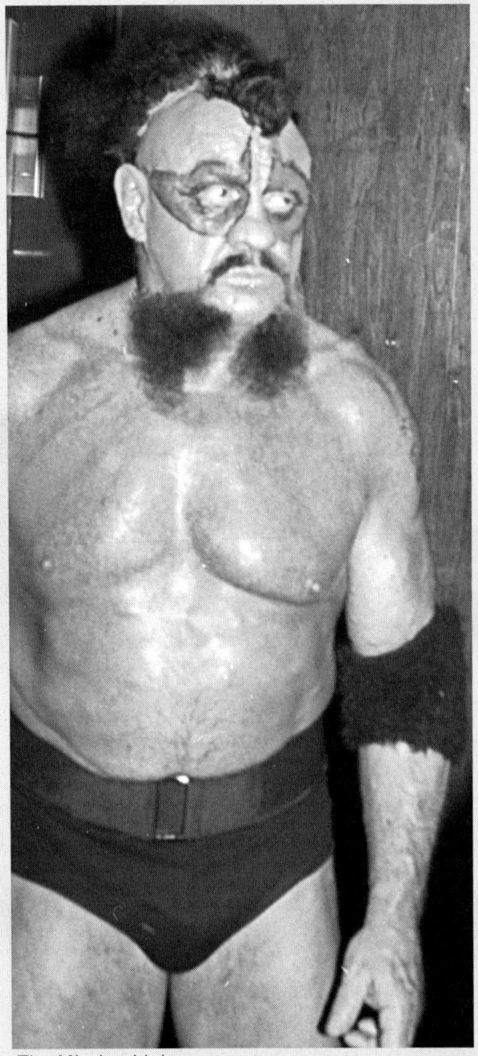
The Missing Link.

On August 31, 1983, in Tokyo, Japan, All Japan hosted a major card for Terry Funk's retirement. Funk would go on to retire several more times through the years and still wrestles today, but on that night, he and his brother Dory faced Stan Hansen and Terry Gordy. In the second main event, Bruiser Brody faced Jumbo Tsuruta. Brody lost the NWA International heavyweight title when he was counted out after 21 minutes and 33 seconds.

From November through early December 1983, Brody and Hansen wrestled again in All Japan's annual tournament, once again making it to the finals, this time facing Jumbo Tsuruta and Genichiro Tenryu. Brody and Hansen won the tournament when Hansen pinned Tenryu at the 16-minute mark.

Chapter X Puerto Rico

Brody first went to work in Puerto Rico in 1984. He worked as a heel and was managed by Larry Sharpe. The only game in town at that time was the World Wrestling Council [WWC] owned by Victor Jovica, local wrestling icon Carlos Colon, Victor Quinones, and in smaller parts, by Gorilla Monsoon and Jose Gonzales.

Dave Meltzer:

Carlos Colon was the local hero in Puerto Rico. In the '70s, they formed this wresting company, WWC. Right place, right time. Carlos was the lead babyface and business was just booming.

WWC held their first card in January 1974.

Dick Steinborn:

Carlos Colon and Victor Jovica had a little Volkswagen that they fitted with a loudspeaker. They would drive through the streets and tell everyone about their wrestling. Those guys started from nothing.

Brody and his AWA and WWC manager Larry "Pretty Boy" Sharpe.

Eddie Gries:

The owners of the WWC were Victor Jovica, Carlos Colon, Victor Quinones, Jose Gonzales, and Gorilla Monsoon. They bought Monsoon out in the '80s Most of it was owned by Colon and Jovica. Brody never owned a piece of that company.

Dave Meltzer:

Jose Gonzales was the booker for the company. Kind of the right hand man. I think he was part owner as well. As Invader he was the number two babyface there, just a guy who had been there forever. He wouldn't have been a star anywhere else but in Puerto Rico. He was that other local hero.

Dick Steinborn:

Gonzales gigged himself every night for Carlos. I was in a tag match with him one night in Puerto Rico and he gigged himself. It was a six-man tag, and I saw him bleeding like nobody's business. It was the worst thing you've ever seen. He grabbed Carlos by the leg and he looked up at him like he was God.

Dory Funk Jr.:

Brody started there through Carlos Colon. May have been through conversations with Terry and myself, but we didn't do the contact. We were pretty close to Colon, and he would talk to us about talent and who would be good for Puerto Rico. Puerto Rico was kind of ... they had really good wrestling talent, but often, talent that was not working steady for one of the feds. They used a lot of outlaw talent in Puerto Rico. Good talent, but renegades.

Carlos Colon:

He was recommended by Ric Flair to work in Puerto Rico. Ric Flair did the contact.

Dave Meltzer:

At that time, Puerto Rico was a real hotbed of wrestling and Brody's style fit perfectly. They were a total blood and guts territory. He was a willing bleeder and a brawler. He was a big foreigner and the Puerto Ricans loved that idea, that sort of a guy against Carlos Colon. Kind of like the Japanese, the big foreigner coming in against your underdog, native hero. He and Abdullah were the prototype as to what those kinds of fans would react to as far as a foreigner as either a babyface or a heel.

Victor Quinones, Carlos Colon, and Victor Jovica, 1987.

Carlos Colon:

You had to be on your toes when you wrestled Brody. He was a hard worker, very intense. You really had to be in shape to wrestle him. You could expect almost anything with Brody. He could throw a hold and then throw you over the top rope, and throw you into the crowd, and hit you with a chair. You just never knew.

Gary Hart:

Puerto Rico was such a dangerous place to work. The fans would cut you. They would punch you. They would hit you with boards. What they really used to love to do was to fill beer cans with sand and stomp them down and throw them at you like Frisbees.

I was always concerned because he was always Bruiser Brody. He had no fear. One night, we were in Trinidad. It was Abdullah, Bruiser Brody, myself, and Dory Funk Jr., and we had a major riot. The four of us were in a little bitty, outhouse-like thing. Just a small room, and thousands of people were congregating around the little area we were at. The bus pulled up to get us in, but none of us wanted to go out. Except Bruiser. He stepped back and kicked that door, knocking it off the hinges. He jumped out into the middle of the people going, "*Huss, Huss, Huss, Huss!*"

They all ran like bastards. Abby, me, and Dory Funk,

jumped on the bus. Brody jumped on and we took off.

Abdullah the Butcher:

Oh, sure it was scary. When I first started going down there in 1960-something, they used to throw great big rocks, but now it's all changed. I'm the babyface there now.

Roger Kirby:

Dick Steinborn, Mr. Fuji, and I were booked in Trinidad one night when we were working in Puerto Rico. The place was sold out. Jose Gonzales [Invader #1] came to the dressing room and said, "*Fuji, I want you to throw the salt tonight.*"

I told Jose, "*That's not necessary. We already have a sellout crowd. Let Fuji beat [his opponent] and throw the salt another time.*"

Jose wouldn't go for it. "*I'm the boss. You do what I say.*"

As I feared, a riot broke out and people started to throw bottles and all kinds of things. Broken glass was raining down on us and I had cuts all over my body. Fuji got the worst of it and wound up with 32 stitches in his arm before I could get him out of the ring and back to the dressing room.

After they swept the glass out of the ring, they called for the main event. Steinborn and I were on top, but we refused to go to the ring. I finally gave in and went out and worked with Jose. I forced him to beat me almost instantly. You couldn't even call it a short match.

The next morning, while we were eating breakfast,

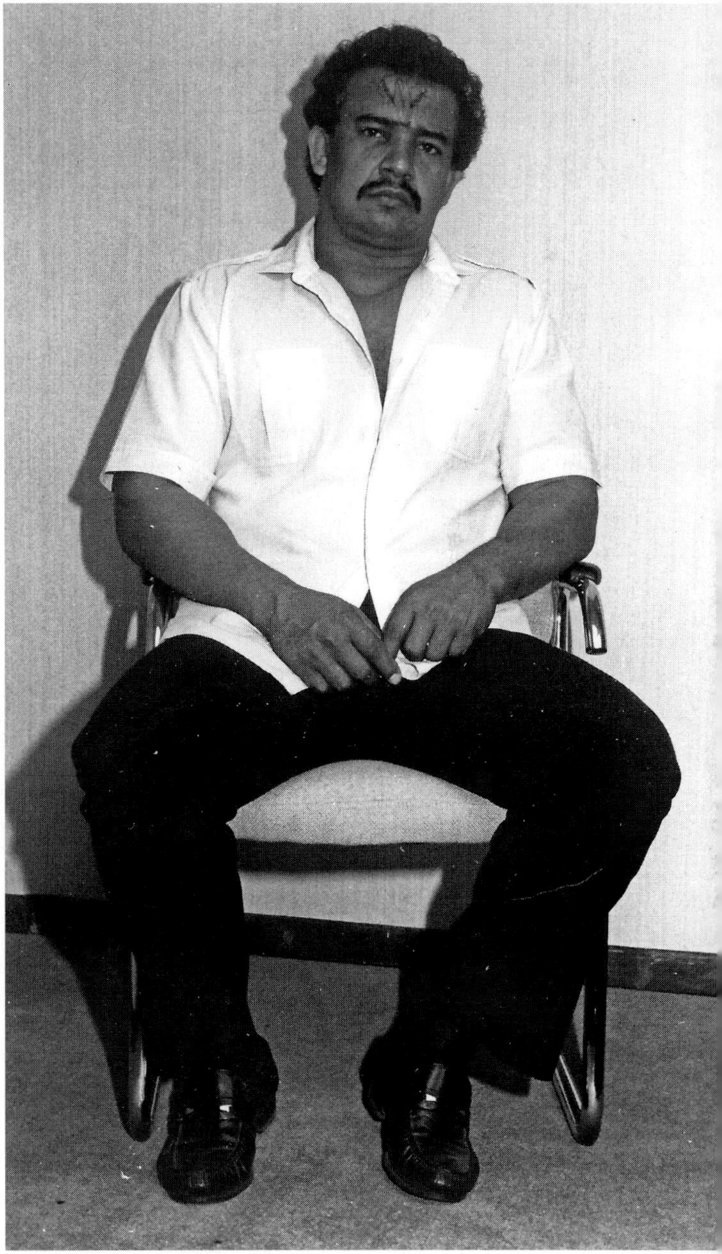

Jose Huertas Gonzales, Invader #1.

Jose and Carlos Colon walked over and fired us on the spot. Years later, of course, Brody refused to do what Jose wanted, too. When I heard about Brody being killed, I thought, "*Jeez!* Steinborn and I could have been a statistic. We were lucky to get fired.

Larry Matysik:

It became a place where if Brody knew everyone was pissed off at him, he knew he could go there and make a few bucks and get out. He didn't like it at all.

Carlos Colon:

If he wasn't in Japan, he was here. He was no problem. He worked here for a long time and we never had any problems with him. We made a lot of money for each other.

In his first match ever, El Exotico was given the honor of getting his butt kicked by his hero, Bruiser Brody.

Leo Sykes:

When they bring you down there, they treat you like a king. They're real polite about asking you to put their people over and you better do it. I'm surprised they let Frank go as often as they did because a lot of times, he just wouldn't do it.

Dave Meltzer:

He was friends with Victor Quinones. That was the guy he went through when he was down there. He didn't have that much to do with the other guys.

Eddie Gries:

Through Victor [Quinones], I was friends with Frank Brody, and whenever he came to Puerto Rico, Brody would usually stay with Victor, or get a hotel room, and Abdullah the Butcher would stay with me. They would communicate by telephone. They couldn't be seen together. It was all kayfabe back then, which Frank Brody broke constantly. He fought with [Mr.] Pogo one night and then he's out drinking with him that night. That drove the promoters crazy.

Frank was a sweetheart. I smoked many a night with him. We were good smoking partners. I loved it. It had nothing to do with his death, though. You got to mention in your book, he loved his smoke. Listen, don't even mention that I helped you unless you talk about Frank and me smoking.

Dory Funk Jr.:

Rabid wrestling fans, fabulous fans. I enjoyed working in front of them. We used to go to Bithorn Stadium, pack that thing with people. How many people does it hold? They used to say 12,000. It's a huge stadium.

Kamala:

Puerto Rico is depressing. You had to fight for your money … they still owe me a lot of money from bounced checks and things like that. I would go over there just to try to pick up a few dollars, but I didn't like it. I liked the climate, but the rest I didn't.

Bruiser Brody takes flight in Puerto Rico.

Dory Funk Jr.:

I had a really great time down there, upwards of 15 years. There was a time when Marti and I used to fly to Puerto Rico every other week and spend 4-day or 5-day weekends. For a while, it was the only place I'd work. It was like a vacation.

In 1984, Vince McMahon and his company, the World Wrestling Federation, began raiding all of the country's local promoters of their top guys. The War of '84 started in the heart of the NWA—St. Louis—and quickly spread. The WWF began touring outside of its "territory" in the Northeast and took its show all over the country. At one time, they even had three groups putting on shows in different parts of the country. McMahon also undercut other promoter's ties with television stations by offering a cheaper, slicker, show, and thereby making his promotion the first major nationwide promotion. Other wrestling promotions had national television shows, but whether you were in St. James, New York, or Santa Cruz, California, you saw the same "WWF wrestling superstars" on television and in person. You shared the same feuds and storylines with every other wrestling fan in the country.

Scott Romer:

St. Louis was the first territory that the WWF came out to crush.

Larry Matysik:

It is a very complicated story. Little do I know, of course, in the background, as we get to the TV situation, and I'm talking to the general manager, Barry Baker at channel 11, all of a sudden the owner, Ted Koppler, calls me. "*Yeah, we really want you back. You know, Larry, we're really good friends with Vince McMahon, and I can't think of a better partnership to be on channel 11 than Larry and Vince.*"

I'm dumbfounded. I was talking to Vince virtually every day. He never said anything to me. He knew what was going on, and I have to say that Brody was the other one I'm talking to everyday, and Frank was the one saying all the way through, "*Don't tell that fucking Vince nothing. Be careful, be careful, be careful.*"

He wanted me to keep fighting while I'm stuck in the middle.

Before I made the deal with Vince, there was an interim in there when we shut down, and before I said yes to Vince because I was ... well, I said yes, then I hemmed and hawed and didn't say yes ... That

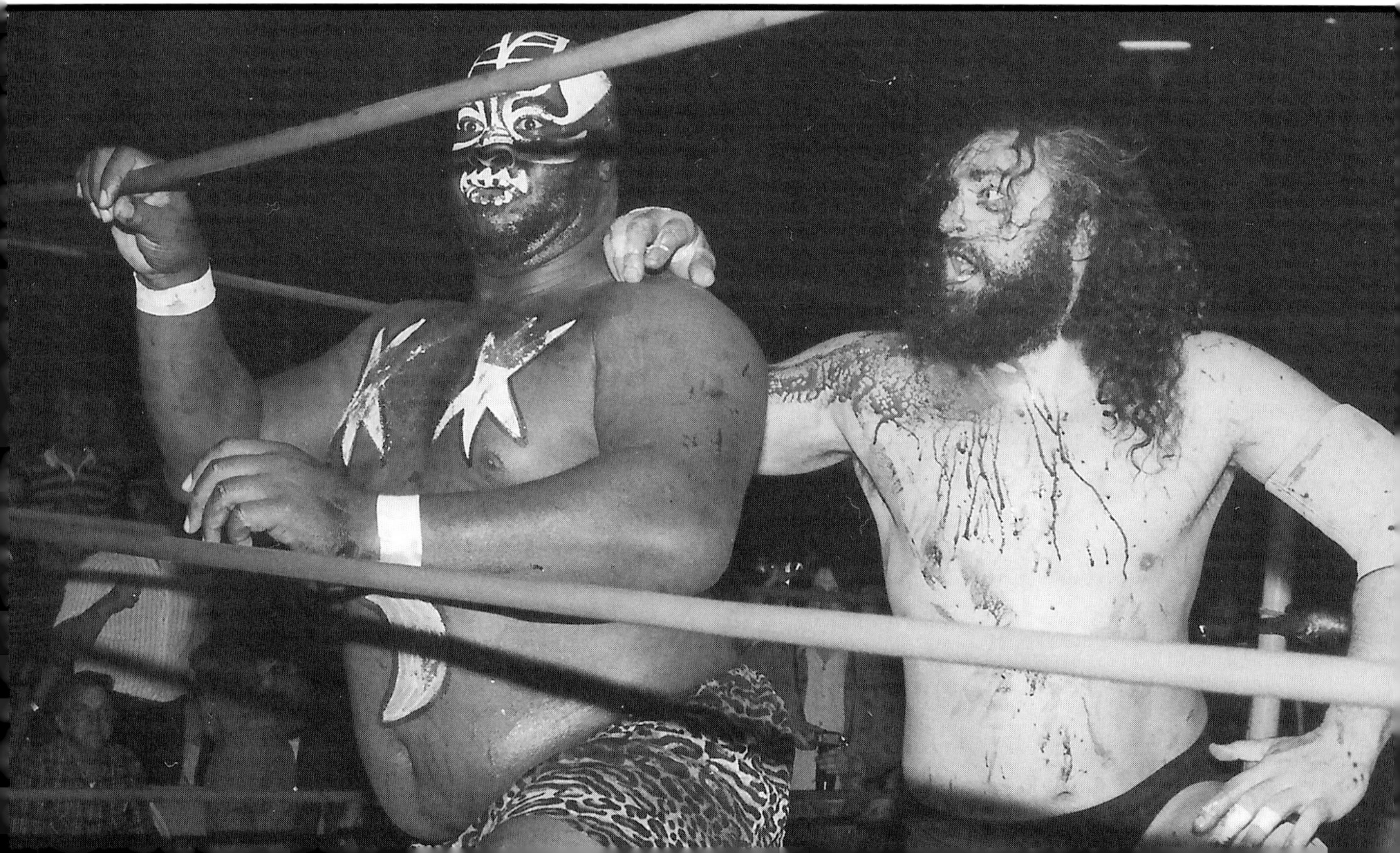

was the time when Geigel, Race, O'Connor … well not so much O'Connor, but Geigel, Race, Crockett, Watts were putting together a show and they were in the Meadowlands. I met at Sam's apartment with Geigel and Race and they wanted me to come back with that operation. "*Hey, St. Louis, do what you want. We want you to do the TV. We're gonna work together.*"

They were telling me all the different ideas they had. And when they left and it was just me and Sam—and I'd known him since I was 16 years old—he says, "*What do you think?*"

I said, "*Some of the things they're saying. I know Crockett and Watts. Those guys aren't going to go for that.*"

And Sam said, "*I think you're thinking the right way. I think the one who's going to win this is Vince.*"

So I knew.

I was doing well with my shows, but pretty much, I was running a one man show, so basically I got forced into the deal with Vince. Vince, of course, over the next year, managed to maneuver around to where I was not making the money I was supposed to be making, in typical Vince fashion. He won. He was smarter than me, he was more ruthless, and he saw the future better.

During that time, Brody and I were running an independent operation until he died. A few months after I went with Vince, I had the opportunity to run a show in Belleville [Illinois], a little suburb of St. Louis, with a guy. I was still in touch with Frank and I was going through bitterness and cyclical depression and everything. Frank's saying, "*Hang in there. It's a dirty fucking business. Everybody cheats everybody, anyhow.*"

So, I called him. "*This guy wants to run a show. What do you think?*"

He says, "*Hey, I want 750 and trans. You oughta take at least 250 or 500. Wadda you want?*"

So I went in the middle with 350 and I call the guy back and said, "*Tell you what. I can book Brody for you. Here's the deal. He gets 750 and trans, I get 350.*"

He says, "*Okay.*"

From that, we started running shows, many places in Southern Illinois, a few Missouri shots. It got to the point where we pretty much put our own stuff together. We would find somebody to front it—somebody you would say is a mark. I'd sell him a show. I'd say, "*Here's the deal. Promoters license, ring, referee, the entire show, six grand. If you make ten grand, we'll pat you on the back and say, 'Great!' You make four grand, we still get six.*"

So we had no financial risk in it. The first $1,500 went to me and Brody, and then we'd go with Greg Valentine, Spike Huber, whoever was floating around. Scott Casey. I can't even remember them all. Just different people that were there, you know. Killer Brooks, Abby, different things like that. Sometimes we had good shows, sometimes we had bad shows.

That was a time when Brody and I talked every day. We rode together a lot when he was in town. I was taking a lot of information I got back to Dave [Meltzer], or that I got from Vince, because don't forget, at that point, Brody and I were probably the only ones, along with Dave, in the entire country that knew when everybody ran their TV. We knew everybody that was fucking anybody. I was with Vince. Brody was running all over the place with

Opposite and Overleaf: Brody wrestles Kamala, the Ugandan Headhunter.

STAR

outlaws. I still had connections with the so-called serious NWA side. Dave had started to develop his connections. We literally talked every day. My wife can tell you many times where Brody and I would be sitting on the phone until three o'clock in the morning.

Bob Geigel:

I never had a problem with him, personally. I got along with him. Physically, I was never in awe. I never backed off from him and I think he respected that.

Larry Matysik:

Brody's theory was, if you lied to him once, that was the end of the relationship, in terms of trusting each other. Geigel fucked him once on a payday. He spent a lifetime fucking Geigel. Not going to show up in Des Moines got Terry Funk going, "*Bruise! Bruise! Bruise!*" In the middle of the ring. Bob Geigel's having a heart attack in the back.

[Brody said,] "*Well, tough shit.*"

[I said,] "*What's it take to get you there?*"

"*About $500 because he lied to me about Kansas City and the payoff, and I want the payoff in Des Moines right there. If it's not there, fuck it. I'm turning right around and I'm walking out.*"

He was just hardcore like that.

Bob Geigel:

I don't remember that time with Terry Funk. We had a show out in St. Louis in the arena one time. We had 19,000 people there. The match was Brody and Flair. When Brody got there, he decided he wasn't going to wrestle. He didn't tell me this, but he told Pat. He didn't tell that to Harley because Harley didn't put up with any bullshit. He showed, but he didn't wrestle. We moved Dick the Bruiser over in his place. Probably had a better match, and we brought the same match back, and we had a full house again. Yeah, I never really had any problem. He was a big strong guy, but I'm really not sure how deep his character went.

Brody and Larry Matysik, St. Louis.

Harley Race:

Bob is the kind of guy who won't say anything bad about anyone.

Ox Baker (wrestler):

Larry Matysik made Brody a lot of money in St. Louis. Larry acted like a big shot to me. He acted like he was running St. Louis, but he wasn't. Sam Muchnik was. So, in the dressing room one time Brody says, "*Yeah he's a great guy. He got me fifty shots around there.*"

I said, "*Yeah, but he keeps acting like he's the big shot,*" and he said, "*I don't like that kind of talk. He's a friend of mine.*"

I said, "*I'm only giving you a true statement.*"

He said, "*Well, we could settle this.*"

I said, "*What are we going to settle? You're my friend. I don't think he's right.*"

No blows were thrown, but 20 minutes later, he came back and we were still friends. We agreed to disagree.

Brody was in and out of Kansas City. His relationship with Bob Geigel, Pat O'Connor, and Harley Race was pretty rocky. They loved the crowds Brody drew, but if it was an off night, and not as many fans showed up as they expected, Brody could be unpredictable.

Kamala:

We talked a lot. Brody seemed like he liked talking with me. Even when we'd be getting ready to wrestle, we'd be sitting side by side, and he kinda liked talking to me. He wouldn't talk to me a lot, but a lot more than the other guys. Brody used to talk about how he lost his weight. [Eat] tuna and drink water, that's how he lost all that weight. He was telling me with the gimmick I had, I should book myself out. "*Don't be tied down to one promoter. That's the way you make money. That's what I do.*"

Ox Baker:

He came through Kansas City a couple of times and wrestled Ric Flair, who was the champion at the time. Brody was old school. The old school was if you thought you could beat him, he'd give you a chance to try it. They don't do that nowadays. I lost nine teeth trying to prove I was tough. Ric Flair was super tough. He said, "*Brody, you couldn't beat me if we wrestled straight up.*"

So they went for fifteen minutes before the fans came in and nobody won. They were both huffing and puffing and they were both red, but Bruiser said to me, "*Geez, I didn't think he was that tough.*"

After that, that night him and Flair went the whole hour, and they wrestled that night, I don't believe five punches were thrown. Bruiser Brody was in fantastic shape.

The Missing Link:

I was wrestling in Kansas City in [January 20] 1983. After I finished wrestling, I got ready to leave, but I decided to watch a few minutes of the main event—Ric Flair versus Bruiser Brody. One hour later, I was still standing in the wings, watching as the referee raised the hands of both men.

Brody and Flair had a great match. They wrestled for one solid hour. And no, they didn't get a hold and sit on the mat for 15 minutes, then get another hold and sit for another 15 minutes. They gave the wrestling fans 60 minutes of mat wrestling—up and down, countering hold after hold, with very few rest holds in-between. Flair was known for being able to walk the walk, and to talk the talk, and he was a great mat worker, but Brody showed me that night that he could stay toe-to-toe with the best of them.

Kamala:

He got me my first big payoff, I know that. We went to Kansas City. I was with the Von Erich's then and I really hadn't made $3,000 in one night, so he took me to Kansas City and said, "*You gonna make some money this time.*"

He didn't just stay in World Class. He booked himself out and told me that's what I should do, because at that time, I didn't have any experience booking myself out. I had been around for about four years. Brody took me to Kansas City and we were in the main event ... and I made $3,000 that weekend. I was flipping like that monkey on Tarzan, Cheetah! I never had that payoff in one night. We used to sell out everywhere we would go.

Larry Matysik:

But one time when we were running opposition, Buck [Robley] was booking for Kansas City. We had back-to-back shows. I was the Friday night show and they were the Saturday night show, and my show on Channel 30 was on. So here I am with the Kansas City booker, Robley, and my top guy, Brody, watching the tape, the night Robley was going to book the other side. But you know Buck was as much on our side ... you know, Buck was a hired gun. We're watching the tape and ... you know, it was Brody against somebody, and he did something where he took a hit and goes down to one knee, and comes up. Robley went nuts. He says, "*God damn. You're serious. You're selling, you're selling!*"

Brody says, "*Well, hey. It's a serious, fucking, fight.*"

Buck says, "*Yeah, but you sold!*"

It was hilarious. That's when Robley knew Brody and I were going to go down the shithole together if that's the way it went. Brody was in no danger. He had plenty of places to go, and he always had Japan to fall back on.

In February 1984, just as he was starting a tour with All Japan, David von Erich died suddenly. Brody had arranged for David to go to Japan and traveled with him, looking out for him as a favor to Fritz. David's death has always been a hotly-debated subject. The autopsy states that von Erich died of enteritis, but many believe that he died of a drug overdose.

Kevin von Erich:

David just looked horrible before he left for Japan. He had been sick for a long time. He had diarrhea. And you know, before he left, I hugged him. I never hugged my brother, but I hugged him that time, right before he left for Japan.

Larry Matysik:

I know when he [Brody] found David's body. It was him and Joe Higuchi. [They] went back from the building and found David's body in Japan. I can tell this story now because it's twenty years later. They found the pills and Brody said, "*Hey, what good*

David Von Erich.

would it do as far as the Japanese people that thought Fritz was a god, to have that."

So he flushed them all down the toilet, and Joe knew it, and Joe didn't say a word.

John Dananay:

This has and will be disputed for years. Brody, as it has been told, told Dave Meltzer that he [Brody] personally flushed drugs [painkillers] down the toilet that were found in David's hotel room. However, the actual cause of death is listed as acute enteritis, which is a poisoning of the intestines, which is very treatable if detected early. David's, by all accounts, was not. David had been having discomfort with his stomach for months prior to his death.

Tony Atlas:

The day before he was killed, I took Brody to the gym with me and he told me about the circumstances behind David von Erich's death.

Scott Romer:

I was on assignment for Gong Magazine. David's funeral was the next biggest thing to hit the Dallas/Fort Worth area since the assassination of Kennedy. It was unbelievable. I arrived early, turned on the TV, and they were running pizza commercials with the Von Erich's on them. They were the All-American family. They wanted it to be like the Brady Bunch, you know. It was so crowded at the service, wall-to-wall people on the inside, and I couldn't even get inside. They had a loud speaker and there was another 4,000, maybe 5,000, people on the outside of the church.

Brody returned to Japan in April 1984. From the 13th through the 25th, All Japan hosted a tournament for the vacant PWF tag team title. Brody and Stan Hansen defeated Giant Baba & Dory Funk Jr. in the final round in the Yokohama Bunka Gym in Kanagawa, Japan.

Chapter XI Red River Jack

On August 16, 1960, Minnesota promoter Verne Gagne and several other Midwestern promoters left the NWA to form the American Wrestling Association [AWA]. Gagne was not only the AWA's head, but he was also its first champion. Gagne held the belt for 15 years, defending it a couple of times a week. He lost it to Nick Bockwinkel in November 1975. Gagne brought Bruiser Brody into the AWA in June 1984, but out of respect to his old friend Dick the Bruiser, Gagne had Brody come in as King Kong Brody.

Nick Bockwinkel:
He, himself, made the inquiry to Mr. Gagne. The promotion asked a number of us our opinion, and his reputation had been established, so at that point, a lot of us said, "*Don't bring him in here.*"

Dave Meltzer:
Verne had been stripped by Vince McMahon of most of his talent, and Brody was a natural one to go to at that point in time. Verne still had a lot of good cities.

In January 1984, Verne Gagne had seriously dropped the ball by letting Vince McMahon lure Hulk Hogan away from the AWA. Gagne paid for his mistake when his gates started to drop as the WWF's expansion rolled across the country.

Larry Nelson:
Verne brought him in because King Kong Brody sold wrestling tickets. It's just that simple.

Brody had worked a deal with Gagne to only work for the AWA on the weekends. Verne Gagne knew Brody could sell tickets even if he wasn't there, so he had no problem advertising Brody on every card, weekend or not. On the night of the weekday shows, he would tell fans that Brody had been unable to make the date.

Nick Bockwinkel:
By that time, Brody had established himself as being a real recalcitrant, and he walked to his own drummer, and for whatever reason, his rep by then was that he had no respect for promotion, other than Japan, which really was his bread and butter, because one could easily bring in close to a quarter of a million dollars a year there. There were those of

us curious as to why he was coming in.

Larry Nelson:

It was still a big territory. He knew he could make money there and Verne knew he could make money with him. So, they would tolerate each other as long as they could. He said to me, "*You'll notice I've been defeated, but I've never been beaten up.*" And he never was.

Larry Matysik:

We would be on the telephone, going over business, or talking about what kind of deal we could do. When he was with Gagne, I'd say, "*You ever think about this? We did this in St. Louis once.*"

He'd say, "*Oh, shit. I could adapt that out here. That's a hell of an idea. How can we involve Verne?*"

Because then they'd all want to do it, if it involved Verne. It was an education. Frank was very smart about the business in a rebellious sort of way.

Nick Bockwinkel:

There are those who kind of like to dictate the flow of a match, and Brody, if he could, would dictate the flow of a match—as would his good friend, Stan Hansen—which would be a thumper and a pounder and a kicker. Ironically, Mr. Brody, if you forced him to wrestle, he could! And he had tremendous talent. As far as I was concerned, he was one of the great talents of the profession. For his size, his speed and agility were unbelievable. A lot of people only got to see the thumping, pounding side, and if you could force him to wrestle, you would see, "*God, this guy can really wrestle and not just pound on people.*"

Vader:

I started out in the AWA. I remember my very first match in the business was with Bruiser Brody, simply because of my size. It was probably the most painful thing I've ever done in my life. He wanted to break me in right. I think he did. After that first night, he eased up a little bit and he was actually trying to teach me a few things. We went around and wrestled maybe six weeks together.

I went right from him to Jerry Blackwell, then I had a run with Stan Hansen for the title. My first three opponents in this business were probably three of the biggest, toughest, meanest in the business.

When I finally got with a normal person, and my first punch, I thought I knocked the guy out. I remember him crawling out of the ring, going to Verne, and saying, "*This guy's crazy. I'm not gonna work with him.*"

Verne sat me down and said, "*Man, what's wrong with you? You never had this kind of problem before. Why are you working so stiff and trying to beat this guy up?*"

I said, "*Look, I've had feuds for the last six months with Stan, Jerry, or Brody. They've been hitting me so hard that I would either be nearly knocked out, knocked out, or couldn't breath, and I just assumed that was the way it was. Now if you're telling me something different, you need to reeducate me because I thought that's the way it was.*"

Magic Schwarz:

I wrestled him at the Showboat in Las Vegas when he worked for Verne Gagne with the AWA. My night with him was probably the wildest night I ever had in my whole career. We were doing television

Left: The classiest man in wrestling, former AWA World Heavyweight Champion, Nick Bockwinkel.

and Sheikh Adnan Alkaissy was his manager. Gagne came into the dressing room and said, "*Okay, look. Tonight, there's not gonna be any chairs used in any matches because the athletic commission has positively said there's absolutely no chairs gonna be hit over anybody's head.*"

So out I go. The bell rings. The first thing Brody does is throw me out of the ring, grabs a chair, and waylaid me. He threw me back into the ring and, kind of like worked me over for about five minutes. What I remember about the end of the match was him picking me up over his head and throwing me into the third row of seats. That was the finish.

The whole time we were in there, he didn't realize who I was because I hadn't seen him in over 15 or 20 years, and I became a wrestler without him knowing about it. After it was all over with, later on that night, we were down gambling at the Showboat in Las Vegas. We were all staying in the hotel. Brody came down and finally realized who I was, and apologized for tearing me apart. Wrestling him was one of the highlights of my career.

Vader:

We were fighting and he booted me, and I went down. He went out and got a chair and hit me in the back, then whacked me in the leg. He was hitting me pretty hard. My leg was sore. It looked like he was breaking my leg. Brody was noted for his realism, God rest his soul. The deal was, I was then going over to [work for] Otto Vanz [in Germany] for the CWA. He broke my leg so I could leave the territory and move on.

Larry Nelson:

I thought, how are the fans ... when I interview this man in the ring, and they know he could squash me like a grape, why would I have the courage to stay in there? And the man knew professional wrestling. He was a giant of a man, towered over me, and I'm walking up with a microphone in my hand. He says, "*I could beat you up any time I wanted to, but you're not worth the trouble! I don't like you, but I'm not going to hurt you because the Sheik's not paying me to beat you up!*"

You understand what he did there? Now I can do my job. I can go ahead and interview him.

He was teaching John Nord. The AWA took John Nord out of their wrestling school when Brody left the territory and called him The Barbarian. They had the Barbarian doing the bark like Frank, but it didn't work. People wanted the real guy, so they brought him back and they paired Brody with John Nord for a short time, and then he left again.

Dave Meltzer:

Verne paid Brody well, but he was always wary of promoters. He had this little radar, and whenever he felt like he was going to get screwed, he'd screw the promoter first.

Larry Nelson:

He would get along with Verne Gagne for a while, but sooner or later, they would snap and he wouldn't be around very long, then he'd come back.

Right: Brody wrestles the The Mountain from Stone Mountain, Jerry "Crusher" Blackwell.

Dave Meltzer:

Verne wasn't used to dealing with someone like Brody. He never did well with guys like him and Hansen, the guys with the Japanese deal. He was used to bullying guys. They left on bad terms all in all.

Spike Huber:

A bunch of us guys were in the back, and you could see it was a sold-out crowd at the amphitheater. We were watching the match and Verne tried to start shooting on Frank in the ring. He went behind him and he was standing up … and Brody just went as hard as he could backwards and ran him into the turnbuckles, knocking all the air out of him. The shoot was over.

Nick Bockwinkel:

Brody was very placid, and seemingly very agreeable, and that was part of his … well, I don't want to say deception, because as far as I was concerned, he wasn't deceiving anybody. He did the same to Paul Boesch in Houston. He did the same to Joe Blanchard, who was one of the nicest people in the world. [Joe] was the promoter in San Antonio, which was his hometown, and [Brody] screwed him over, in some fashion or another, by not being professional. Not being a quality person and fulfilling his obligations to a promoter, to a crowd at any arena. So he had already done that to Blanchard and Boesch. For me to suspect him [of doing] the same thing to Verne Gagne? There was nothing to suspect. If somebody would have said, "*Ten dollar bet,*" I would've said,

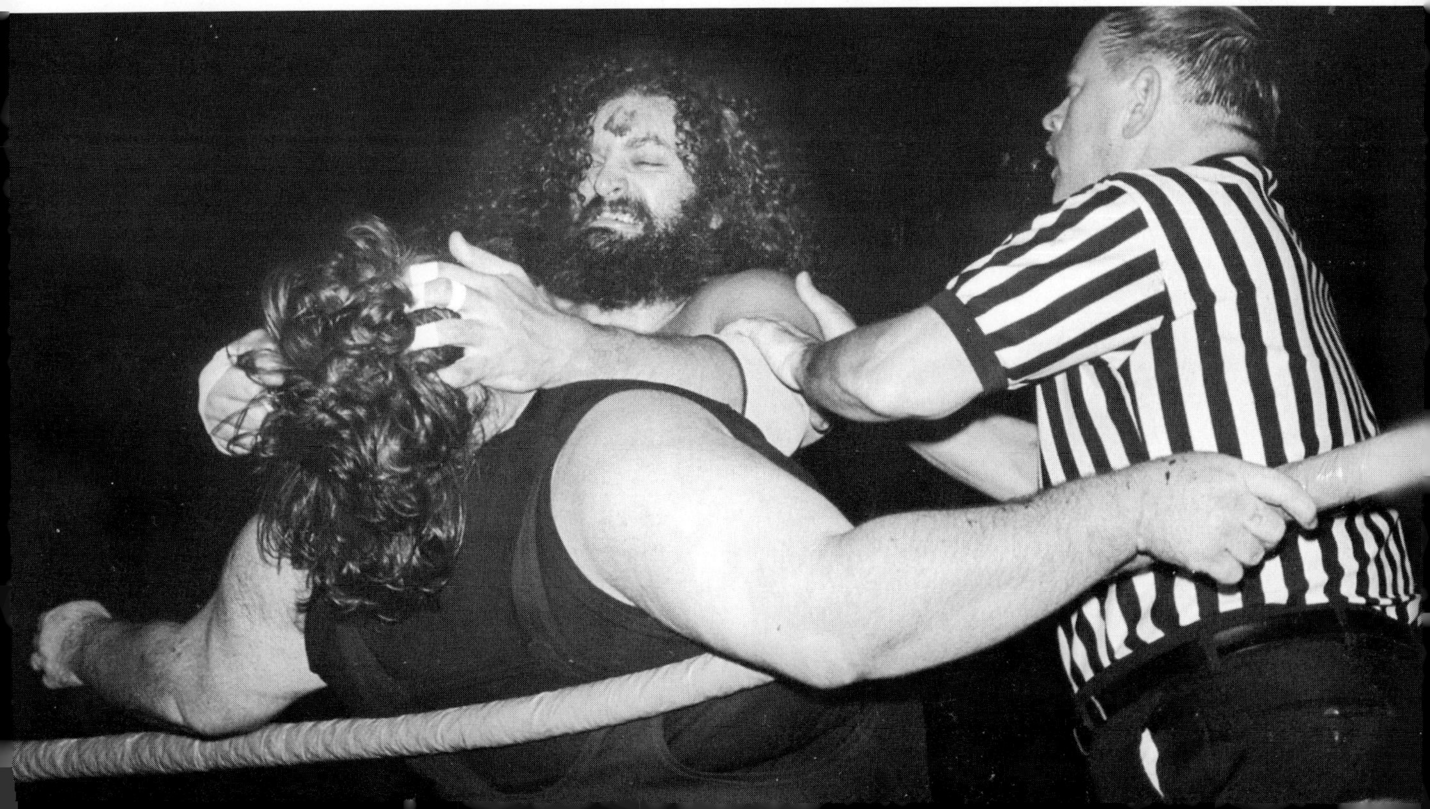

"*Hah. Make it twenty.*"

Scott Romer:

I went out with him after an AWA show and he was full of all kinds of hostility at Verne Gagne. Verne Gagne and the Bruiser ran an AWA show together in Indianapolis and probably drew less than 1,000 people. A terrible crowd.

Brody was all, "*Fuck Gagne. Screw him. I had to leave my family to come to this crap town. After my expenses, I'll be lucky if I've made a hundred bucks!*"

Nick Bockwinkel:

And then he proved himself to be consistent. I was one of the people who said, "*As a promotion, don't bring him in.*" Why? 18,000 people, St. Paul Civic Center. He and [Jerry] Blackwell are partners in a tag match. I don't even remember who it was against, but all of a sudden, he just jumps down off the apron and walks back to the dressing room.

Why'd he do that? You tell me. This was the first time Mr. Gagne had seen that. Oh, wow! I'm sure his eyes opened up real wide, and of course, that was the last night that he wrestled with the AWA. But why would he even do it, anyway?

The AWA's owner and first champion, Verne Gagne.

Dave Meltzer:

He and Blackwell were friends. They worked independently together afterwards, but he saw the writing on the wall. They were going to beat him, so he figured it was time to leave, and he figured he'd beat Verne to the punch.

Larry Nelson:

I remember that match with Jerry Blackwell. Verne Gagne had decided to change the finish to the match, halfway through it, which was going to be Frank getting beat up, and he simply left the ring.

Brody left the AWA, but he did return one other time for a special event. On April 20, 1986, in the main event at AWA's WrestleRock, Brody and Nord the Barbarian faced Brody's old tag-team partner, Jimmy Snuka, and Greg Gagne in a steel cage. The AWA, like all of the competition, eventually fell to Vince McMahon and the WWF.

Things were changing in Japan as well. All Japan had hired thirteen new wrestlers in 1984. Brody had been touring there steadily for six years and he was now the old hand. Brody's radar went off. It was time to go.

Dave Meltzer:

The Road Warriors came into All Japan in March of '85, and because the Road Warriors were new and so big at the time, he may have sensed that instead of him and Hansen being number one, the Road Warriors, because of their newness, would become number one, and they would settle into a new position. Plus, the New Japan offer came. If he jumped, he'd be fresh. Riki Choshu came over, too, and All Japan was just so loaded with talent.

James Beard (referee):

Bruiser was teaming at the time with Killer Brooks, and there was noise that he was considering moving from Baba's group to Inoki's. Baba's people wanted him and Killer to put over their top tag team in a big showdown. Bruiser refused, and he and Killer stayed locked in their dressing rooms with no intention of cooperating. A lot of pressure was applied and Baba sent his representatives to talk to the two American outlaws, but all urging and begging went to no avail. Bruiser wasn't going to budge. When things got really tense, Killer told Bruiser he was willing to put the Japanese wrestlers over. Bruiser told him in no uncertain terms that no tag team partner of his was doing any such thing. So, the standoff continued.

Killer Tim Brooks:

Bruiser and I were tag team partners with Baba's group [All Japan]. We were scheduled to wrestle on TV on the last night of the tour. [March 9, 1985, 7:56 time] It was also the last night that Bruiser was going to work for Baba's group, but nobody knew that.

We were going to be tag teaming in the Sumo Palace [Ryogoku Kokugikan] against [Yoshiaki] Yatsu and [Riki] Choshu, Baba's two up-and-coming stars. They asked us to do the favor [lose the match]. Bruiser wasn't gonna do a job, whether he was leaving or not. Not for those two. If Bruiser was gonna do a job, it would be for Baba, and that would be just about it. He wouldn't do it for anyone else but the boss.

We stayed on the bus for a long time. When everybody else went inside, Bruiser said, "*We'll stay on the bus.*"

A while later, they sent somebody out and they said, "*The office said to come in.*"

Bruiser said, "*You go tell 'em we're stayin' on the bus.*"

Again, they left us for awhile, then came back out with the finish. Bruiser said, "*No, we cannot lose.*"

They left and came back with another finish. Bruiser said, "*No, we can't lose.*"

The next time, they came with another finish and a message. "*Bruiser. You're not losing. We're asking Killer Brooks to lose.*"

Bruiser said, "*Killer Brooks can't lose. He's a main eventer who wrestles all over the world and he's my tag team partner. If Killer Brooks loses, it'll make me look bad, too.*"

Bruiser didn't want our team to lose because he was switching groups, and even though I was doing the job, it would make him look bad.

James Beard:

Finally, after a long period of time and things getting nowhere, it was coming up on match time. Other incentives [upfront] were offered and Bruiser agreed to wrestle. From the opening bell, Brody and Killer beat the hell out of the Japanese tag team, much to the dismay of Baba and his officials. It was obvious Bruiser intended to leave an impression as he left the company.

Killer Tim Brooks:

We argued back and forth for a long time. It was pretty nasty. When we finally went to the ring for the match, nothing had been settled. After the match started, Bruiser told them [Yatsu and Choshu] to just grab their best hold and do whatever. Whatever happened was going to happen. We had a tremendous match. It was damn near a shoot. Of course, the Japanese boys were gonna pick on me because I was the weakest link, but every time they would go to try to beat me, or do something to me, Bruiser would come in and give them a big boot to the face to get them off. It got nastier and nastier.

Halfway through the match, Bruiser told me, "*Go ahead and do it for 'em.*" He continued on to say, "*After you do it, get your ass of the way in a hurry because I'm gonna take my chain and beat the hell out of everybody.*"

After a few minutes, I told Yatsu, "*Hey, take the fall on me.*"

So they did—1-2-3—and here came Bruiser with that chain. He whacked both of them and they scooted out. He whacked some of the young boys at ringside. Of course, they ran, too. He even went into the audience and hit a couple of people. It was all on TV. He went crazy. Of course, he kept his heat. That was quite an experience. True story.

Really and truly, it was okay for Bruiser because he was switching over to the other group, but it was a hard thing for me to do because I was left there. I always made good money there. The argument made it look like I didn't want to do business, and sure enough, that was my last trip over there. I had been there about 20 times, but I was trying to be a good tag team partner and a good friend of Bruiser, and it ended up costing me.

I'm not saying that I regret it because I don't, but I was dead in the middle. I had to make a choice and ... I have to make a statement. Bruiser was my very best friend in the business. [Roddy] Piper was right close, but Bruiser was probably a closer friend than Piper. Piper and I were tag team partners in the Pacific Northwest. Roddy was a real good friend, and still is, of course.

As his partner, Bruiser didn't want me to do the job, but you just don't do shit like that in Japan. It's a dishonor to the company and to Baba. I paid for it, but do you know what? I don't care. I just don't care, because the promoters practically always got their way, and I had denied them before, in the States. A lot of times I would leave territories, or send their belt back and say, "*I'm gone. I'm not gonna do what you want.*" That hurt me. I think if I had done everything they wanted me to do, I could have gone a little higher in the business ... but I don't know. Some of the guys let the promoters do everything they wanted, let 'em completely control their lives, and there's some others who will only go so far before they start denying. I don't really know which way is the best to go. I walked out on Lebell in California. I walked out on Fritz a couple of times, and Joe Blanchard. I walked out on Cowboy Bill Watts, too. He was the most difficult to work for.

Abdullah the Butcher:

He wasn't being treated right. Why did I jump from All Japan to New Japan? I wasn't being treated right. When you're drawing people, money, you want people to respect you.

Stan Hansen:

I think because of how I came up. I went to New Japan, then I came over [to All Japan], and because I was the new guy, and Brody had been there a little bit, maybe I had more opportunity. But I always thought of us as one. I think Brody wanted to basically try to see if he wanted to be the number one. He wanted to go over there and he wanted to pop New Japan, and he wanted to go and be in that good position. Whether that was ego, or whether that was just opportunity, or whether that was just wanting to know if I can do it—I don't know. We had no bad feelings about that. I knew it was going to happen. I warned him. I said, "*This is not Giant Baba you're dealing with. This is a whole different group of guys*," and sure enough, he had problems from day one.

On a New Japan card on March 21, 1985, at Korakuen Hall in Japan, Beethoven's Symphony No. 5 rang out through the arena. Unannounced and unexpected, Bruiser Brody rushed out of the dressing room, wearing a suit. He carried a bouquet of flowers and his chain. He was there to challenge the New Japan champion, Antonio Inoki.

Dave Meltzer:

He got huge money at the time. It got up to $17,000 a week and I think, maybe, it even got

higher.

Kamala:

You don't have to worry about the money when you go to Japan. Whatever he tells you, you gonna get. You gonna get it, and you get it in cash.

Dave Meltzer:

Baba was always easier for him to deal with than Inoki. In All Japan, it was always about keeping the business strong, whereas in New Japan, he was getting the big money to lose to Inoki and to keep Inoki strong. He didn't want to do that.

Dory Funk Jr.:

Yeah, he had a big match coming up with Inoki and he studied the wrestling match between myself and Inoki that took place in December of '69. He asked me for the tape. He studied the tape in preparation for his match with Inoki. It's kind of an honor that he did.

Brody and Inoki's first matches drew huge crowds. Brody-Inoki had been sort of a dream match in Japan, something nobody thought would ever happen, but there they were in the ring, face to face. The Japanese media showed video of Brody running and working out. Magazines showed photographs of him training with legendary NWA champion, Lou Thesz.

The problem with the Brody-Inoki matches from the start was that neither man would give the other an inch. Their egos were too big, and the matches look almost like old-school legitimate wrestling matches at points. They really look like they are trying to outwrestle each other. At first, it was pretty exciting to watch them go back and forth, but by time they had wrestled each other four or five times, it became pretty boring. Nobody won, nobody lost.

Brody and Hansen had another chance to team up when the two of them toured Australia in April 1985. Brody

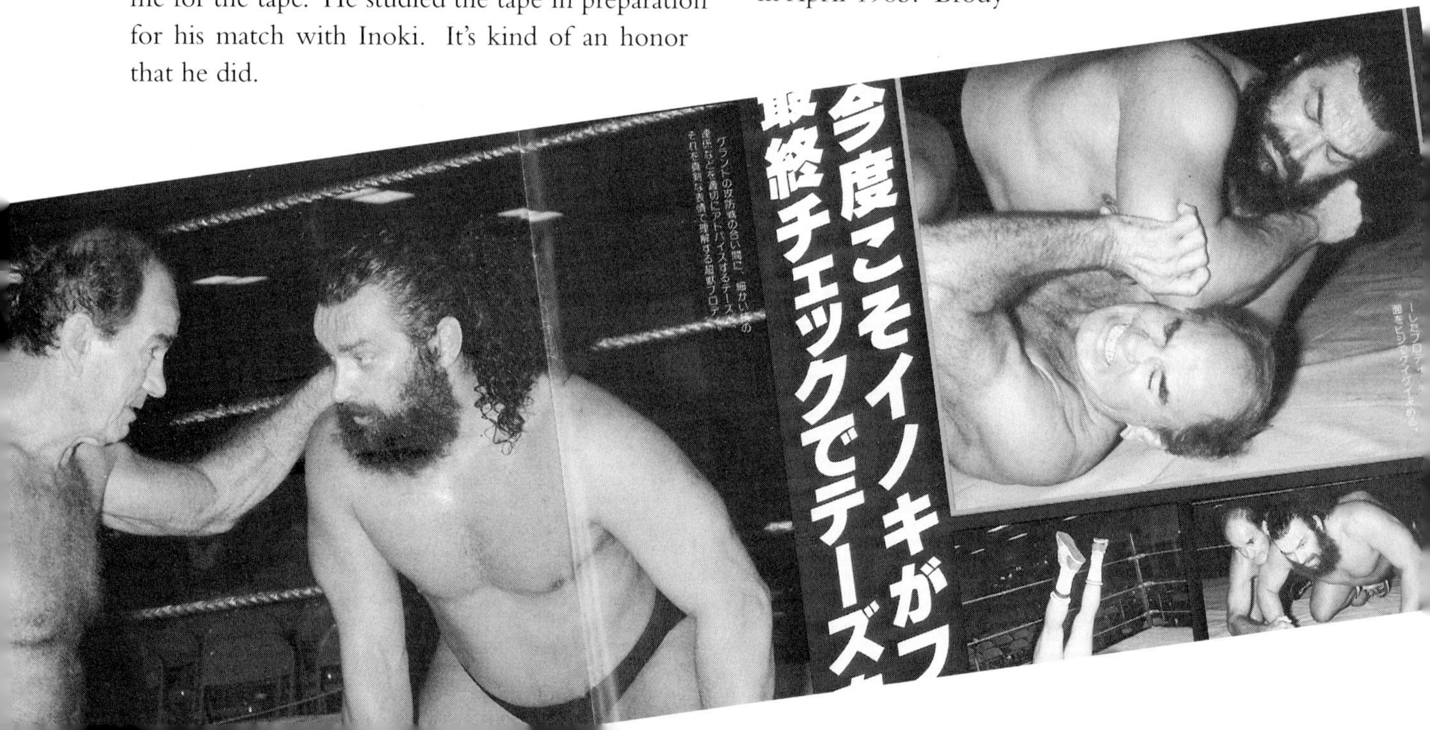

left the tour early. Some say he had problems with the promoter.

Stan Hansen:

Shortly after Frank jumped to New Japan, we got booked into Australia by Larry O'Day, the promoter at that time. Frank had been there years before, in 1977, after he finished up in New York.

Gary Hart:

The day after Bruiser went to Japan for a 12-week tour, I introduced One Man Gang [George Gray] to the Texas wrestling fans. My story was that Bruiser Brody knew that One Man Gang was coming, so he left town. I didn't harp on it constantly, but every couple of weeks over the 12-week period, I would mention it. "I'm sure you noticed that Bruiser Brody disappeared when the One Man Gang arrived."

When Bruiser's tour of Japan was over, I immediately booked him against One Man Gang. No angle, no interview. Nothing. We turned people away at the door. That's how well Bruiser Brody was over with the people.

Ox Baker:

He was making top money in Australia. All the guys were getting like a $900 guarantee. He was getting $1600 or $1700, and yet, he beat the promoter up because he didn't think he was getting paid enough. I think Brody just wanted to come home. That's how he did it.

Back in the states, Brody was moving around the country, working for different promoters. In the early part of the summer, he found himself in promoter Jerry Jarrett's Memphis promotion. The storyline was that local babyface/local god, Jerry "The King" Lawler, was having trouble with the territories leading heels, Randy Savage and David Schultz, so he called in Bruiser Brody for a little help. Within weeks, Schultz was gone, Savage began a feud with Jerry Oski, and Brody turned on Lawler. They wrestled a series of tag matches with Lawler teaming up with Austin Idol, Bill Dundee and Jay Youngblood at various times, and Brody teaming with Kareem Muhammed. Lawler and Brody wrestled a series of singles matches, as well. In typical Brody fashion, the matches all resulted in disqualification finishes with no real winner, but they were bloody, insane matches.

A Memphis institution, announcer, Lance Russell.

Lance Russell:

He was only here a very short time. We had a lot of bad guys there. It may be a toss up between him and Stan Hansen, but he may be the baddest dude that ever came through the Memphis territory, and I've seen a lot of bad guys.

Brody had become so popular in some places that he found it hard to get over as a heel. No matter what he did, or how bad he was, some fans just insisted on loving him. He was working as a heel on Texas All Stars in San Antonio and as a face for World Class in Dallas.

Left: Bruiser Brody vs the legendary Lou Thesz.

General Scandor Akbar:

When Brody came back to Dallas, he was the big crowd favorite. We had some good matches against him. Kamala had some good matches with him.

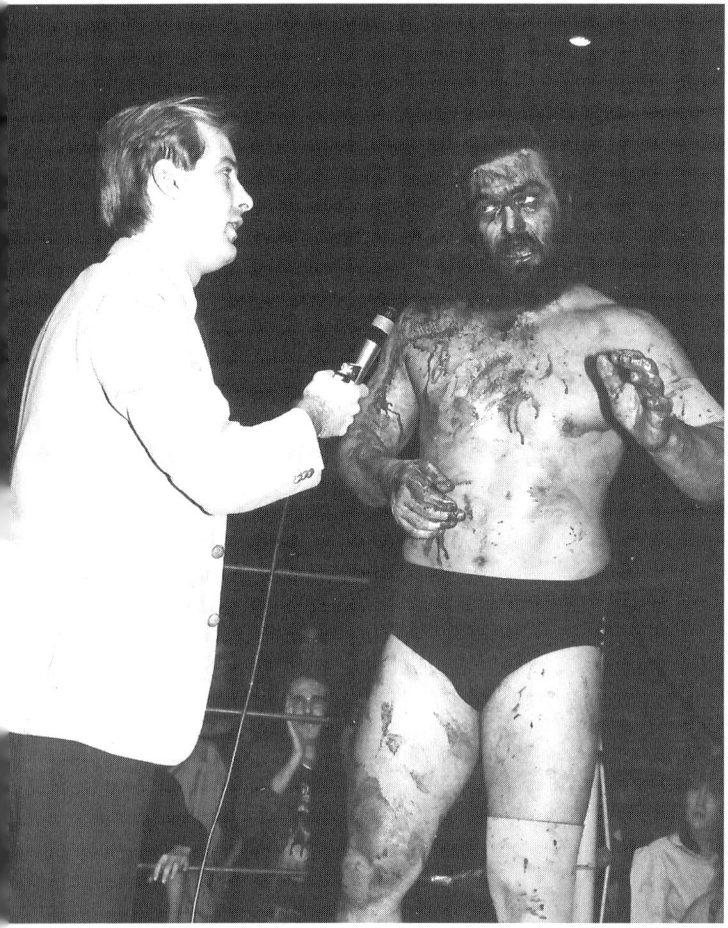

Abdullah the Butcher:

All promoters are tough to get along with … not only Fritz, all promoters.

Above: Brody apologizes to the fans for getting beat up.

Larry Matysik:

The man he had the most respect for, clearly, was Fritz.

Kevin von Erich:

I think a lot of people didn't like Brody because they didn't like my dad, and they were so close. My dad sure liked Brody, though. One time, he [Brody] was in the dressing room. After I had a match with a guy, I came back thinking it was a pretty good match—50/50. Brody says to me, "*You gonna let him get away with that?*"

I didn't know what he was talking about. "*He made a fool out of you. You've got to stand up for yourself.*"

He got me so mad that when the guy came back to talk, I punched him and beat him up. Well, I found out later, the match was good. Brody was just mad at the guy for something else and got me to do the dirty work.

Meanwhile, manager Gary Hart had brought his "*Million Dollar Man*" into San Antonio. He gave the moniker to Brody because Hart claimed it cost him a million dollars to get Brody to work for him. Brody didn't have a lot of respect for the management in San Antonio. He and Joe Blanchard never saw eye-to-eye, and now Blanchard's money man, Fred Behrend, was running the territory. Brody never had much respect for Behrend and he had no problem with helping to kill his business.

Dusty Wolfe:

This was all in the summer of '85. Joe [Blanchard] had already sold out to Fred Behrend. I don't know if he was calling it USA All-Stars yet, or if it was still Texas All Stars. It was Fred's [business] and [Buck]

Robley was booking, and basically, Fritz had worked a deal with Brody, which he then worked it through with Robley, and Mark Lewin. If they came in and killed San Antonio, and put Fred Behrend out of business, Fritz would move in and they would all have a job with Fritz. So they did. It was at the Freedom Coliseum. Basically, they went out and did one or two moves, and then Brody grabbed Lewin in a nerve hold and they stood in that hold for 45 minutes.

I wasn't in on the scam, but Robley always took care of me. Brody always took care of me, so I would have followed them if it had all taken place. Two days later, Brody and Lewin were in Dallas. Buck was fired, and I lasted another two weeks, until Chavo [Guerrero Sr.] took over, and then I was gone.

I didn't know what they were doing at the moment. Robley had said something to me earlier in the dressing room about how, "*We've seen this before, haven't we?*"

Yeah, because Brody had burned his bridge in Kansas City before. I didn't put two and two together because I hadn't been around but three years. Then Brody and Mark went out and did what they did, and I was still kind of at a loss. I didn't say anything to Frank afterwards, because, hell, I knew better. But, I was looking at him, and he said, "*Don't worry, kid. It'll all work out.*"

And it still didn't click. Over the next week, from what little bits and pieces I was hearing, it all fell into place.

Whatever anybody else says about Frank, he looked out for me. He would call me and get me bookings ... call me and get me overseas.

Brody's time in New Japan was also coming to an end. The fans were growing tired of Brody and Inoki wrestling to draws. Brody wasn't going to budge and Inoki was growing increasingly frustrated.

Dave Meltzer:

The first two Brody-Inoki matches did huge business, but they ended up burning it out because neither would ever lose to the other. Brody was never willing to put Inoki over, and obviously, Inoki was never willing to put Brody over. He had two tenures there and they both ended up blowing up.

In the short term it was great, but in the long term, he just couldn't get along with New Japan. They weren't as organized [as All Japan] and Baba was just easier to get along with.

The first time he [Brody] left, he walked out before the finals of the tag team tournament after he had a fight with Seiji Sakaguchi in the ring, and I guess he was going to lose in the final of the tournament, so he and Jimmy Snuka just got off the bus. They were in the main event of the big year-end show and they just went home. I forget how much money it was, but something like $30,000 to $40,000 for a tour, but they left the day before and didn't get a dime. It was quite strange.

Seiji Sakaguchi was Inoki's booker. He handed Brody and Snuka a note before they boarded the bus en route to the tournament finals on December 12, 1985. Brody and Snuka were scheduled to win the tournament and Sakaguchi had changed the outcome. They would be losing.

Jimmy Snuka:

"*Hey, that's not the plan. It was the other way around.*" They switched it on us real quick. Business is business. We work hard for our living. They was monkeying around, brother. "*Take your money, brother. We don't want it.*" We split.

When the bus arrived in Miyagi, Japan, Brody and Snuka were nowhere to be found.

Ox Baker:

They had just gotten back from Japan. Brody had beat one of the Japanese guys up in the ring, so Brody and Snuka took off early from Japan and went to Hawaii. Vince McMahon had a crew over there with the Hawaiian group. Brody and Snuka were just there visiting someone in the locker room—could have been Big John Studd—and they were renegotiating to go back to Japan. So the boys in the locker room were downing Snuka, and finally Brody says, "*Vince, I want to tell you one thing.*"

"*What's that?*"

"*If one more of your guys knock Snuka, I'm gonna whip everybody in the dressing room and throw 'em out in the street.*"

Snuka said, "*It's all right.*"

He said, "*It's not all right. You're my friend.*"

Jerry Grey (wrestler):

I first met Brody in 1986 in Hawaii. He worked with the Sheik in a tag. The reason he liked me at first was because he and King Curtis were standing on Honolulu Beach right near where Curtis had his umbrella rentals. I only knew King Curtis slightly, but referee Bill Alfonso asked me to see if the King had some weed. I walked up to Curtis and Brody, both of whom looked like monsters, and asked about pot. Curtis looked nervous and said, "*No, brother. It's all dried up here. There's no more marijuana here.*"

I noticed another guy standing beside them and talking to them. Curtis informed me that he happened to be the Chief of Police on the island. Brody died laughing ... one of the only times I ever saw him laugh. He said, "*I like you. You have big balls to ask something like that in front of a cop.*"

In the states, Brody continued working a lot for Fritz von Erich in Dallas, with a couple of shots in Kansas City, Hawaii, and Puerto Rico. Meanwhile, Antonio Inoki sent representatives to the U.S. to try and lure Brody back to New Japan.

James Beard:

Brody used the media to enhance his position, saying that Inoki had asked him to lay down for him. Brody, sounding like the idea of this hurt him deeply, told the Japanese media he would never do such a thing, and that Inoki had dishonored him in asking. At that, Bruiser left Japan and headed back to his home in San Antonio.

Inoki sent his representatives to talk to Brody and, like Baba had done, begged him to reconsider his position. Bruiser would have none of it, remaining indignant that anyone would think he would consider anything as underhanded as throwing a match. He continued to use the Japanese media to his advantage, and Inoki was feeling the pressure to do something to accommodate the big American wrestling God.

Finally, an offer he couldn't refuse was on the table. Inoki had offered him $100,000 to return to Japan and fulfill his contract by wrestling him. One match—$100,000. Brody agreed, but with one stipulation—half the money would be paid up front and he and his wife would meet Inoki's people in Hawaii for the pay off. This was agreed on and the meeting was set up.

As agreed, the Japanese representatives flew to Hawaii and handed Bruiser his down-payment for coming to Japan to wrestle Inoki. Bruiser took the money and handed it to his wife, who boarded the next plane back to Texas, $50,000 richer. After seeing his down-payment safely in the air on its way back home, Bruiser boarded his plane … and flew straight back to Texas, much to the dismay of Inoki's representatives. Bruiser used the Japanese media to explain that once again, he had been urged to lay down for Inoki, and once again, he had refused.

Brody did relent and his last tour with New Japan was in September 1986. In his last match, fittingly enough, he and Inoki wrestled to a 60-minute draw.

Jerry Grey:

A few months later, I toured Japan with Brody. He really liked my work. He taught me how to work the Japanese style and not let them get away with anything.

During that time, Frank was on the outs with Antonio Inoki and the New Japan office because he held them up for $40,000 for two shots. He told me and Kevin Kelly [Nailz], a tough guy, and [Jim] Duggan, to stand by the ring and watch his back because Seiji Sakaguchi and the young boys had been instructed to jump in and stretch him. Well, they never got the chance because we had his back.

Dave Meltzer:

Things were really tough for him, physically, for that year after he left New Japan, before he went back to All Japan. I was surprised he never went to the WWF, but I really think he was saving that for the end, figuring that was his last big run. He was beat up. He was in his forties by then. He had elbow problems. He had hip problems, knee problems.

On May 17, 1986, Brody won the World Class Championship Wrestling [WCCW] TV title from Rick Rude via disqualification in Fort Worth, Texas. Brody dropped the title in June because an injury made him unable to defend it. Chris Adams was given the belt. Around this time, Brody stepped into a role he never would have imagined himself. Fritz von Erich asked Brody to be his booker.

Dusty Wolfe:

Towards the end of '86 is when Frank took over the book at World Class. He kept it through the first part of '87. He was good. He knew what he was doing. I think Gary Hart took over early '87.

Spike Huber:

He was the booker there around '87, and he had a great grasp of the business as a booker. They brought him in when the territory was on its last rung, you might say. His ideas were great.

John Dananay:

Brody was hired as WCCW's booker because neither Kevin nor Kerry showed an interest in doing this, and Fritz respected Brody so much, he became one of Fritz's top "go to" guys. He, in a lot of ways, replaced David von Erich as the one wrestler Fritz could go to for sound advice. Fritz also considered Brody to be a lot like him, a throwback to yesteryear.

Jerry Grey:

When Brody was booking World Class for the Dallas office in '86, he really wanted me to come in. I had been on the road for eight years straight, working all the territories, and had finally got my spot to come home to Florida. I regret that I never went to Dallas for him, but at the time, all I wanted was to be home.

Gary Hart:

Brody wasn't—and it's hard for me to say this—he wasn't a good booker. He wasn't very good dealing with people. He had no concept at all of television production and structuring a show. He didn't understand that the most important match of the evening is the first match. He didn't understand how to position people for the future. He was a very short time booker and, oddly enough, I followed him and took back over the job. I didn't want the job [originally] and I encouraged him to take the job. He told me, "*Gary, I really have no background in this. I really don't know how to put a television show together. I really don't know how to build to the future and have a long term view.*"

He was out of his element. At the time, the talent he had was also secondary. A good matchmaker needs to be very good at resupplying your talent. You need to be very good at picking the guys that fit the chemistry of what you already have. That is something that takes years to understand. Brody just didn't have the background and I don't think he really wanted the job.

One of the golden rules that I learned from Jim Barnett is to watch every match. If you can watch them from the arena, watch them from there. If you have to, watch it on a monitor in the back, but you must watch the matches. If you don't watch the matches, you don't know who the people are excited about. And there are little nuances. When guys walk down the aisle, are they halfway down the aisle before they're noticed, or are they noticed at the top of the ramp?

Bobby Fulton:

He [Brody] had a lot of charisma. In the Kansas City Memorial Auditorium, there was a stage. The wrestlers would stand in the darkened wings while the matches were going on. One night, Brody tried to sneak his way across the stage. The people were watching the match in the ring, but when Brody reached the middle of the stage, one of the fans spotted him. Within seconds, the fans had quit watching the match and were chanting, "*Brody! Brody! Brody!*"

Tony Atlas:

Oh, yeah. Me and Brody almost got into it. You could talk to Skip Young. Skip Young was surprised because I was the first person Brody ever backed down from. I was gonna fight him in Fort Worth, Texas. It was me and the Ultimate Warrior. We was tag team partners.

George Scott was the one that asked me to come down there. He called me into the office one day. I guess he had it out with the Von Erich's. You know, George Scott, when he ran a place, he had to have total control of it, so it was very hard for George to do what he wanted to do when they're making him change everything, so George ended up leaving, and Brody ended up with the book.

I talked to George and Brody right there in the office, and both of them assured me, "*Don't worry. Ain't nothing gonna change with you. Everything is cool.*"

Tony Atlas.

Brody booked me for about the first week that he had the book. After that, I didn't get booked. The Ultimate Warrior wasn't getting booked. Brody told me one day, "*Come to Fort Worth. Don't worry. I got a lot of bookings for this one.*"

I guess he figured I wasn't going to show up, but I'm down in Texas with no money. I just had a divorce, my wife cleaned me out, just lost a job with Vince, I'm down in Texas starving to death, and I'm two months behind in my rent! I was about to get evicted. So I explain all this to Brody. I say, "*If you guys don't want me, let me know. There are places I can go.*"

"*No, no, no, no. Don't go nowhere, Tony. You're okay. We're just leaving you off things for a while so when you come back, you'll make a big splash. It's gonna happen in Fort Worth.*"

I was living in Eunice, Texas, so I drive to Fort Worth and I'm not on the card. This guy named Earl Evers says, "*Well, you know you got to talk to Brody, you know. I don't have anything to do with it.*"

So I go to Brody. He tried to ignore me. That's when the hollering and screaming started. So finally, someone went and got the cops, and the cops came into the dressing room and escorted me out. I was banging on the door. "*Bring your ass out here, Brody! I'll whoop you!*"

I was going nuts. I went back, packed all my shit, and went to Puerto Rico. About two weeks later, in walks Brody. Is that not weird?

Spike Huber:

He got along with everyone there okay.

Percy Pringle (manager):

I had opportunities to work with Frank numerous times through the years. The memories that stand out in my mind the most was when he was booking World Class during the latter years of the 1980s.

I had an office in The Sportatorium, where, in addition to my on-air managerial duties, I handled the merchandising of the novelties, the program, WCCW Fan Club, etc. Many afternoons, Frank and I were the only ones in the building. I learned so much from him, not only about the wrestling business in general, but about writing, as well. Many don't realize that Frank had a degree in journalism, too.

One Friday night, a big red-headed kid that was being trained by Buzz Sawyer stopped by the office wanting to get a chance to wrestle for the first time. Frank put him off for a few weeks, but then had a change of heart and told the kid to bring his stuff the following week. When the night came around, Frank gave me a wink and that smile of his, and told the kid he would be wrestling him [Frank], and to wear a mask. "*We'll call you 'Texas Red.'*" He then added that he was going to send me to the ring with him as his manager.

Well.... what a welcome wagon 'Texas Red' received at the hands of Bruiser Brody. Frank beat him all over the building, breaking several chairs over his head before he finally pinned him in the middle of the ring.

A few years later, in November of 1990, 'Texas Red' made his debut in The World Wrestling Federation as "The Undertaker." Joining him just two months later, in January 1991, was myself as his manager, "Paul Bearer."

I managed The Undertaker in his very first pro match at The Dallas Sportatorium, then enjoyed an almost 14-year run with him all over the world as his manager in The WWF/WWE.

If you ask The Undertaker today about that night against Bruiser Brody, he'll tell you that the only reason Frank sent me to the ring with him was to show him the way back.

John Dananay:

Like a lot of wrestlers/bookers, he tended to put himself over a bit much, but it wasn't like he didn't deserve it. He was one of the few faces in WCCW, besides the von Erich's, to draw money, and he had a tremendous feud with Gary Hart at the time, so he certainly brought a level of excitement to WCCW, which needed it, considering during this time Gino Hernandez and Mike von Erich had passed away. Kerry was out indefinitely with his ankle injury from his motorcycle injury, etc.

Larry Matysik:

I talked to Brody all the time. I helped him book shows there, come up with ideas. He wanted it and he didn't want it. I think he knew when he took it ... gosh, 18 years ago. I kind of remember him and he knew it wouldn't last, but he was intrigued by the idea.

Gary Hart:

The day that I went in to inform him that I would be replacing him as matchmaker and booker, I think was one of the happiest days of his life.

The Midnight Rider, the Yellow Dog, the Giant Machine. One of my favorite storylines is one that has been used over and over in virtually every territory in the world. In late 1986, Brody and Abdullah the Butcher were in the midst of their worldwide, cross-country, bloodbath of a feud. On one of their many stops in Dallas, Texas, at the Reunion Arena on Christmas Day, the two wrestled a Loser Leaves Texas match in a steel cage, and with the help of a fork and his manager, Gary Hart, Abdullah won the match. Brody had to go.

Brody headed to Canada for a couple of shows against Abdullah the Butcher, and then on to Florida, where he wrestled in one of the most talked about "shoots" in wrestling.

Sir Oliver Humperdink:

I had a bounty out on Lex Luger when he came back in. I think it was $15,000 I had out on Luger.

Lex Luger had firmly established himself as a star in Florida and was about to begin working for the Crocketts when Florida booker Hiro Matsuda scheduled him in a series of matches with Bruiser Brody. Luger, however, refused to put Brody over in any of the matches, worried about his reputation as he headed into a new company. It is a common courtesy for most wrestlers, who were about to move out of a territory, to lose their matches and make the wrestlers there look good. Brody didn't usually subscribe to that custom and Luger refused to here. Matsuda was furious and Brody … well, he acted like Bruiser Brody.

Gary Hart:

Bruiser had told me on more than one occasion, "*When you send me to Florida, tell the booker that I don't want to wrestle Lex Luger because I have no respect for him.*" He just didn't like him. I relayed the message to the office. The office, of course, went against my suggestion and everybody knows what happened. They went against our better judgment … and you know the story.

Dave Meltzer:

There was a TV match before the famous match where Brody beat Luger up a little bit.

In this television match, it is obvious there is heat between Brody and Luger. Luger no-sells for the first quarter of the match until Brody loosens him up with a series of stiff kicks. Brody and Luger also wrestled in a six-man tag team match. Brody teamed with Bad News Allen and the Cuban Assassin against Luger, Kendall Windham, and Ron Simmons.

Howard Brody (Photographer, promoter):

I was working for Gold Belt Wrestling magazine at the time. Once a week I would go down to the War Memorial Auditorium or the Sunrise Musical Theater or the Miami Beach Convention Center and take pictures and interview the guys for the magazine. This particular week Bruiser Brody was going to be there and I was still pretty green and had just started working for the magazine. So, I went into the office and into the back and Brody's in his little dressing room, him and Humperdink. He's taping his fingers up and I tried to interview him, but he was really, very quiet. One of these things we were going to do in the magazine was a computer match between him and Hogan. Humperdink said something like, "*Yeah, I'd like to see that,*"

Brody looked at him and smiled and said, "*Yeah, me too.*"

I don't know what was going on there but they had something on the side.

I asked him about his background and he talked about West Texas State. I was asking him questions, and he was kind of shrugging off a lot of the questions and then he said, "*If you really want to know what Bruiser Brody is all about, just watch the match tonight.*"

The two then met in a cage match in Fort Lauderdale, Florida. The match started off normally enough, but a couple minutes into it, Brody shut down and refused to budge for any of Luger's offense. He just stared at Luger. After a couple of minutes, Luger pushed referee Bill Alfonso, climbed over the cage, and left. It was a surreal sight.

Jerry Grey:

Frank didn't like many guys, so I'm glad that, for whatever reason, he liked me. He was a great worker and he had one of the best looks ever. We were also in Florida together when the Brody versus Luger match took place in a cage. Luger was, and is, a prima donna, so Brody decided to teach the musclehead a lesson. I saw it happen. Luger was scared to death when Brody didn't sell Luger's shitty punches. Brody stormed after Lex, but he never touched him because Luger jumped over the cage and went back to the dressing room. Funny!

Craig Cohen (videographer):

I was the time keeper that night in Fort Lauderdale at the War Memorial Auditorium, but I was also the one that filmed the match. I actually worked for Florida Championship Wrestling at the time. I filmed a lot of stuff.

There is a lot of talking that goes on during the match. The first two or three minutes are kind of normal, but at one point, Luger is pounding on Brody. Brody is just standing there looking at him with that goofy look that he had—that cross-eyed, Bill Murray kind of look. That was it. He completely stopped selling.

Luger throws about two or three fists to the chest in a row and Brody just stands there and looks at him. Luger looks at Bill Alfonso and says, "*What's he doing?*"

And then Brody just starts pounding on Luger. I

Above: Brody decides not to cooperate with Lex Luger. These pictures are from the only known set of photographs taken that night.

don't think he hurt him. Luger was too strong to be hurt like that. We used to joke in Florida that Blackjack Mulligan would expose the business every time he threw a punch. Luger wasn't much better, but he was trained by Hiro Matsuda, so he had good training. He was just something to look at, as opposed to being a good worker.

Luger kept looking over at Alfonso, "*What's going on?*" Then he would talk to Brody and say, "*What are you doing?*"

Brody wouldn't answer him. So, when he [Luger] had an opportunity to climb out over the cage, he did. He just flew out of that cage. Depending on what generation of the tape you have, you can hear me talking. Even a couple of my best friends down here don't know it's my tape. They used to talk about the tape. I'm going back fifteen years ago, but they would say, "*I got a great copy of the Brody-Luger shoot match. You got to see this.*"

But they didn't know it was my voice on the tape. What I actually say is, "*Hey, Dana! Wasn't Luger supposed to be the babyface in this match?*"

Dana was the ring announcer. He goes, "*I have no idea what the hell is going on.*"

Humperdink was standing there with his mouth open. You really didn't know who was in on it and who wasn't.

Sir Oliver Humperdink:
The thing with Luger wasn't really a shoot. It was more of a rib. Luger was very green, and I don't talk bad about anybody, and everybody gets ribbed just like he did. The guys he was traveling with and hanging around with in the dressing rooms were telling him what an animal Frank was. "*He'll break you in half and romp and stomp you.*"

Luger's listening to all this. "*Oh, really?*"

Finally, on the night of the cage match in Ft. Lauderdale War Memorial Auditorium, Brody just stopped selling, and Luger went over the wall. Frank looked at me and I looked at Frank. "*I don't know.*"

Bill Alfonso was the referee. They just pumped Luger so full of stories.

Lex Luger (wrestler):

I was brand new. I was green. I was like, "*My gosh! Why did he stop wrestling?*" I couldn't get the door open, so I climbed over the cage and went back to the locker room. Afterwards, "*I guess I'll go over and talk to him and see if we're going to have a fight, or whatever happens.*" He was nice as could be. That was all it was, totally blown out of proportion.

Yeah, he was ribbing me. He just stopped working. He was real nice afterwards, shook my hand, gave me a hug. He embarrassed me. At the time, I didn't know what was going on. I was scared to death, I'll be honest. I'm not ashamed to say that. He was a big scary guy and I was brand new to the business. I didn't know if he was going to cut me or what he was going to do. "*I'm getting out of here.*"

Craig Cohen:

When Luger jumped over the cage, he left. He didn't go to the back. He left. He couldn't have talked with Brody, anyway. They were in different dressing rooms. One was on the left, one was on the right. Believe me, there was no conversation.

Bad News Allen:

It was funny because I worked with Brody the next week in Lakeland. It was actually supposed to be Lex Luger. They called me from the office and had me on the speakerphone. I could hear Humperdink in the back just laughing his head off. He [Luger] went to the office. "*I can't work with him. The guy is crazy. He says he could give me a boot to the face and I'd have to have plastic surgery.*"

Matsuda was talking to me, and I could hear Humperdink just rolling in the background. He [Matsuda] said, "*Allen, can you do us a favor?*"

I said, "*Yeah.*"

"*We want you … when you go to Lakeland, we're gonna put you in a match with Bruiser Brody. You get along with him, right?*"

I said, "*Yeah. I get along with him well.*"

He says, "*You saw what happened the other night with Luger.*"

I said, "*Yeah, and he deserved what he got.*"

Here's a guy who's been in the business a long time, knew what he was doing, and you go, out of respect, you ask him, "*What do you want to do?*"

He'll tell you what he wants. "*Okay, you do this, this, this, I'll do this, this, this.*"

Well, he [Luger] went and told Brody, he says, "*Yeah, we're gonna do it this way. We're gonna have the match this way.*"

I'm lookin' over thinking, "*This ain't gonna be pretty. This is NOT gonna be pretty.*"

As soon as they went out there, I ran out there because I knew Brody was gonna kick his ass. I knew it. He went out there and beat the crap out of him … he [Luger] ran out and ran back to the locker room. I'm on the floor, rolling, because I knew this was coming up.

Dave Meltzer:

Jim Crockett was freaking out when he heard about it. "*What's your guy doing to my next big star?*" But I think Brody knew Luger was only going to be in the territory for another day or two, so he figured it was his job to look strong, and Luger's was to look weak because he was leaving.

Sir Oliver Humperdink:

It wasn't a shoot. Stories, as they're passed down, they get a little embellished.

Jerry Grey:

One other thing he did for me in '86. We were working Tampa TV. I was working with jobber Luis Astea and I was supposed to go over [win the match], but Astea intentionally threw himself over the top rope when I was shooting him through the middle. If you throw somebody over the top rope, you automatically lose the match by disqualification. Astea wanted to win, so he went over the top, making it look like I threw him over. The referee had no choice but to change the finish in the ring and disqualify me.

When I got back to the dressing room, Hiro Matsuda, who was the booker, was furious. I argued with him and tried to tell him that it was Luis' fault. Brody got tired of hearing Hiro run his mouth about the finish being fucked up and stood up. He told Hiro, "*Jerry didn't do anything wrong. Even if he did, nothing ever goes perfect, so just shut up about it.*"

Hiro just walked out. Hiro was a big shooter, but even he didn't want to test King Kong.

From the Red River Valley comes Red River Jack.

Within a few weeks after Brody left Florida, a new wrestler named Red River Jack appeared in the World Class area. He was about 6-foot-6, 300 pounds, and billed as being from the Red River Valley. He wore cowboy boots, jeans, and a white mask, with black, curly hair spilling out from the back of the mask.

Gary Hart:

Red River Jack was a personal friend of Bruiser Brody. He was from New Mexico, right across the mountain, and he was coming into the Texas area to fight for the honor of Bruiser Brody, who was chased out of town by Abdullah the Butcher and Gary Hart. The great thing was that he had his hair sticking out of the mask.

Bruiser had about sixteen acres of land there in Boerne, and he had a nice little creek and some Arroyos, and some mesquite trees there, and all his interviews he would do around a little campfire, making coffee. He'd have a horse over there and we would play the Willie Nelson song, "On the Road Again." It caught on bigger than shit and I would scream, "*It's Bruiser Brody!*"

Occasionally, when the refs back was turned, Brody would pull the mask up and wave at the people. People just went crazy. They loved it. Even though it was a copy of something that had been done before, it had never been done in Texas, and they loved it. I really think that was the last big business in Texas.

During one match in early 1987, Red River Jack tagged with the Dingo Warrior against Nord the Barbarian and Jeep Swensen. In the middle of the match, Brody appeared at ringside to prove he was not Red River Jack. A wrestler named Rick Davidson was under the Red River Jack mask that night.

In May 1987, at the annual Parade of Champions, Gary Hart got his chance to prove that Red River Jack was indeed Brody. Bruiser Brody was allowed back to WCCW for one match. If he could beat muscle-bound Jeep Swenson, he would be allowed to return for good. In a "Battle of the Dinosaurs," Brody showed much more defense than he normally did. Swenson beat on him for the first couple of minutes of the match, until a boot to his face stopped him dead in his tracks and Brody beat on him for the next couple of minutes. Using a chair that Swenson had brought into the ring, Brody beat Swenson's back and chest, then pinned him. After the brutal-but-short match, Brody was reinstated into the ranks of WCCW.

Later on the card, Red River Jack and Spike Huber wrestled Abdullah the Butcher and Eli the Eliminator. If Red River Jack's team won, he would be allowed five minutes in the ring with Gary Hart. If Hart's team won, Red River Jack would be unmasked. If Brody was found under the mask, he would be banned from wrestling for life. In another short-but-brutal match, Spike Huber pinned Eli the Eliminator, so Red River Jack had five minutes in the ring to beat the hell out of Gary Hart. Hart tried his best to escape and the two fought their way back to the dressing room.

Red River Jack made a few more appearances, even tagging with Bruiser Brody, before he disappeared into the sunset.

When Brody left his job as booker in World Class, he was pretty down. His connections in Japan were lost. His connections with many U.S. promoters were delicate, at best. His body was beaten up. He made a plea to an old friend to try and get him back into the graces of Giant Baba.

Dory Funk Jr.:

I booked him over there. I don't know if it was 1987. I was working for All Japan. He had had a successful run with New Japan, I believe, and he let me know that he was interested in going back to All Japan. He had had some difficulties. He called and asked me to talk to Mr. Baba … and he came back to All Japan.

Abdullah the Butcher:

Baba's territory was dropping and they needed two people—Abdullah the Butcher and Bruiser Brody. As soon as we walked in, and the territory was dead, we exploded. We were giving the people what they wanted. You cannot say, "*Why did they call him back?*" Because he was a professional. He done what he had to do. Whoever he was working for, he'd give him 100%. That's all I can say about Brody.

Stan Hansen:

It was good for him to come back. It didn't work out with New Japan, and he went back, and he basically lost the job in Japan for a few years, and finally Baba brought him back. It would've been really good and he'd probably still be there doing something.

Dave Meltzer:

And when Brody came back, he came back for a lot less money than he left, to get back into good graces with Baba.

In what many consider a dream match, Bruiser Brody wrestled against his tag team partner, Stan Hansen, on November 22, 1987, in Tokyo, Japan. It was the only time in history that Brody and Hansen were on opposite sides of the ring. Brody and Jimmy Snuka faced Hansen and Terry Gordy in the Real World tag team tournament. Both teams were counted out of the ring at 9:27.

Ed "Moondog" Moretti:

We were on an All Japan tour together, and a couple of nights, I got to be his tag team partner. We'd be sitting on the bus, or on the bullet train, and he'd be reading the Wall Street Journal, or we'd be talking about stamp collecting. His son collected stamps and I'd send him some stamps from Canada.

Brody beat Jumbo Tsuruta in Tokyo on March 27, 1988, to win the NWA International heavyweight title for the third time. It was the last title Brody would hold. His matches with Tsuruta were always great and that match was no exception. Tsuruta was great at mixing up Japanese submission wrestling with American high impact moves. That was because he was trained by the Funks in Amarillo. Tsuruta was also big for a Japanese competitor. He could give Brody a good run for his money.

The beginning of the match was great, with Brody moving around and reversing armbars like a junior heavyweight. Tsuruta controlled most of the early match with submission holds. They went back and forth inside and outside the ring for several minutes. Tsuruta had the upper hand after a piledriver, suplex, and a kick from the top ropes, but when Tsuruta tried to bound off the ropes and tackle Brody, Brody put him in a bearhug and fell backwards, clotheslining Tsuruta with the top rope. Brody delivered his big running knee drop and pinned Tsuruta.

On April 19, 1988 in Sendai, Tsuruta won their rematch and regained the NWA International heavyweight title. Brody went for his big kneedrop off the top rope and Tsuruta rolled out of the way. Tsuruta followed up on Brody's mistake with a suplex and pinned him in the middle of the ring at the 20:33 mark.

Brody's last match in Japan was three days later—April 22, 1988. He and Tommy Rich lost to Genichiro Tenryu and Ashura Hara in the Kawasaki City Gym in Kanagawa.

Chapter XII Abdullah the Butcher

Abdullah the Butcher, the Wildman from the Sudan, is a bloodthirsty, maniac known for carving up the flesh of his opponents with a fork. He has been an icon in Japan since 1970. Outside the ring, Larry Shreve is a pleasant restaurant owner from Atlanta, Georgia, by way of Windsor, Ontario, Canada. He owns and operates Abdullah's House of Ribs and Chinese Food.

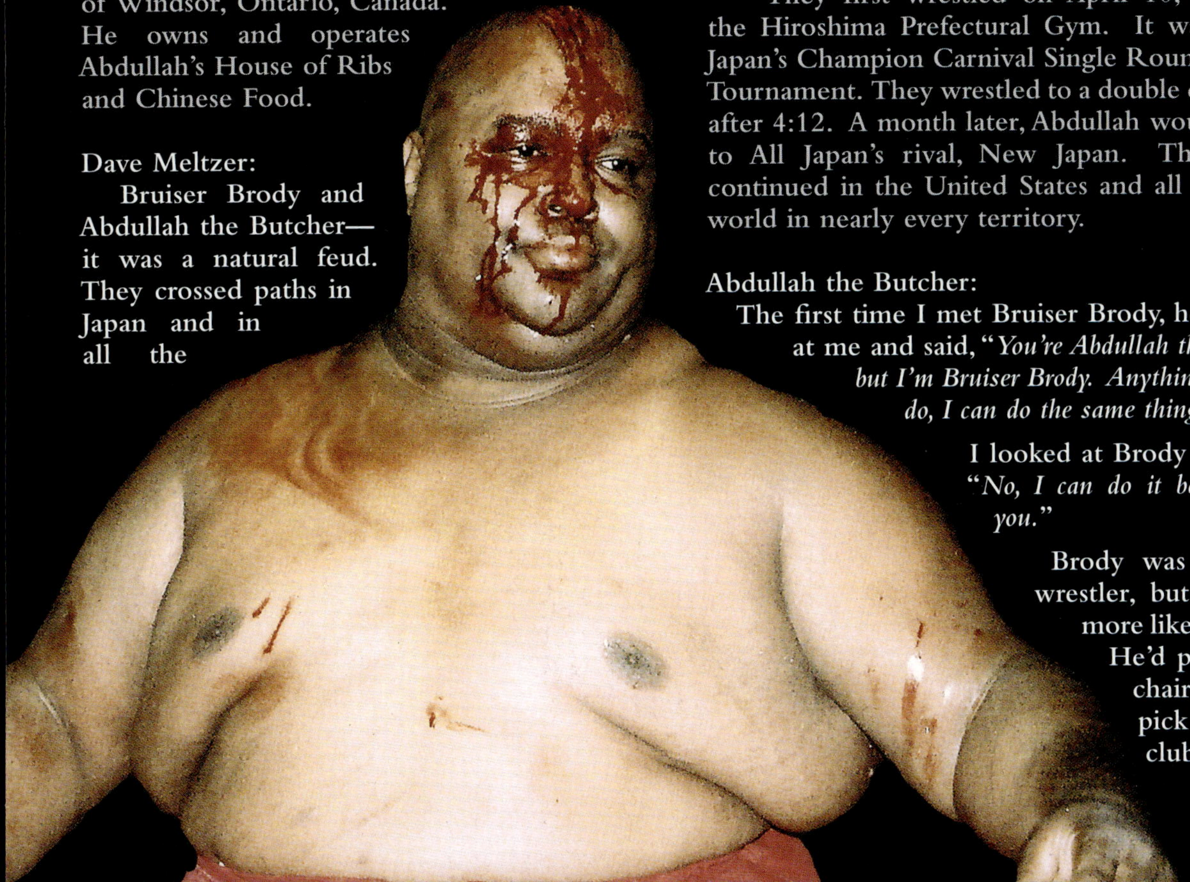

Dave Meltzer:
Bruiser Brody and Abdullah the Butcher—it was a natural feud. They crossed paths in Japan and in all the independents.

Larry Matysik:
Oh yeah, made a lot of money with that [Brody vs Abdullah] ... sold out like three different spots with that one. Made a lot of people a lot of money with that one.

Abdullah and Brody almost crossed paths early in Brody's career. Abdullah made his first trip to Dallas in late August 1977, but Brody had left the territory just one month earlier after losing the Texas Brass Knuckles title to Fritz von Erich. The two would have to wait almost four years before they finally met in the ring.

They first wrestled on April 10, 1981, at the Hiroshima Prefectural Gym. It was in All Japan's Champion Carnival Single Round Robin Tournament. They wrestled to a double countout after 4:12. A month later, Abdullah would jump to All Japan's rival, New Japan. Their feud continued in the United States and all over the world in nearly every territory.

Abdullah the Butcher:
The first time I met Bruiser Brody, he looked at me and said, "*You're Abdullah the Butcher but I'm Bruiser Brody. Anything you can do, I can do the same thing better.*"

I looked at Brody and said "*No, I can do it better than you.*"

Brody was a good wrestler, but he was more like my style He'd pick up a chair. He'd pick up a club. He'd pick up whatever he could get his hands on. That's what Bruiser Brody done. In the ring, he was a violent man. Outside the ring, he was a good man.

Do you see? We were professionals. We gave the public what they wanted. They wanted to see violence, and we gave them violence. Me and Brody, we started the hardcore. This stuff these guys are doing with the barbed wire and all this stuff. Number one, I started it, then Brody got into it. We done what we had to do. We were professionals. If we had to take a bottle and break it over somebody's head, we done it. And we didn't care what we done. A lot of times, when you're in the ring, we didn't know what we done. A lot of times, we psyched ourselves out before we got in the ring, and we'd come back [to the dressing room] and say, "*Damn, you done this,*" and we'd have to think, because when you're in that ring, doing crazy stuff, you're mind changes.

J Michael Kenyon:

He and Abdullah became cult heroes. Brody could gear himself down to Abdullah's pace. Abdullah has a relentless pace, he just moves slower. He could move a long time at that pace and. of course, bleed buckets for a long period of time. And, of course,. Brody could also bleed. They were wonderful together.

Larry Matysik:

We talked about blading one night. He told me, "*I'm a blade freak. I don't know. I guess we're all S&M guys or something. If you don't get it good, if it sounds like a scrape, you know you didn't get it good. It's not gonna bleed good. But, if you get it right, it's like tearing paper. You can hear it when you go through your forehead.*"

Gary Hart:

Bruiser was one of the few guys that could wrestle Abdullah on multiple occasions. Abby was the type of guy that was really good for two or three shots, but no promoter and no wrestling fan wanted to sit in the audience, over and over, and watch him take out the fork and open up white guys and make them bleed. Brody was one of these guys that no matter where you put him with Abdullah, they knew Abdullah was going to get an ass kicking. I think that is what really helped that feud. The audience knew that Brody wasn't going to succumb to the fork, and lay down and wallow in his own blood. He was going to get up and kick Abdullah's ass.

Abdullah really liked Brody, so he would actually take a few bumps. He would fall down for Bruiser Brody. They truly liked each other because they made money together.

The last time I was booking in Dallas after Brody left as booker, Abdullah and Bruiser came to me and they said, "Gary, we would like to have a cage match on Christmas night in the Will Rogers Coliseum."

So, I said, "*Okay. Well, who's going to do the favor?*"

"*Aww, don't worry. We'll figure out something.*"

I said, "*Boys, this is a cage match. You can't*

ave a countout. You can't have
ı disqualification. There's got to
ɔe a winner and there's got to be
ı loser."

"Don't worry Gary. We'll figure
t out."

So, at the time, I was managing
Al Perez, and I thought, "Why
lon't I go with two cage matches?"

I was leery of Bruiser and
Abby because Abby ... he really
didn't want to lose at all, and
didn't want him to beat
Bruiser Brody in Fort Worth,
Texas. That was my strong suit
with Bruiser. I always took
very good care of him because
knew Bruiser could do a
favor for somebody, like when
he did for the Great Kabuki.
He made the Great Kabuki
overnight. So, I knew that
and I didn't want to harm that
persona that he had. I made
t a double cage match and I
had Kevin [von Erich] and Al
Perez right before Bruiser and
Abby. Perez and I did the favor
for Kevin. That way, at least I
would get one good win out of
the damn thing.

So I'm coming back to the
dressing room after the Perez
match, and the music is playing
for Bruiser. He and Abdullah
are sitting back in the dressing
room, talking, and I said, "Boys!
The bell's ringing. The music's
playing. Go to the ring."

Well, we haven't figured ou
what were going to do yet."

And I said, "Guys, you go
to get in the ring now. They'r
playing the music."

So Butchey said, "Hey, cham
Why don't you get involved?"

I said, "Fuck both of you guy
I'm telling you right now. Go
to the ring. I don't give a dam
what you do, but if someone doe
not do a favor for the other, I wil
never use either one of you guys in
Texas again."

So, they went out to the ring
and finally, after about 15 o
20 minutes, Bruiser Brody did
the job for Abdullah.

Dave Meltzer:
The first time I saw them
cross paths was in '87 in All
Japan. Abby was with TNT
and Brody was with Snuka
They tore up the building.
was there, the fans running
around. They took it all over
the country. It was the big
independent match.

Carlos Colon:
Down here [in Puerto Rico
it was a continuation of wha
they were doing in Japan—
hardcore, blood-and-guts type
of matches. Between Brody
and Abdullah, they changed
wrestling. They made all o
wrestling more hardcore style

Abdullah the Butcher:

We wrestled all over the world. We were in Israel, Japan, Australia, Puerto Rico, all over. Name it, we been there. They kept asking us to come back over and over. When we wrestled in the Middle East, all the Muslims came to me. "*Abdullah!*" Giving me this and that. "*Abdullah, you don't let him beat you!*" It was a play. Me and Brody wrestled there in the same building five times and sold it out five times. We were professionals.

Bobby Fulton:

We were all working in Tel Aviv, Israel. Bruiser was working with Abdullah. Their matches were so bloody and intense. A guy with an English accent walked up to several of us and said, "*That stuff isn't real, is it?*"

About that time, Brody grabbed a piece of barbed wire and wrapped it around Abdullah's head. He jerked it, like you'd jerk a rope, and it looked like the top of Abdullah's head came off. The blood went flying. The guy looked at me and said, "*That was real.*"

Malak Al Rahim
(Jim Vasaldua, wrestler):

I think one of my best memories of Frank, and this shows his lighter side, was one day when Juan Reynosa [referee] and I drove down to Brownsville, Texas, for a show at a high school gym. This is when Southwest Championship Wrestling was touring the valley in Texas and did a lot of high school gyms.

That night's main event was Frank and Abdullah the Butcher. From the get go, the match was a free-for-all. In and out of the ring, chairs and chains flying. The match went on for almost 30 minutes. Once the two climbed back into the ring, Frank threw Abdullah into the ropes. From my position at the corner of the ring, I could see the middle turnbuckle strip. Frank hoisted Abdullah into the air and body slammed him in the middle of the ring. Now picture this. With those two in the middle, you're looking at over 600 pounds! Once Abdullah hit the middle of the mat, the whole damn ring collapsed! I remember thinking to myself, "*Holy shit!*"

Juan fell out of the ring and he looked over to me as to say, "*What the hell just happened?*"

Through it all, in the middle of all this broken

Kevin Von Erich saves Brody from a double team by Abdullah and his manager, Gary Hart.

lumber and ropes, through Frank's heavy beard and long curly hair, I could see a smile that could tame a lion! Even Abdullah was trying to stay professional, but you could hear a chuckle. The two of them finally made their way out of the mess they had just created, and you could see a smile from ear to ear on both their faces.

Once in the locker room ... I had gone to the locker room to see if they were both all right, and they jokingly blamed Juan and I for the ring falling apart. The four of us laughed about it for the rest of the night.

Even when SWCW held its shows in the Junction for TV tapings, we would always tell Frank to take it easy in the ring. We never let him live it down. It was funny.

George Napolitano:
This ECW extreme mentality, where everything's wild and crazy. Before we had ECW, we had Bruiser Brody. Brody and Abdullah the Butcher were doing that style. It's what they were doing 25 years ago.

Abdullah the Butcher:
Hurt? Many times. Split open here, here, here. They have a tape where they're stitching me up. Brody's been hurt many times. Brody was getting up, and he'd stand and wait a couple minutes. I'd say, "What's wrong with you?"

He said, "You do the same shit, but you don't want to tell nobody."

'Cause some days, your legs just hurt.

I pinned Brody once, and Brody pinned me once ... in all the time we fought.

Bruiser Brody and Abdullah the Butcher's last one on one battle. Anyone who has seen the match will remember it for this scene. Brody chokes Abdullah for several minutes with the television cable. Abdullah looks near death but comes back and the two have one of their classic battles. The match took place in Cantanyo, Puerto Rico on Wednesday, July 13, 1988. It was Brody's last taped match.

A. BUTCHER

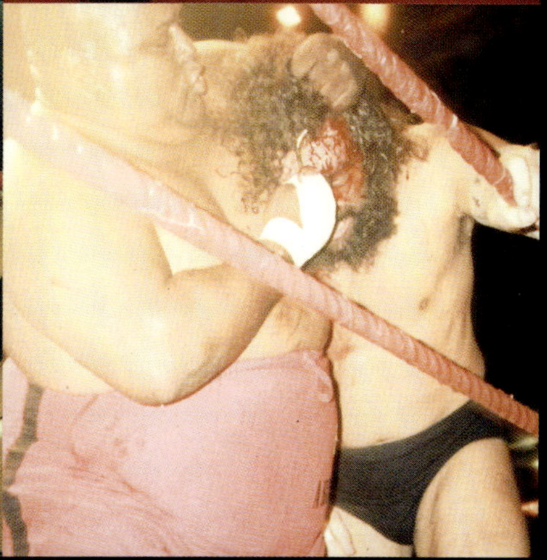

Bruiser Brody vs. Abdullah the Butcher
February 20, 1987
Hiram Bithorne Stadium, San Juan, PR

I've chosen this particular match because it is a great example of the tornado-like fury the feud between Brody and Abdullah often times took. Their feud is also referred to by many as a precursor to the hardcore style that predominated independent wrestling throughout the nineties and even in many parts of the country today. This match is a great example of that. It would hold up in any ECW pay per view. I also love the crowd. The Puerto Rican wrestling fans have got to be the most energetic and wild in the world. I've heard stories of kids gathering bags of rocks and even spark plugs outside the arenas to throw at the heel wrestlers. The events in Puerto Rico were often times held in stadiums with the ring in the middle of the field and only armed military personnel allowed on the green. The fans watched from the bleachers. But in this match there were seats set up on the green, pretty close to the ring and Brody and Abdulah just bulldoze through them. The military is mixed up in the fans. The cameramen struggle to get shots. The whole match is an insane mess. It's perfect.

From talking with fans that were there, the match was pure chaos from the get go. Brody and Abdullah wrestled outside the ring for several minutes before the bell even rang. Brody was a bloody mess from Abdullah's ever present foreign object.

Abdullah stabs Brody, hits him with a chair, and smashes his skull into a ringside truck. After about five minutes the combatants finally get in the ring. Abdullah continues to stab Brody's face with his foreign object until Brody delivers a onslaught of kicks along with the screams of the crowd. Abdullah is on the ropes. Brody's boot comes off in the melee. He goes to pick it up as a weapon and finds Abdullah's weapon on the mat. He picks that up instead and Abdullah's head is soon a bloody mess as well.

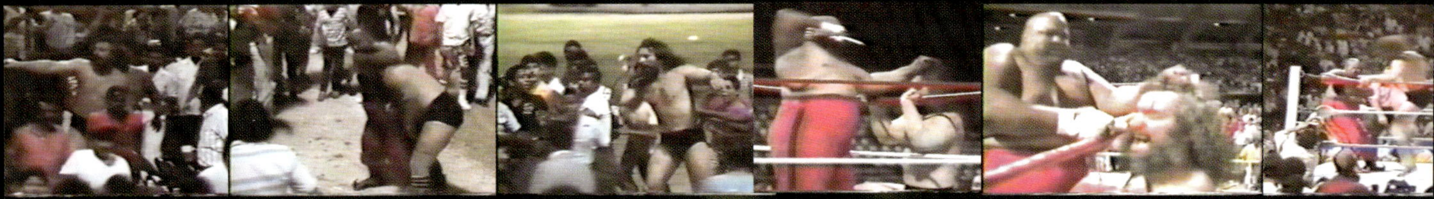

The two men only stay in the ring for about two minutes. When Brody bails out Abdullah makes an insane leap, something I have never seen him do, onto Brody's back and the two take it back out into the crowd again. The fans are just rabid and it is surprising they don't attack either man.

The rain starts coming down, as well.

With each shot Brody delivers, the crowd lets out screams of adulation. Air horns go off constantly, and the announcer directs a family to the front gate to pick up their lost child.

The audience is so excited and scared. They follow the wrestlers around the coliseum as the two men beat, kick, gouge, and tear at each other. Along the way Brody's other boot is lost.

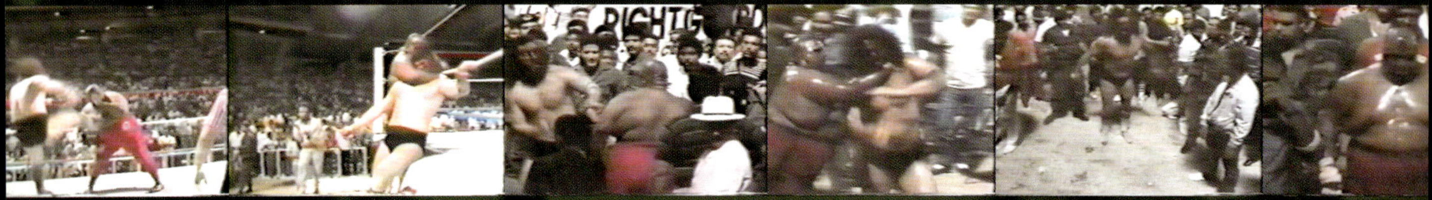

Brody double axe handles Abdullah's head, Abdullah head butts him and takes off into the raging sea of fans. Brody barks after him and heads off in another direction. He looks lost in the mass of people. Both men wander around the coliseum floor, bloody and wet. The match is over.

Chapter XIII
The Rebel

J Michael Kenyon:

He was like Jim Londos, who was originally an independent crossroader who traveled all over the country with Ray Steele through the '20s. They would work towns and Londos would fleece the Greek merchants all through the town. They would all think he was going to win the match, but he'd put his opponent over and they'd have rematches. He went to jail a couple of times for that, or he had to leave town real fast. He was an independent wrestler in the true sense. I think Bruiser Brody was an independent guy, much like Londos. He worked everywhere in the world, but he was his own guy. It can't be stated enough just how much of an independent spirit and mind he was.

Abdullah the Butcher:

He didn't care too much about promoters because they lie.

Dave Meltzer:

It was a tough way to make a living then, as it is today—$750 a shot and trans. You don't know what you're dealing with, promoters underpaying you, wrestlers not of your level.

Brody and Andre the Giant.

Bruno Sammartino:

He was basically quiet and respectful when he was in the WWWF, but I heard later on that he was kind of like me, a rebel, standing up for himself and for the boys. I was glad to hear that. There aren't many men who will stand up for what they believe in, let me tell you. And Frank, apparently, was a stand-up guy.

Dave Meltzer:

When promoters were hurting and they needed something to pop the territory, he could do that. The flip side to that was he was going to control his own finishes and, eventually, he was going to be going back to Japan, so it was a short term fix.

Bill Watts:

He just ... he had no credibility, and so therefore, promotions that were not stressed financially or in trouble, they weren't dealing with him. The solid promotions quit dealing with him.

Chris Benoit (wrestler):

He was one of the first guys, in my opinion, to make it big just doing independents. He never went to any one territory. He went to all the territories.

Dave Meltzer:

When wrestling was starting to constrict and a lot of the old territories were going down, he was the number one indie guy. He was responsible for making independent wrestling a little healthier. Certainly his style was a forerunner to what came later as a cult style of ECW.

J Michael Kenyon:

I spent most of my life up in the Pacific Northwest. He never was billed as a top of the card talent up there, but one night on a WCW show—I guess it was still the NWA in those days—[Ric] Flair, Dusty Rhodes, the Road Warriors, and the Koloffs were on top. The opening match of the night in the Seattle Center Coliseum, the one-fall, 15 minute opener, some guy came into the ring, and then down the aisle comes Bruiser Brody. Completely unannounced, unbilled, he went into the ring, squashed some guy in about five minutes, growled at the crowd once, and then left.

Allen Bolte (wrestling announcer):

Brody was flown in for a couple of events for Roy Shire in San Francisco. A battle royal and I think one other event.

Ole Anderson (wrestler, booker, promoter):

I brought Bruiser Brody into Atlanta. He was a guy unto himself. He came out to do an interview with a light bulb in his mouth. I asked him, "*What the hell is that supposed to be about?*"

"*Well, the people think I'm crazy.*"

"*No, they don't,*" I corrected him. "*The people think you're nuts—not desperate nuts, mean nuts, or 'I'm-gonna-kill-somebody' nuts—just goofy. Get the light bulb out of your face and don't do it again.*"

Bruiser Brody and his smoking buddy, Fast Eddie Gries during a WCCW tour of the East Coast.

Frank Goodish in the Mid-South territory. The photo to the left is a play on a famous publicity shot with Andre the Giant. Frank holds up Vikki Williams and Joyce Grable.

Dory Funk Jr.:

I know that he used to train out in front of our apartment. Really, a lot of his training was cardio and aerobic at that time. He used to do step-ups on anything he could find strong enough to support him. He'd tear chairs up, benches, and things like that. He'd do hundreds of step-ups.

Larry Matysik:

Aspirin and squats. That was life for him on the road. Aspirin and squats. He did a million squats. He didn't lift heavy anymore. He'd pretty much given up lifting heavy, but he wanted to keep that flexibility. Many afternoons, we'd be at the hotel room and he'd be doing them. I fell asleep on the bed one day when he was doing squats, before we went to a show, and when I woke up, he was still doing squats. No weight, just straight up squats on a chair, and deep, real deep.

Joe "Jody" Hamilton (wrestler, The Assassin):

When I had my Deep South show on channel 69, I did a parody on Joe Pedicino and Boni Blackstone. I taped a segment for my show where I dressed my son, Nick, in a fat suit and slicked his hair back, making it look greasy. He pulled up in a van in front of the studio, opened the sliding door of the van, and dozens of pizza boxes fell out onto the parking lot. The viewers could see that his ass was as wide as the door opening, and as he backed out of the van, he lost his balance and fell flat on his ass. The only man who was strong enough to pick up that amount of weight was the Assassin, so I walked out to help him get to his feet.

I used Nick's sister-in-law, Janet, to play the part of Boni, who was the princess of pancake makeup. Janet had the same hair color and was about the same size as Boni. As she stepped out of the van, she looked into the mirror and patted herself on the face with a purple, powder puff that was as big as the steering wheel of a car. Her head was engulfed in powder as it billowed into the air. We got more calls about that skit than anything else we had ever done. Everybody loved it and commented on how funny it was. Pedicino and Boni didn't like it at all. In fact, I was told that Pedicino hyperventilated and they had to take him to the hospital. They thought he was having a heart attack.

Shortly after it aired, Bruiser Brody came in to do interviews for Pedicino's show. Brody was on a lot of the tapes that Pedicino aired, so he wanted him to do some promos. Pedicino said, "*You have to see this, Bruiser. It's absolutely terrible.*"

He played the tape of my skit for Brody, expecting sympathy and understanding. Instead, Brody sat and laughed until tears were rolling down his cheeks. Pedicino lost his cool and said, "*You wouldn't think it was so funny if it made your 12-year-old son cry.*"

Brody said, "*If I had a 12-year-old son that bawled over something like that, I'd beat his sissy, little ass.*"

Dennis Stamp:

Outside of Stan Hansen, he didn't hang out with anybody that I know of. He'd ride with anybody, just for a ride. He didn't hang out much at all. A lot of the guys played the girls pretty hard. I don't even remember him doing that at all.

Ox Baker:

In San Antonio, there was a gang of Mexican guys that were all extras in a movie Bruiser Brody was in. They put some explosives around a guy's waist. It was supposed to be a scene where somebody shot him with a shotgun. When they set the charges off, it would blow him backwards. Bruiser Brody was standing up there. The guy made a mistake and got himself with his back almost to a wall. When they shot the explosive in his waistband off, it blew him back through the wall. The guy is lying there—muddy, dirty—you know, in shock. Brody walked up to him and said, "*Come on. We're going to do the scene again. We gotta do it right this time. I gotta get home for supper.*"

The guy got up. "*Sorry. I didn't want to make you miss supper.*"

Here the guy almost got blown in two.

Bill Watts:

To me, if you're a whore in one place, you're a whore in another. To me, he was a whore. There's guys that have a lot of ability, a lot of strength, a lot of great things, but they're short in principle. I think the business has a certain principle and you had to adhere to the principle. I had times that I was very upset with the promoters and walked out right after a match, but I fulfilled the match. I never left the town hurt, with the individual that I left the town for. If I left, I left it the way it should have been. I had several cases like that early on in my career. But, it didn't sour me. I didn't think every promoter was a thief. I realized the system, and there was a system in negotiation, but once you accepted a major deal, you had to live by it.

Dory Funk Jr.:

Yeah, I wrestled Bruiser Brody three weeks before he died in San Juan, Puerto Rico. I wrestled him in the tournament. In fact, I won the match against him.

Adrian Street (wrestler):

I was wrestling in Ohio. Bruiser was wrestling against the Iron Sheik and I was with the old Detroit Sheik [Ed Farhat] in singles matches. I went in the ring first, and then the Sheik came out doing all this, and it took him three-quarters of an hour to get to the ring. I was face, he was the heel. He came in the ring and tried to stab me with that lollipop stick with the blade on it. I knocked it out of his hand, picked it up, and stabbed him with it. He bled all over the place. I'm working with the stick, and who should run up behind me, kick me in the back? It was the Iron Sheik. It was very funny. They were trying to stomp on me with those big, curly boots, and I'm diving between their legs.

I dived out of the ring, ran back to the dressing room, and grabbed Bruiser Brody and brought him to the ring. We jumped in. I'm fighting with one of them, he's fighting the other. We're swapping over, and we went outside of the ring, then jumped back in, and got on the mic and said, "*Okay, you bloody camel jockeys. We'll get you next time,*" and all that. We got up a hell of an angle for Bruiser Brody and myself to tag against the Detroit Sheik and the Iron Sheik. We made this big angle to come back against those two, but in the meantime, Bruiser went to Puerto Rico and he never came back.

Nick Bockwinkel:

Most promoters have dealt with these big, gregarious, male, macho, testosterone-laden animals, and a lot of the promoters were wrestlers. A lot of them thought they could control this wildebeest, so they would take that challenge on. Now, from what I understand, he had been going to Puerto Rico for some time, making some good money. The sad thing that happened in Puerto Rico was he again decided to jack around the promoter, and he just ran into a promoter who's ego was probably as big as his, and he pushed the buttons hard enough, and one of the buttons pushed back.

So, when someone says, "*Isn't it sad what happened to Brody in Puerto Rico?*" I think, more sad than what happened to Brody, is what happened to a mother and child in San Antonio, Texas. Their father, their provider, their husband, got removed from their life, that's what's sad.

The second sad thing is that Brody is gone. It's sad what Brody ultimately did to himself.

Gene Lewis:

He told me he was going to take more time off and spend more time with his family. We had planned a big picnic in Dallas for all the guys to get together. Two weeks later, he was killed.

DE PUERTO RICO

© EL VOCERO DE PUERTO RICO, 1988

VOL. 8 NUM. 5289 SAN JUAN, P.R.

MARTES 19 DE JULIO DE 1988

35¢

PRIM

Nú

El precio de EL VOCERO fuera de NY, Boston, Hartford, Fila

Tragedia entre luchador

INVADER

A BRUISE

EMIO

SEGUNDO PREMIO

TERCER PREMIO

eros Lotería de Santo Domingo

a, Norte de NJ y Chicago, es de 40₡ diario y 50₡ sabatino.

UNO MATA

R BRODY

Chapter XIV
If Heaven Ain't A Lot Like Dixie

J Michael Kenyon:
They say the good die young. Maybe that was the case with Frank Goodish, too.

Harley Race:
I'm sure I'm not the first one to tell you this, but his attitude got him in trouble. When he went to Puerto Rico, I told him, "*If you don't change your attitude when you're over there, you won't live to get off the island,*" and he didn't.

General Skandor Akbar:
You might want to mention this. When he got killed in Puerto Rico, I was here [Dallas] and I was helping in the office a little bit. We had him booked for that following Friday and I had called Barbara, his wife. She said, "*Ak, I've got it down on the calendar. He'll be coming in from San Juan.*"

We always put one of the main events on the marquee outside the Sportatorium, and this marquee read, "*Bruiser Brody returns versus The Angel of Death.*" That turned out to be the truth.

David Sheldon, aka the Angel of Death, was to be Brody's first scheduled opponent when he returned to Dallas. In a strange twist of fate, in 1993, Sheldon was scheduled to be Kerry von Erich's next opponent, but Kerry died before the match took place.

Tony Atlas:
We were supposed to be there for a week. Whenever we went [to Puerto Rico], it was for a week. We had three more trips to make that time and we were at Bayamon.

In the summer of 1987, Bruiser Brody had become a babyface in Puerto Rico when he saved Invader #1 [Jose Gonzales] from Jason the Terrible and Abdullah the Butcher. This set up his feud in WWC with Abdullah.

Eddie Gries:
I have that great match where Brody takes that television cable cord and wraps it around Abdullah's neck for ten minutes.

Brody was still marching to his own drummer. Neither promoter Carlos Colon, nor his right hand man, Jose Gonzales, could control what Brody did in the ring.

Eddie Gries:
Watch the Brody match when he is partners with the Rock's father, Rocky Johnson, against Mr. Pogo, who's his drinking buddy, and Kendo Nagasaki. He takes the kendo stick away from them and beats the shit out of them, while Rocky just stands there, jumping up and down, chewing gum, and having a good time. He wouldn't give them their kendo

stick back. Well, after the match was over, Carlos Colon came charging into the dressing room. It was me, Abdullah, and Brody there. He started yelling and screaming at Brody. He says, "*I had that tag team match … those two Japs, I built them up for six months, the strongest tag team on the island, and you, in one match, totally destroyed them. All that work for nothing! You can't do that to me!*"

This was one of the reasons why he got into trouble. He went against the promoters.

Eddie is referring to another great Brody match, which took place in Roberto Clemente Stadium in San Juan, Puerto Rico, on January 30, 1988. Brody beat the hell out of Nagasaki and Pogo. The two Japanese wrestlers looked like kids next to Brody. He gave them about 30 seconds of offense in the whole match and just kicked the hell out of them, beating them mercilessly with Nagasaki's kendo stick. That kendo stick was not an ECW kendo stick. It didn't bend, or give, or splinter into pieces. It held strong as Brody beat the hell out of them. After the match, both Colon and Gonzales were incensed over Brody's actions in the match. Colon had spent a lot of time building up Pogo and Nagasaki to the Puerto Rican fans, and all his work had been undone in a matter of minutes. Brody explained that the Japanese press had been at ringside and he needed to look strong, or he would be in trouble with All Japan. Colon and Gonzales didn't buy it. They didn't forget it, either.

Tony Atlas:

I was married to a Puerto Rican girl at the time. I had a place down there. I was set up nice. I had no plan on leaving Puerto Rico. I said, "I'll just stay here until something in the States happens for me."

He just became super nice to everybody. Like a month before he died, he did a complete 360. Even though he was that way, you liked him. I never disliked him. I just got mad at him that time in Texas when he … you know. But if you ever met him, he was the most likeable guy you ever met in your whole life. I think a lot of the stuff he did, he did to impress. Not so much that he wanted to do it, but the people he was surrounded with.

George Napolitano:

I was supposed to be there that weekend in Puerto Rico, but something came up.

Eddie Gries:

That Wednesday night; Brody and Abby wrestled. Abdullah also had that match where he beat the shit out of that one kid, and then Brody comes in with the stretcher. You notice he comes out with the stretcher with Gonzales.

Tony Atlas:

The day before the murder, he [Brody] rode with Jose [Gonzales] to the town.

Eddie Gries:

Thursday night, they go wrestle somewhere, and he actually came back in the car with Gonzales. They were wrestling as partners. They were both babyfaces. Friday night, they're in Ponce, and its Abdullah and Dan Spivey versus Carlos Colon and Brody. Well, the lighting wasn't that good. I didn't take too many pictures. I'll see him tomorrow night. Frank said he'd take a lot of pictures with me on Saturday night.

(Pro Wrestling Illustrated, December 1988) is only because I said to Frank in the dressing room, "*Can I get a couple of still shots from you?*"

He says, "*Eddie, we'll do it all tomorrow. Let's get this one out of the way.*"

So, that was the end of that match. I took one or two shots, then we went to eat—me, Quinones, and Brody—and that was it.

Dutch Mantell:

The only time I ever talked to Brody at length, talked to him for more than five minutes, was the day all this happened. I was down in the hotel lobby waiting for Abby.

Tony Atlas:

On Saturday, when I went outside to meet my ride, I saw Brody and Dutch Mantell sitting on the steps of the Panama hotel. I said, "*Brody, where's your ride at?*"

He said, "*Well, Jose is supposed to pick me up.*"

I said, "*You're more than welcome to ride with me. I've got my buddy coming by to pick me up. I could tell the guy at the front desk to tell Jose that you already got a ride.*"

He said, "*Yeah, if you don't mind.*"

I said, "*No, I don't mind.*"

The last two photos of Bruiser Brody alive. In his last match he teamed up with Carlos Colon and faced Danny Spivey and Abdullah the Butcher in Ponce, Puerto Rico, on Friday July 15, 1988.

So, Brody got in the car with my buddy and his wife. Brody sat in the front seat, his wife slid over, and me and Dutch was sitting in the back seat. When we got to the building, Victor Jovica, Carlos, and Jose were sitting in like a football huddle, like in a circle.

It was that evening, July 16, 1988, before a show at Juan Lobriel Stadium in Bayamon. The wrestlers were in their locker rooms getting ready. The stadium was not packed. Business was slow.

Dutch Mantell:

That evening, Gonzales was wilder than usual. He had a slimy way of asking—no, telling you to do something that you didn't want to do. I was told to juice big that night, and I told him, "*Hell, no. I'll blade myself if I'm going to do anything.*"

Bruiser Brody was scheduled to wrestle Dan Spivey.

Tony Atlas:

I was showing my art to the guys. I do portraits, and Brody asked if I could do one of his son. After awhile, when me and Brody were talking, Jose got up and walked out of the room, and came back a few minutes later. I didn't even notice the towel draped over his hand. Jose came and stood in front of the shower and said, "*Brody.*"

Brody turned, holding a picture in one hand and his pouch in his other hand, and went behind the door with Jose.

Going into the shower stall was a common way to get a little privacy in the locker room.

Dutch Mantell:

Atlas, [Bobby] Jaggers, Ricky Romero's kids [Mark and Chris Youngblood] were there, along with [Hercules] Ayala and TNT. TNT and Ayala would later testify that Gonzales cut Brody, and I was proud of TNT. He was yelling, "*We have to go to the police and tell them Jose did it.*"

I was pondering what Gonzales and Colon had told me, and the way the locker room was. The showers were centered, and in the back, separated from the main locker room by a smoky glass window. I was in a walkway on the other side and directly in front of the smoky glass. We all heard a scream.

Tony Atlas:

Within no time at all, we heard a little scuffling, then we heard, "*UUUUHHHHHRRRRR! UUUUUHHHHHRRRR!*"

Twice. When I heard it the second time, I ran to the shower and pulled open the door. Carlos was right beside me. And I saw Brody bent over. When I looked up, I saw Jose with the knife in his hand, as if he was getting ready to cut Brody's throat. I grabbed Brody and pulled him back by the waist. When I pulled Brody back, the knife came down and cut off his ponytail. Carlos shot in front of me, grabbed Jose, and pinned him up against the wall. Then Brody looked at me and said, "*Brother, I'm hurt.*"

I pulled him back and laid him down on the ground, and I straddled him. I said, "*Don't worry, brother, ain't nobody gonna mess with you no more tonight.*"

Carlos started to come over, and I threatened Carlos. "*Don't you come over here.*"

He said, "*I ain't got nothing to do with that. That's between these guys.*"

Then I saw Jose walking out the door, unescorted.

Dutch Mantell:

Brody's main chest wound had blood that was bubbling, so I figured his lung [peritoneum] had been sliced open. He kept asking Tony [Atlas] to take care of his wife and kid. He knew he was dying, but could talk. The police were disorganized and got there well before the ambulance, and knew nothing about emergency care. Even Jose and Colon were standing over Brody while the police questioned us all. That was sick. We all knew Jose had done it, and then ran out the back way.

Eddie Gries:

Gonzales had run out after he stabbed him and then came back like nothing had happened.

Tony Atlas:

We tried to tell the cops on the scene. They just laughed, thinking it was a wrestling angle. Somebody had to call the radio station so they could announce that we needed an ambulance.

Then Carlos says, "*I need to talk to him.*"

So, I kind of unstraddled Brody and let Carlos talk to him. The only thing that Brody said to Carlos was, "*Take care of my son.*"

Carlos said, "*Don't worry. I'll take care of your son.*"

Dutch Mantell:

I tried to clean and compress the wound to stop the bleeding.

Tony Atlas:

Then we waited about forty minutes. We had just got there and the people was coming in, because it happened just at the beginning of the show. The fans was still coming into the arena.

The Youngbloods was in tears. I was in tears. The rest of the room was getting dressed.

The lady [medic] had some old guy with her. He couldn't lift Brody and she couldn't lift Brody, so I picked him up and carried him down the stairs to the ambulance, but nobody else would help. The funny thing is, there were all these white guys standing around, and the one black guy carries him. When I lifted him up, he said, "*Don't drop me brother.*"

I said, "*Don't worry, brother. I got you.*"

The lady said, "*Is anybody going to the hospital with him?*"

I jumped into the back of the ambulance and there was a friend of mine—Hurricane Castillo Jr. I grabbed him by his shirt collar, and it was probably the greatest feat of strength I ever did in my whole life. I yanked him up into the ambulance as they were pulling off. I needed an interpreter. His eyes were as big as two 50-cent pieces. I said, "Brother, I need you to talk for me."

He said, "*Okay, I'll talk for you.*"

Eddie Gries:

I was riding to the matches with Abdullah and we actually passed the ambulance on our way there. We got there late, and since the good guys and the bad guys had dressing rooms on opposite sides of the arena, I was the only one that could go back and forth, because I was the photographer. I know for a fact that Gonzales did not mean to kill him. He wanted to teach him a lesson.

Abdullah the Butcher:

Well, the truth, I didn't see it. I could sit here and tell you other things, lies that I seen it. I don't want to sit here and lie. To me, it's not worth it. I knew there was a fight, and that's all I know. I don't know what happened. I didn't see anything go down. The only thing I knew was after Brody went to the hospital.

Tony Atlas:

I held his hand and I knew he liked country music, so I sang the old Hank Williams hit:

If heaven ain't a lot like Dixie, I don't wanna go.
If heaven ain't a lot like Dixie, I'd just as soon stay home.
If they don't have a Grand Ole Opry, like they do in Tennessee.
Just send me to Hell or New York City, it would be about the same to me.

When Tony Atlas returned from the hospital, he and Dutch Mantel wrestled their scheduled match against Bobby Jaggers and Dan Kroffatt. On the following night [Sunday], there was a card scheduled for Mayaguez. Several of the Puerto Rican wrestlers, who hadn't heard the news, made the trip to Mayaguez, while most of the American wrestlers refused to go. There weren't enough wrestlers there to fill the card, so Carlos Colon cancelled the show.

Tony Atlas:

When we got to the hospital, they took Brody and laid him on a table. I took his shoes off, and when I did, I could see that his feet were turning blue. So, then I got all hysterical. I started looking for a doctor. There was stab patients all over the room. Stabbing in Puerto Rico, they treat that like a head cold because it happens so frequently, but I didn't know that. We was always over in the tourist area where everything was beautiful. When I finally got a doctor, he said, "*Be there in a minute.*"

I headlocked that doctor and took him in there. I sure did. He said, "*Let me go. Let me go.*"

I said, "*You're going with me.*"

So, I took him to Brody and he said, "*So, this is your friend?*"

I said, "*Yeah, this is my friend. Look at him.*"

The doctor spoke English. He asked Brody, "*How are you doing?*"

Brody said, "*I'm just sitting here, waiting on you, brother.*"

So, I sat outside for a while and then they told me Brody was stable.

Abdullah the Butcher:

I've heard people say that I called Brody at the hospital, but I didn't, 'cause if a man's at the hospital, how can you call him? I was waiting for him to come out. Everybody was waiting for him to come out.

Bruiser Brody's last posed shot. Wednesday, July 13, 1988 in Cantanyo, Puerto Rico.

Tony Atlas:

Carlos Colon came to my room and asked me, "*What room did Abby say Brody was in?*"

I told him, and as soon as he left, I realized Brody was dead.

Larry Matysik:

The doctors told Barbara that he must have been taking aspirin, which he was. He was living on aspirin. He had that broken elbow for a long time. He had already lost the feeling in two fingers on his right hand because he worked with a broken elbow for so long. They couldn't stop the bleeding because his blood was so thin, and I know he was from when he worked with me. Aspirin, aspirin, aspirin. People worried about drugs. No … aspirin, aspirin, aspirin, aspirin.

Brody died in the early hours of July 17, 1988. He had been stabbed twice, once in the thorax and once in the abdomen. The autopsy states that the cause of death was from hypovolemic shock, or shock caused by severe blood loss.

Dutch Mantell:

Those butchers at the hospital did experimental, observational surgery on him that caused more intense bleeding, then I got the call he died around five a.m. the next morning. I called Mrs. Goodish and told her she better come down a few hours before he died—that the rumors she heard were true. It really was bad.

Abdullah the Butcher:

I think Carlos Colon's wife called Brody's wife.

Tony Atlas:

The next day, I was working out in the gym, and some off duty cops come up to me. "*It's a shame what that crazed fan did to Brody.*"

I said, "*What?*"

And I told them the truth. They said I should go down to the station, so I did. I brought Sika, the Wild Samoan, with me. Sika didn't see it. He was over in the heel dressing room, because the heels and the babyfaces didn't dress together. I just wanted him with me. With Sika, I felt like I had the U.S. Marines with me. I figured nobody would mess with me if Sika was with me.

Sika Anoai (wrestler):

I don't wanna talk about that. We were all sad about what happened. Brody was the one that got us that job down in Puerto Rico. We were wrestling in Japan and he said we should go there.

Dutch Mantell:

Tony Atlas and I volunteered to go to the cops, but the cops acted ignorant, like they couldn't understand a word Tony told them. I credit TNT and some others for having the guts to tell the cops it was Jose, too, since they were regulars.

Tony Atlas:

I told the police exactly what I saw, and who else was in the dressing room. I said, "*Go ask that guy, and ask this guy.*"

They went and asked them people and they all said, "*I don't know nothing. I didn't see nothing. I didn't see nothing!*"

Made me look like a big, 'ol liar.

Abdullah the Butcher:

I was picking up a ticket. This lady who I talked to [on the telephone] many times ... I had never seen her. She came to me and she says, "I'm Bruiser Brody's wife."

That's how I met her. Sad day.

Eddie Gries:

I was there with Abdullah, trying to get out of that place. We wanted to get out of there as fast as possible. We were scared. All of us were scared. We met his wife and son at the airport, and then Colon's wife came and picked her up.

Tony Atlas:

That night, TNT came to my room and says I got to get out of Puerto Rico. I told him, "*I'm leaving tomorrow.*"

He said, "*NO! Right now.*"

Dutch Mantell:

I couldn't leave right away, and I got the hell out of where the other wrestlers were staying, for my own safety, and got a condo elsewhere on the island.

Tony Atlas:

I had to leave the girl. She didn't want to come with me. I wanted her to, but she says, "*No.*"

After I told her what happened, the first words out of her mouth were, "*I hope you kept your mouth shut!*"

I said, "*No, I told them everything.*"

She said, "*Shit, you better get out of here.*"

I said, "*Okay. Get your things ready. It'll probably take us a week to get out of here.*"

She said, "*No, you better get out of here. I'm not leaving my family just because you don't know how to keep your mouth shut.*"

Dutch Mantell:

So I stayed in my condo room, looking out the window, and I was one nervous, scared, son-of-a-bitch. I kept dreaming Colon and Gonzales would climb up the stairs to my room, and a couple times, I thought I heard my door open. I jumped out the window in fear for my life.

Larry Matysik:

I can remember when everything was happening, and she [Barbara Goodish] had to go down there. God, I remember she called me from down there in Puerto Rico and saying, "*Did Frank ever talk to you about being cremated?*" Which, he had. On one of those many rides, somehow it came up.

I don't think Abdullah had anything to do with his cremation. That's all bullshit. Frank and I had talked about this on the road and I remember him saying, "*I'm going for the burn, brother. I'm going for the burn.*"

That's what they were doing in Australia. He said, "*They're right. If anything ever happens to me, I'm going for the burn.*"

I thought he told her, but she asked me, and I said he had, and she said, "*That's what I'm going to do.*"

Abdullah the Butcher:

They were friends of mine, like Brody. Brody was a friend. Invader is a good friend of mine. Carlos Colon is a good friend of mine.

Killer Tim Brooks:

I had a lot of good times with him. The last time I saw Bruiser was about a month before he died. He came through Dallas quite often. I didn't go to his funeral because I had to work and I couldn't get out of it. To tell you the truth, I really didn't want to go. I absolutely hate the way he was killed. I don't think the business is worth anyone getting killed over.

Eddie Gries:

Meltzer called me. Apter called me. "*You got pictures? Can you write me something? You got anything?*" This

Opposite: Bruiser Brody strangles Invader I, 1986.

and that.

Tony Atlas:

Everybody knows he [Gonzales] did it for revenge. Everybody in that dressing room knows that. It's no big secret. He pleaded self defense, and then, when Brody's record came up, they said, "*Oh, yeah. This guy.*"

They looked at all the stuff he had done and ... you know. It's kind of hard defending a guy like that, so Jose just pleaded self defense.

Dutch Mantell:

I believe, in my heart, that Brody and Invader had had trouble previously, but it was forgotten. Brody beat him up in the ring, but see, Brody beat a lot of people up in the ring. That was the way he worked. He just beat the dogshit out of you. But I don't know if that was the problem. I think Brody had bought into this company [WWC]. Gorilla Monsoon had owned some stock here at one time, and somehow, Victor Quinones was involved in this ... he took stocks from Monsoon, and I think Victor Quinones and Bruiser Brody were like good buddies. What I think happened, and I can't confirm this, but I think Brody had somehow had a percentage of this company here in Puerto Rico, and the Invader was in a position where he was in either a booking position, or he owned part of the company, and that's where the clash came. Then again, I don't know why it happened. I think probably the most infamous day in the history of professional wrestling.

Eddie Gries:

There's a Brody tape I put together where Brody just destroys the Invader. Absolutely, it's on the Brody tape I did. If you're thinking revenge, it could be for that match.

Terry Funk:

That was Brody's way. It worked at that time. I don't mean that badly or anything. He was a strong guy. He was a tough guy, and he could push people to the limits, and it was successful for him. Who would have thought that it would turn out the way that it did? We didn't know that the one guy was off the edge, because if he wasn't off the edge, he wouldn't have done it. This guy had a great deal of problems. It was very difficult for him, because for some people, it was easy to change things, to come up with matches, but to him, he'd think about it and think about it, and think about it, and think about it, and spend all of his time and drive himself nuts. "*How am I going to do this?*" And he'd go ahead and give it to Brody, and Brody would just tear it apart and say, "*We're not going to do that. We'll do it my way.*"

So, it had this guy like ... crazy, and Brody would take over in the ring, and physically, just wail his ass. Physically abuse him in the ring. There's nothing wrong with that. That's part of it. It's not a death sentence. I'm just being honest about Frank.

Wife of a professional wrestler:

It was a $400,000 pot deal gone bad.

Abdullah the Butcher:

Whoever said that, they're a liar. I've never seen Brody with any drugs. I'm not going to hang with somebody who's dealing with drugs. Jose. I've never seen him with any drugs. A lot of people are going to say things about a man who's not here, and that's what I told you before when we talked. I said if you want me to lie to you, I'll lie to you, but everything I tell you is the truth. I'm not going to try and condemn a man when I know for a fact that I've never seen him with nothing. I've never seen him or Jose with any drugs. You talk about other people, okay, but I would never condemn this man for that.

A lot of wrestlers might watch something in the ring, blow by blow, but for somebody to tell a lie and say Brody was selling drugs … excuse my language, but they're a goddamn liar. And for Jose, the same thing. I've never seen anything. This is the first time I'm hearing it from you. I've never heard it from nobody else that Bruiser Brody or Invader ever sold any drugs.

Dutch Mantell:

I'm not dodging and I'm not ducking, but I don't know what happened. I don't know what caused it. I don't know what preceded it.

Dennis Stamp:

All I know is that it couldn't have happened unless Colon wanted it to happen. A fly doesn't land on the wall down there without Colon knowing.

Bill Watts:

You know, Brody created his own bullshit.

Nick Bockwinkel:

It was just a matter of time, and needless to say, the gentleman down there was found not guilty by self-defense. All you had to do was show pictures from some of his matches and the jury, along with a sharp attorney, could imagine what took place. But, Frank did that to himself. He brought it upon himself. I don't know what chip in his computer was not sitting in its slot correctly, that made him function the way he did.

Tony Atlas:

The story was out, after Brody's death in Puerto Rico. He was supposed to leave Puerto Rico to go to Japan. They was waiting on him there, too. If it didn't happen in Puerto Rico, it was most definitely going to happen in Japan. It was his time, anyway. Isn't that weird? Jose could have saved himself by just ignoring Brody and letting him go to Japan, and they would have done it for Jose. Isn't that weird? If Jose was a little more patient, Brody would have got his a week later in Japan.

Nick Bockwinkel:

Ultimately, eventually, yes. Tony is probably one of the more mild-mannered, soft-spoken, easy-going guys. To find that I'm in agreement with Tony, that's fine. It's good company. It's rather validating.

Personally, I think Gonzales reached a breaking point. He had been a steady mid-carder in the WWWF in the '70s when Brody came in and immediately got a top spot against Sammartino. I'm sure there was jealousy there. When Brody and Gonzales wrestled in the Nassau Coliseum, Brody just beat the hell out of him and Jose swore revenge.

Brody and Gonzales didn't cross paths again until 1983, when Gonzales' boss, Carlos Colon, decided to bring Brody down to Puerto Rico on a recommendation from NWA World Champion Ric Flair. Gonzales was the booker, but Brody refused to listen to him. Terry Funk has said that Gonzales had a lack of imagination and always struggled to come up with original booking ideas. When he did, Brody wouldn't listen and did what he wanted.

In March 1987, Gonzales' son drowned. I have been told by contemporaries of his that he was also using a lot of drugs at that time.

Also, in 1987, Brody became a babyface. Gonzales had always been the number two babyface under Colon, and now Brody was a babyface on the rise. Would it be a repeat of the WWWF days?

In 1988, after Colon and Gonzales had built up the tag team of Kendo Nagasaki and Mr. Pogo for months as a super badass team, Brody disassembled them and made them look like wimps in minutes.

Gonzales was arrested two days after the stabbing incident on charges of First Degree Murder and a weapons violation. The alleged murder weapon, a knife, was never found. Gonzales was indicted in November 1988 on charges ofVoluntary Homicide. In January 1989, he was acquitted of those charges.

In court, Gonzales didn't take the stand, but Colon testified that there was a dress code in WWC locker rooms, and Brody constantly refused to pay heed. While this sounds like a lame excuse with everything else, it's easy to see Jose Gonzales going off the deep end and seeing the threat of physical violence as his only recourse. Nonetheless, I would still have liked to have seen Jose Gonzales executed for the murder.

Stan Hansen:

I went to Frank's memorial service. John Studd and I were the only people there from the wrestling business. Oh, yeah. Larry Matysik was there. I'm sure more of the guys would have been there, but it was after the fact. John and Frank were good friends. We all went back to New York in '76 when John was with [Killer] Kowalski as the Executioners. We were all kind of cut from the same cloth. Of course, in his own way, John tried to emulate Brody's style of work. You might say Brody was his inspiration.

Dave Meltzer:

As far as the trial goes, none of the eyewitnesses were there to testify. Gonzales didn't testify on his own behalf. I don't know too many people that take that trial seriously.

Dick Steinborn:

Sadly, my friend Carlos Colon got on the stand and said, "*He was on marijuana. He was on cocaine. He was crazy.*"

Eddie Gries:

And the trial was political. The district attorney was in one party and the prosecutor was in another party. They were in opposite parties and didn't want to work with each other or something. He wound up walking out on self-defense.

My wife and I (she speaks Spanish) called the Records Department of the court of San Juan, Puerto Rico. We talked to close to twenty people. We were continually transferred and given different phone numbers to call. After suffering through hours of that kind of treatment, a woman told us she would go and look through the boxes of files and we should call her back in three hours. When we called back, the woman started whispering to us. "*The files should be here, but they are not. Something has happened to them. Don't call here again.*" Then she hung up. I believe the transcripts of Jose Huertas Gonzales' trial were destroyed.

Abdullah the Butcher:

Oh, yes! Why should I stop going to Puerto Rico?

Sir Oliver Humperdink:

Never begrudge a guy for trying to feed his family. While I didn't think it was right, I'd never judge any of the guys that went back.

Tony Atlas:

Believe it or not, I went back and worked for him [Carlos Colon] last year. Abdullah convinced me of it. Yeah, about a year or two ago. But, it just wasn't right. Jose was there, and he came up and shook my hand and everything. Yeah, it just wasn't right.

Abdullah the Butcher:

I've been with Colon for a long time. Why should I stab a man in the back to go work for another [opposition] promotion [IWA] for a few dollars extra? When I go to bed at night, I can go to sleep. I don't have to worry about double crossing guys for a couple bucks. Japan was different.

Road Warrior Animal (wrestler):

That's one reason we've never gone back to Puerto Rico.

Road Warrior Hawk:

That's why we won't go back. Not for that promotion.

Jerry Grey:

What happened in Puerto Rico makes me sick. I've been invited many times to work there, but I never will.

Dave Meltzer:

You could really trace the downslide of wrestling in Puerto Rico to the death of Bruiser Brody. It just never regained its popularity that it had had at that point.

Dory Funk Jr.:

I wasn't there. Didn't see it happen. I know the people involved, and that's about it. I could repeat to you what I've heard other people say, but that wouldn't even be factual. As you know, so many people say different things.

Larry Matysik:

I think he [Gonzales] just had a grudge for a lot of years and it built. I know Frank had done a number on him in the ring about two years before that. They fought about, guess what? Money. Puerto Rico was known for being horrible on the money. They would often tell you one thing, and then you'd get the check, and it would be for half of it, or it would bounce.

Road Warrior Hawk:

Is this going everywhere? Is this going to Puerto Rico? Jose Gonzales, suck my butt. If I ever get in a

shower with you, I'm stabbing you to death.

Gary Hart:

I was in Atlanta with Al Perez. I remember, as I was coming back across the street from the restaurant where we had been eating, the Road Warriors and Paul Ellering were standing in front the La Quinta Hotel. I said to them, "*Why do you guys look so damn sad, man? We have the day off.*"

And they said, "*Bruiser Brody was killed.*"

I said, "*What? How? Car wreck, plane crash? What?*"

They said, "*No. He was stabbed to death in a dressing room in Puerto Rico.*"

It was such a shock. The death of Gino [Hernandez] hurt me. The Von Erich boys hurt, but Bruiser was someone that was invincible. You never thought that anything like that could happen to him. He was Bruiser Brody. It was such a shock. Bruiser and I were super tight. His little boy was one or two years younger than my youngest son. When Brody would be in Dallas, he would stay at my house with me, and when I would be in the valley in Boerne, I would stay with him.

Chapter XV Coroner's Report

External Exam:

This is regarding the cadaver of a white man of the established age of 42 years. His body is devoid of clothing and is wrapped with a white sheet, that once it is removed, you can appreciate a body in the state of development and nutrition that is average, measuring 76" of height, and with a weight of 300 pounds. The cadaver is rigid and has lividity in the posterior corporal region. The head is normal in configuration and the hair is long and wavy with some white hair, also with a beard and moustache. The iris of the eyes are clear brown and the pupils are dilated and the same. In the face, you can appreciate at the level of the forehead multiple, old, linear scars with marked engrossment. The lips are pallid and edematous. On the body, you can appreciate a tattoo on the shoulder of the right arm and there are old scars on the left upper arm, on the left forearm, and on the third medium and posterior of the left leg, and a linear abrasion that was nearly healed. There is also a contusion in the third anterior superior of the left leg muscle of two centimeters in diameter and another one in the third anterior inferior of the right muscle of three centimeters in diameter that are nearly healed. There are needle marks on the right side of the neck, on the flexor of the right arm and on the left wrist, and an old surgical suture scar on the right side of the hemithorax of five centimeters of length, another surgical wound on the hemithorax of 22 cm of length due to the tracheotomy. In the left side of the hemithorax there is another old surgical suture wound of three centimeters of length. In the medium abdominal line, there is a surgical suture wound that extends all the way up to the right side of the hypochondrium of 29cm of length due to the exploratory laparatomy and there is a small surgical suture wound that is open on the right side of the abdomen that is 2cm of length that has been put in as a drain.

The major discovery of interest you can appreciate is two wounds done by a bladed weapon that left two incisions and penetrated the thorax and the abdomen that has the following location and characteristics:

Wound "A":

Bladed incision is located and penetrated the right side of the hemithorax, 55" from the left heel and 3" from the center of the body. The wound is orientated towards the oblique, the borders are clean and separated in the form of double parenthesis that in it's extreme has a notch, and it's total length is 2¼". The internal examination reveals that the instrument that produced the first wound when contacting the corporal surface went in and out, up and down, and right to left. Following the trajectory it is evident that after lacerating the skin, the cellular tissue situated under the skin, and the muscular plane, it fractured the 6th rib on the right side in its anterior aspect, lacerated the diaphragm that has been surgically repaired and produced a laceration of the left lobe of the kidney 3cm deep. This wound produced a hematoma in the right hemithorax finding in the right hemithorax 200cc of blood and in the abdominal cavity 500cc of coagulated blood.

Wound "B":
Wound incision punctured and penetrated the left side of the abdomen, 46" from the left heel and .5" from the median line of the body. The same is oriented in a horizontal of the clean borders that are separated in the form of double parenthesis 2 ¼" of length, and at it's end, continues with a small superficial incision on the right side of the abdomen of 1.5cm of length that only enters the skin. The internal exam concluded that the instrument that produced the wound, once it contacted the body, it had a direction of up and down, side to side, right to left, and after the laceration of the skin and the cellular tissue was subcutaneously lacerated, the muscular plane and aponeurotic of the abdominal wall was lacerated. The incision goes to the abdominal cavity, but it does not interfere with organs of the same, making the penetration of the instrument approximately 2".

On the right side of the back and to the level of the infraclavicular region, you can appreciate a superficial incision wound, orientated towards the oblique of 5cm of length that only penetrates the skin and the subcutaneous cellular tissue and the region of the left scapula. There is another superficial incision wound orientated towards the oblique of 1cm of length that only penetrates the skin. On the dorsal of the left hand there is a small superficial incision wound from defending and located on the 4th level metacarpal

vertically oriented and 1" length that penetrates only the skin that forms a small hanging (piece of flesh from it.

While opening the cranial cavity, you do not see evidence of trauma lesions. The brain weighs 1,400 grams and is considerably pallid. The cerebral hemispheres are symmetrical and the meninges are thin, clear, and transparent, letting us see the cerebral circumvolutions of normal configuration. The arteries of the base of the brain are distributed normally and do not show any significant change in their walls. The cerebral sections, bridge, and cerebellum only show signs of being pallid.

In the neck, you can appreciate the thyroid glands of normal shape, configuration, and normal appearance. The larynx also has a normal appearance and the cervical column is also normal. In the walls of the thorax, you can appreciate an extensive surgical wound in the fifth intercostals muscle of the right side due to a tracheotomy, with another small open wound in the eighth intercostals muscle of the right side to put a tube into the chest and into the left hemithorax. Also, there is an open surgical wound in the fifth intercostals muscle on the left side to put the tube in the chest.

The exam of the abdominal thoracentesis organs you can appreciate pallid lungs augmented of size. The right one weighs 900 grams and the left one weighs 850 grams, while we sectioned the lungs liquid is abundant within them and through the bronchial tree. The pericardium cavity once sectioned shows 20 cc of pericardium liquid of clear yellow color

The heart is augmented of size and weighs 520 grams. Once sectioned, you can appreciate the concentric hypertrophy on the left ventricle which has the coloration of grayish whitish and the valves show no significant changes. The coronary vessels show yellowish plaque on their walls, which makes it thicker, and that looks from light to moderate in color, being marked on the right coronary, you can appreciate 2 cm from it's origin a great plaque build up that blocks 50% of his lumen. The liver weighs 1,900 grams and, apart from the wound of the bladed weapon described before, shows yellowish coloration and light consistency which is diminishing comparable with changes of fat. The spleen is permeable and there is 10cc of bile in the interior of the spleen which has normal appearing mucus. The spleen is augmented and weighs 250 grams, and its capsule is bluish greenish and once it is sectioned it shows a firm consistency. The adrenalin glands have normal measurement and appearance, but pallid in color, and the pancreas is also pallid and augmented from its normal size. The kidneys weigh 260 grams each. Once sectioned, there is good delimitation of the corticomedulla and the superficial surface looks pallid. The urethra has a normal quality and distribution and the bladder has no content of urine.

Once examined, the gastrointestinal and the gastro cavity, there is barely any content of yellowish liquid and the gastro mucus is pallid just like the intestines.

DIAGNOSTIC SUMMARY:

1. The wound made by a sharp object in the thorax and in the abdomen produced:
a). Fracture of the sixth rib on the right side.
b). Laceration of the right middle diaphragm and liver.
c). The right hemithorax and the massive hemoperitoneum.
2. Incision wounds on the back.
3. Incision wounds of self defense on the left hand.
4. Status post exploratory laparotomy with diaphragm sutures.
5. Pulmonary edema.
6. Cardiomegaly (520grams) with left ventricle hypertrophy and arteriosclerosis of the coronaries of light and moderate grade.
7. Kidneys with change of fat.
8. Pallid organs.

Cause of death:
Hypovolemic shock because of bladed weapon wounds on the thorax and abdomen.

Manner of Death:
Homicide.

Final Note:

The cadaver is a white man and he is 42 years old, according to the information from the family. In the hours of the night of yesterday, July 16th, and finding him in the Stadium Juan Ramón Loubriel of Bayamon, was wounded with a bladed weapon, and being transported to the Rio Piedras Medical Center, where he was surgically attended to, and passed away in the dawn hours today July 17th.

The autopsy gives evidence that the cause of death was hypovolemic shock due to incision wounds penetrated in the thorax and the abdomen.

Author's note: The autopsy also includes two toxicology reports which show that Goodish's body was free of aspirin, alcohol, cocaine, morphine, heroin, quinine, codeine, methadone, talwin, and amphetamines. The autopsy was performed by Dr. Ophelia Vera, who has since died.

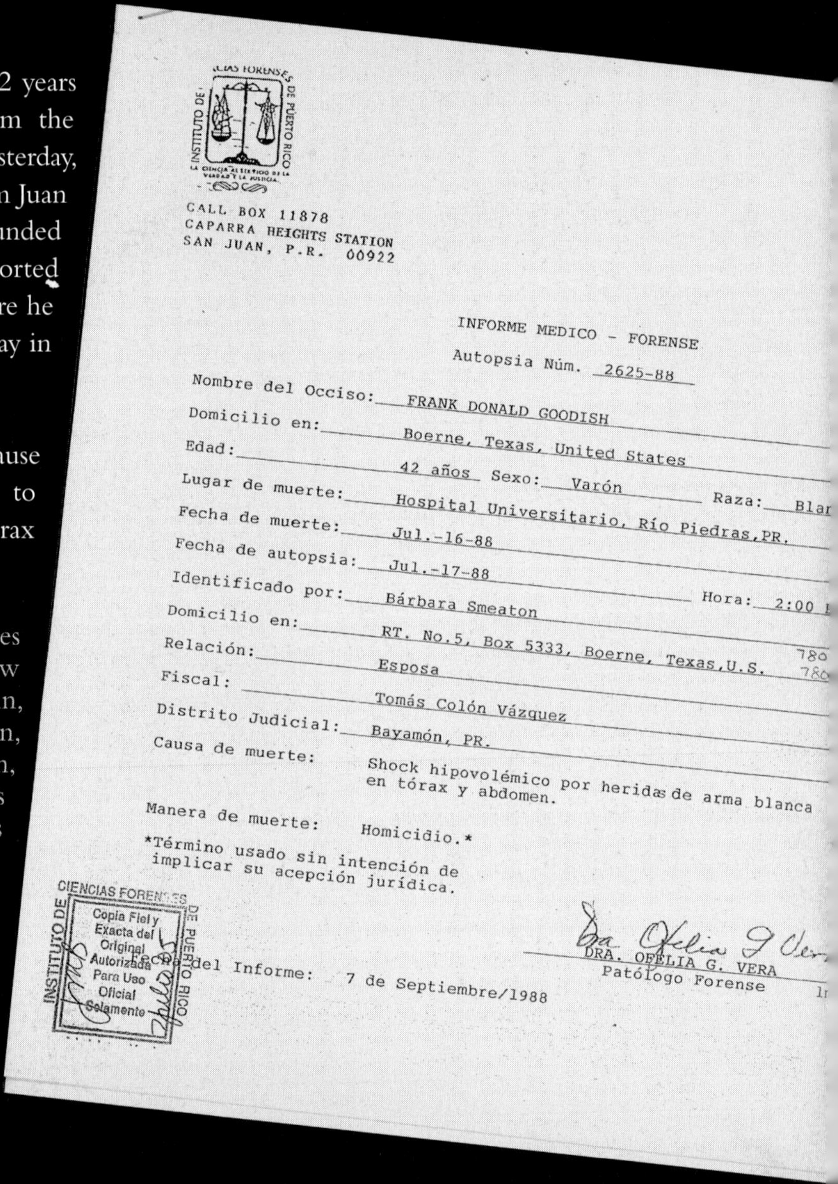

INSTITUTO DE CIENCIAS FORENSES DE PUERTO RICO

CALL BOX 11878
CAPARRA HEIGHTS STATION
SAN JUAN, P.R. 00922

INFORME MEDICO - FORENSE

Autopsia Núm. 2625-88

Nombre del Occiso: FRANK DONALD GOODISH
Domicilio en: Boerne, Texas, United States
Edad: 42 años Sexo: Varón Raza: Blan
Lugar de muerte: Hospital Universitario, Río Piedras, PR.
Fecha de muerte: Jul.-16-88
Fecha de autopsia: Jul.-17-88
Identificado por: Bárbara Smeaton Hora: 2:00
Domicilio en: RT. No.5, Box 5333, Boerne, Texas, U.S. 780
Relación: Esposa
Fiscal: Tomás Colón Vázquez
Distrito Judicial: Bayamón, PR.
Causa de muerte: Shock hipovolémico por heridas de arma blanca en tórax y abdomen.

Manera de muerte: Homicidio.*

*Término usado sin intención de implicar su acepción jurídica.

DRA. OFELIA G. VERA
Patólogo Forense

Fecha del Informe: 7 de Septiembre/1988

INSTITUTO DE CIENCIAS FORENSES DE PUERTO RICO
Copia Fiel y Exacta del Original Autorizada Para Uso Oficial Solamente

Chapter XV Replay

All Japan held the first annual Bruiser Brody Memorial Night at Nippon Budokan in Tokyo, Japan, on August 29, 1988. All of All Japan's wrestlers gathered at ringside while Brody's widow, Barbara, and son, Geoffrey, held a large portrait of Brody in the ring. The ringside bell rang ten times in salute to the fallen warrior. On the wrestling card that night, Brody's longtime tag-team partner, Stan Hansen, faced Brody's arch-nemesis, Abdullah the Butcher, in the main event.

Abdullah the Butcher:
It was heavy, a horrible night. Stan is a friend of mine. Everybody took it hard. Any time a wrestler dies, or whatever happens ...

Dutch Mantell:
Thank God there are some decent people in this business of ours. I want everyone to know that although Frank was a rascal, he was loved, and shouldn't have gone this way.

Dave Meltzer:
When he died, it was such a huge news story in Japan, like a John Lennon thing almost. For months after his death, it was a huge news thing.

Scott Romer:
Larry [Matysik] also did a few Bruiser Brody memorial shows in St. Louis, after Brody died. Barbara and the son were there at the first one, and at the very end of the show, somebody interfered in the match. Mrs. Brody got in the guy's face and kind of shocked the heel, and he got pinned by the babyface. She did that little angle.

In August 1990, Frontier Martial Arts Wrestling [FMW] promoter, Atsushi Onita, traveled to Puerto Rico to schedule a talent exchange for his upcoming one year anniversary show.

Scott Romer:
About 13 years ago, I received a call from my agent, Jimmy Suzuki, who wanted me to meet him in San Juan to do photos for the Japanese press. I told him no problem and he sent me a round trip ticket. I took a taxi to the San Juan Inn and met Jimmy, [Atsushi] Onita, Cage, and another Japanese photographer. I also met and hung out with Fast Eddie Gries, an American who also had a home in Puerto Rico, and Victor Quinones, part owner at the time of WWC.

Onita rented a limo that took us to the WWC offices, where they also edited the wrestling TV tapes. When we arrived at the WWC offices, I remember Gonzales, Quinones, and Colon, all had their own offices. My job was just to keep on shooting photos of a worked situation where Onita and Gonzales both sign a contract for Gonzales to work in Japan for Onita's group. So I'm shooting photos of the contract signing and Gonzales's wrestlers attack Onita, and Onita gigs like crazy. I got the shots necessary and Gonzales and his henchmen leave the offices. Meanwhile, myself, Onita, and the other Japanese press stayed. Then Onita tries to blade his stomach. He grimaced in pain as he tries to draw blood from his stomach, but only got a trickle. So he takes the blood from his head, and blood that dripped on the floor, and rubs in around his stomach, and has me take photographs of him as though he had been stabbed. So I'm taking photos of him as he rolls around the floor holding his gut.

Photographer Scott Romer and Brody.

Next, an ambulance is called to the office and I'm taking photos of Onita being carted away to the hospital. The police show up and detain me. They asked me questions on what I saw . I was like Sergeant Schultz in Hogan's Heroes and "saw nothing." Next, the limo drove us to the hospital where I took photos of Onita in the hospital. Onita tried to convince the doctors to stitch his gigged stomach, which didn't need stitches. They finally put one stitch in the wound and let Onita go.

Next, the limo took us to the drugstore and Onita bought crutches, BAND-AIDs, and a sling. He then taped his head, put on the sling, wore sun glasses, and we drove to the San Juan Airport for more photos. So I'm taking photos of Onita limping around the airport, arm in sling, and bandaged up.

Jimmy Suzuki then took my film and flew to Miami to send the film to Japan. When I asked him why he had to fly to Miami, instead of sending it Fed Ex from Puerto Rico, he told me how important the shoot was, and in Puerto Rico, their airborne shipping system was all screwed up and they might lose the film.

The next day, I took a rental car to a spot show. I have no idea where. Pogo was with me and he insisted on driving. I'll never forget the winding narrow roads and how close the cars going the opposite direction came to hitting us head on. Upon entering this worn out arena, I saw poor people on the roof of the building peeking through a window to watch the matches for free. Little children would curse the heels and give them the finger.

Once inside, I was in the dressing room for the Americans and Japanese that were all heels. I remember seeing Kim Duk, who I hadn't seen in over 15 years. Fast Eddie Gries comes running into the dressing room and tells me Jose Gonzales wants to see me el pronto. I follow him to Gonzales's dressing room, and upon spotting Jose, he says,

"*Amigo, come follow me.*"

He takes me to the shower area, and at that time, my heart was racing and I almost peed my pants. He says to me, "*I hear you were married to Dick the Bruiser's daughter.*" I told him I was, but now I am divorced. He said when he first started wrestling around 1969, he worked for Dick the Bruiser. He then asked me how I liked the angle with Onita. I told him everything went fine and that the hospital

would only put one stitch in Onita's stomach. He said, "*What do you mean?*"

I changed the subject and told him Jimmy Suzuki had to rush the film to Miami to send it to Japan, and would be back tomorrow. I got the hell out of Jose's dressing room and photographed the matches. I'll never forget how over Jose was with the fans. The next day, I picked Jimmy up at the airport and took him back to the San Juan Inn. We get a fax from Japan and the stabbing angle is on the front page of the Japanese newspaper, blaming Gonzales for trying to kill Onita during a contract signing.

After hanging in Puerto Rico for a few days, I went back home to Indianapolis. About a week later, I get a Gong Magazine with [a story on] the whole stabbing incident, and on the bottom of the page, *Photos by Scott Romer.* To make a long story short, I had no idea that I was going to be involved in that angle. The Japanese press didn't want to blame themselves for the pictures, so they used me. I didn't know the angle was going to happen and was told to just keep on shooting. Then, I hear the Japanese equivalent of 20/20 or Inside Edition heard about the set up and exposed the whole angle on national TV in Japan. I have kept silent about this unorthodox angle, and now, after 13 years, let the truth be known.

Don't get me wrong, Jose Gonzales was going to work in Japan for Onita's Group. He was only under the assumption that we were going to take publicity

Atsushi Onita after his press conference with Jose Huertas Gonzales.

photos—photos of the contract signing, heel Jap gets beat up by Gonzales and his henchmen, etc. Publicity photos like that appear all the time in the Japanese publications.

Jose didn't have any idea Onita was going to take it a step further and do the stabbing angle. Jose and everyone else left the building, leaving Onita and the rest of us [there], and that's when the photos of Onita juiced and holding his gut like he was stabbed were taken. Could you imagine what would have happened to Gonzales if he didn't find out about the angle and showed up in Japan? The Japanese fans would have killed him. First, their star American, Brody killed, and then an attempt to kill their other star, Onita.

Dave Meltzer:

The Onita/Gonzales angle was the worst ever. This was only a year or so later, with the idea of a big stadium show, and Onita would get revenge on Gonzales, who was so hated in Japan as the guy who killed their hero, Bruiser Brody. They did the angle, and they had the photos, but the press was so negative to the bad taste of the angle that Gonzales never came to Japan, and they never did the payoff.

Of all the tasteless angles that have been done in wrestling in the last 20 years, that's a hard one to top.

On November 23, 1999, Dory and Terry Funk auctioned off Bruiser Brody's boots and furry ring jacket in Japan. The money went to Brody's widow, Barbara, and son, Geoffrey.

Adam Windsor (wrestler):

We went over to Japan. It was actually a tag team match with Dory and Terry, and it was the first time they were back together as a team in ten years. On that night, as well, they were auctioning off Bruiser Brody's wrestling boots and his ring jacket. The jacket was the one he wore to the ring in his last match. The boots were the ones he was wearing when he died. The boots still had blood on them.

My job that night was to accompany Dory and Terry to the ring and to carry Bruiser Brody's boots and ring jacket with me. I was told how I was supposed to take them to the ring, how I was supposed to hold them, where I was supposed to put them, give them to whoever, but nobody told me that I was actually supposed to bring them back from the ring. So the match happens and Dory and Terry win, and we're on our way back to the dressing room. When we get to the dressing room, Terry looks at me and says, "*Where are the boots, Adam?*"

And I'm like, "*I'm not sure.*"

Terry really wasn't that pleased. I didn't know. I was supposed to have brought them back from ringside. So, Terry was kind of going berserk, so I thought, "*I'll go off and try and find the boots.*"

I went to where the entrance ramp was to go down into the arena and I hung out there for awhile, and the next thing I know, the boots appeared and they're in Dory and Terry's hands. But it was pretty scary. Nobody told me to bring them back from the ring.

On July 16, 2005, WWC in Puerto Rico held the First Annual Bruiser Brody Memorial Cup. Wrestlers like Abdullah, The Sandman, Sabu, and other hardcore wrestlers participated.

Carlos Colon:

The Bruiser Brody Cup is a 30-Man Battle Royal. Come as you are. Everybody's going to come in their street clothes and bring any kind of object they want. It's going to be held in two separate rings. Fifteen men in one ring, fifteen in the other, and the two winners will meet at the end for the First Bruiser Brody Memorial Cup. There's going to be eight other matches, too.

Jose Gonzales had left the company, so relations with many [wrestlers] stateside were warming up. Colon appeared at a couple of fan conventions and even made an appearance on Dory Funk Jr.'s BAM wrestling show.

Carlos Colon before WWC's First Bruiser Brody Cup on July 16, 2005, the seventeenth anniversary of Brody's murder.

Sabu won the First Bruiser Brody Cup. The event was held at the Juan Lobriel Stadium in Bayamon. The same venue where Brody was murdered.

Chapter XVI Legacy

Larry Nelson:

There were the babyfaces. There were the heels. Only one Bruiser Brody.

Abdullah the Butcher:

If Brody was here, we'd still be going. Brody was a professional 100% in this business. People believed in Bruiser Brody and Abdullah the Butcher, Terry Funk, Stan Hansen. People seen the battles and they say, "*Bruiser Brody. You can't touch him.*"

Gene Lewis:

People remember characters and Frank was a character.

Magic Schwarz:

Frank was a real nice guy when he was out of his Bruiser Brody character. He went out of his way to help people. He was very respected. It's a shame that he met the end that he did.

Jerry Grey:

I partied with Frank in Japan. He was lots of fun. When he was with his friends, he was mild and calm.

Stan Hansen:

Bruiser Brody and I, I must say ... and I don't brag a whole lot, but I must say we were probably the most dominant tag team ever in pro wrestling. I'll say that. Nobody could run with us. We were both 300 pounds and we wrestled like junior heavyweights, and we never stopped, and people just couldn't keep up.

Dory Funk Jr.:

Did he influence me in standing up to promoters? Well, I respected the way he held himself and he took a real hard line attitude. Yeah, maybe he does influence me somewhat. I don't take as hard line an attitude as Bruiser Brody, but he might have taken me from a certain level and then to another level. Yeah, I did respect so much what he did, the way he handled himself, and how he did it, and the reason he did it. He did it to make sure he was going to provide for his family. In hindsight, would I go as far as Brody? I don't think so. He was very successful at the way he did it. I don't know; maybe it ended his career short, maybe it didn't. I don't know.

Dave Meltzer:

He was the prototypical brawler; the great brawler of his era. They had a poll of the Japanese wrestlers of who was the greatest foreigner of the 20th century, and Brody got more votes than anybody.

Dory Funk Jr.:

In his life—who he was and what he did—there's nothing deep. It was rather simple. He wanted to look good and he cared about his family. He did push. He pushed hard, and all he was doing was

The Madman from the Sudan, Abdullah the Butcher, in his restaurant, 2001.

pushing hard for the money so that he could take care of himself and his family. That's a pretty honorable thing to do. He did push more than most, and at the time, I respected him for it, and he may have changed my way of thinking. I didn't pattern myself after him, but he was someone to study and learn from. I did learn from watching him as he took his career through the wrestling business.

One of the world's most respected wrestling journalists, Dave Meltzer at his home, 2001.

Dave Meltzer:

He changed Japanese wrestling in a lot of ways. Toughness became really important. Believability became really important. He popularized that brawling outside the ring, using chairs and things like that.

Wrestling historian, J Michael Kenyon

Dory Funk Jr.:

Maybe the fans identify with him because he was a renegade. He didn't conform. He didn't conform to Crockett, to McMahon, Colon, Inoki, Baba, or anybody. Nice guy, but he didn't conform at all. That may have given him an identity with the wrestling fans as being different from most of the other wrestlers, and just like me, I'm no different from the fans. I was a fan of Bruiser Brody.

Photographer, George Napolitano.

Sir Oliver Humperdink:

I've got a photo of me and Bruiser Brody on the way to the ring. It's still hanging in my living room and it means a lot to me … an awful lot.

Larry Matysik:

But why'd he get along with Sam? Why did he get along with Baba? Why'd he get along with me, who was probably considered the straightest person in wrestling at that point? Because we all kept our word. Where unfortunately for him, maybe I or Sam had been a little … well, they lied to you once, you'd say, "*Well, let's try to work this out, deal with it, get over this hump.*"

No, there were no humps with Brody. You lied to him, he's gonna fuck you. Bottom line.

There was no grey in his life on that matter. It was black and white. If you're my friend, I will kill for you. He did a number on a guy once in a dressing room because the guy said something about me, and Brody beat his ass—destroyed him. That's loyalty.

"Moondog" Ed Moretti.

business was a dream to me. I never saw the dirty side of it. Brody filled me in and kept me okay.

Larry Matysik:

No, it's funny. How could this guy that was such a rebel, such a complete rebel, how could he get along with … well, I certainly was no name in wrestling, but people knew me as Sam's guy, and I was straight. I was honest. I was clean, didn't drink. How the hell could he get along with someone like me? How could he get along with Sam Muchnick if he was this animal, out of control all the time?

We talked a lot about that, that whole dual personality thing. A lot of wrestlers don't understand. "*I'm Frank Goodish and I'm Bruiser Brody.*"

And, he could turn it on and off. Once, up in St. Louis after Sam retired … Sam was more of a baseball writer. He'd always buy a table at the baseball writers dinner. He'd have different friends there. I was there a lot, and one year,

Chavo Guerrero:

He was a philosopher. One time, after the matches, we were eating and having a few beers. I said, "*You know, if I was to die today, I'd be satisfied. I was the world champion. I got a Porsche. I was married to a beauty queen from El Paso. I got a boy. I got a girl. I had a boat.*"

He says, "*You're wrong. You can't just take from life. You got to give back.*"

I say, "*Fuck you, man.*"

We get in the bus and he just looked at me. In about three days, I said, "*Hey, brother. You were right. I'm sorry.*"

He said, "*I knew you'd come back. I knew you'd come back.*"

My dad taught me the good things about the business. This

Gene Lewis, AKA The Mongol, AKA Cousin Luke, AKA Molakai, etc.

Chris Benoit.

Brody went as a guest. Brody and me, Sam, Don Lenhardt, who at that time was scouting for the Boston Red Sox, George Silvey, who was scouting for the Giants, two different lawyers, Bob McGlynn and Pat Byrd, who was a democratic power in the state of Missouri. Brody gave them another side. He fascinated them. It was incredible.

As far as that dual personality, here is a completely different group. These were not wrestling people. You didn't say "*fuck*" every six words to get their attention, which is what you have to do with wrestling people. That's a Bob Geigel story, by the way. Geigel always said you had to say "*fuck*" every six words or they don't think you're serious. But here Brody was with these people at the baseball writers dinner—very coat and tie, very serious, and very straight sport—with people coming up to him for the autographs, and he's getting as much play as the people on the podium. And here were these lawyers, and this political power, and they're fascinated because he's telling them stories and weaving this little personality thing. Yeah, fascinating, truly. One of the most fascinating personalities, I understand, though. I've heard it, and he told me sometimes when he did things, and I was kind going, "*Oh Christ, why did you do that?*"

Gary Hart and Bruiser Brody.

Dave Meltzer:

I'm sure if he would have lived, he would have ended up in the WWE. Wrestling would have changed in many different ways, and I'm sure he would have ended up working in ECW with all those guys towards the end of his career.

Chris Benoit:

His style, too. So many people that came after him took a piece of his style and molded it into their own style. He's looked up upon by all the guys I know. If you mention Bruiser Brody, everyone's got a story to tell ... when they were young watching him, or one of the matches they had seen him in.

Gary Hart:

Bruiser was one of my very best friends and I miss him to this day. When I heard he died, I just went off by myself for a while. I couldn't bring myself to go to Bruiser's funeral. That doesn't mean that I don't have respect or feel pain for his family. It was just something that I couldn't bring myself to do. I didn't go to the Von Erich's funerals, either. I just couldn't do it. I'd rather pretend Bruiser was in Japan, and think that maybe he'll call me tomorrow and ask if I had any dates.

Rest in Peace
BRUISER BRODY
Frank Goodish
June 18, 1946—July 17, 1988

Photograph Credit

Every effort has been made to trace the ownership or source of all photographs for the purpose of giving proper credit. We regret any inadvertent error concerning the atrribution of any photographs and will be pleased to make the proper acknowledgments in any future printing.

Howard Brody: 154-155

Eddie Gries: 123, 124, 125, 126, 127, 160, 166, 167, 168, 186, 187, 190, 193, 215

Michael Hawkins: 79

Pete Lederberg home.bellsouth.net/p/PWP-flwrestlingpix: 6, 5, 22, 50, 53, 55, 67, 68, 69, 70, 71, 122, 135, 213

Mike Lano wrealano@aol.com: 85, 143, 178-179

Dominick Marcello: 81

Bob Murphy/Wrestling Warehouse prowrestlingwarehouse@yahoo.com www.prowrestlingwarehouse.com: 157, 161, 163, 212

George Napolitano: 1, 4, 5, 6, 7, 8, 65, 74, 75, 76, 78, 80, 86, 90, 98, 113, 116, 139, 164, 165, 169, 174, 176

ht: Frank Goodish, 1976.

Thomas Nores: 136, 210, 211

Mike Rodgers: 162, 215

Scott Romer
www.scottromerphoto.com:
17, 19, 91, 92, 93, 95, 96, 102, 103, 104, 105, 106, 107, 108, 114, 117, 118, 119, 128, 130-131, 146, 172-173, 198, 203, 205, 208, 217, 218

Tim Roper: 73, 209, 210, 211

Luis Santiago: 207

Al Vavasseur
(Courtesy of Chris Swisher)
www.csclassicwrphotos.com:
14, 55, 58, 59, 60, 61, 84, 175, 177

Courtesy of:

Fred Ekmark: 45, 46, 47
Gary Hart: 112
Michael Hawkins: 77, 83
Karin Heymer: 29, 31, 32, 37
Nate Kruk: 2, 24, 25, 26, 27, 28, 216
Donald Nagy: 24
George Napolitano: 182-183
Marie Neece: 34, 38, 64, 214
Dan Nixon: 42
J.R. Obrecht: 111
Scott Romer: 204
Marge Splatt: 24
Scott Teal: 36, 52, 54, 62, 110, 140, 151

Far left: Frank Goodish, 1968.
Above: Bruiser Brody and Grizzly Boone, 1988.
Left: Bruiser Brody and Road Warrior Hawk, 1986.
Next page: Frank Goodish and the Hi-Y Club, 1963.
Last two pages: Bruiser Brody before, during, and after a match.

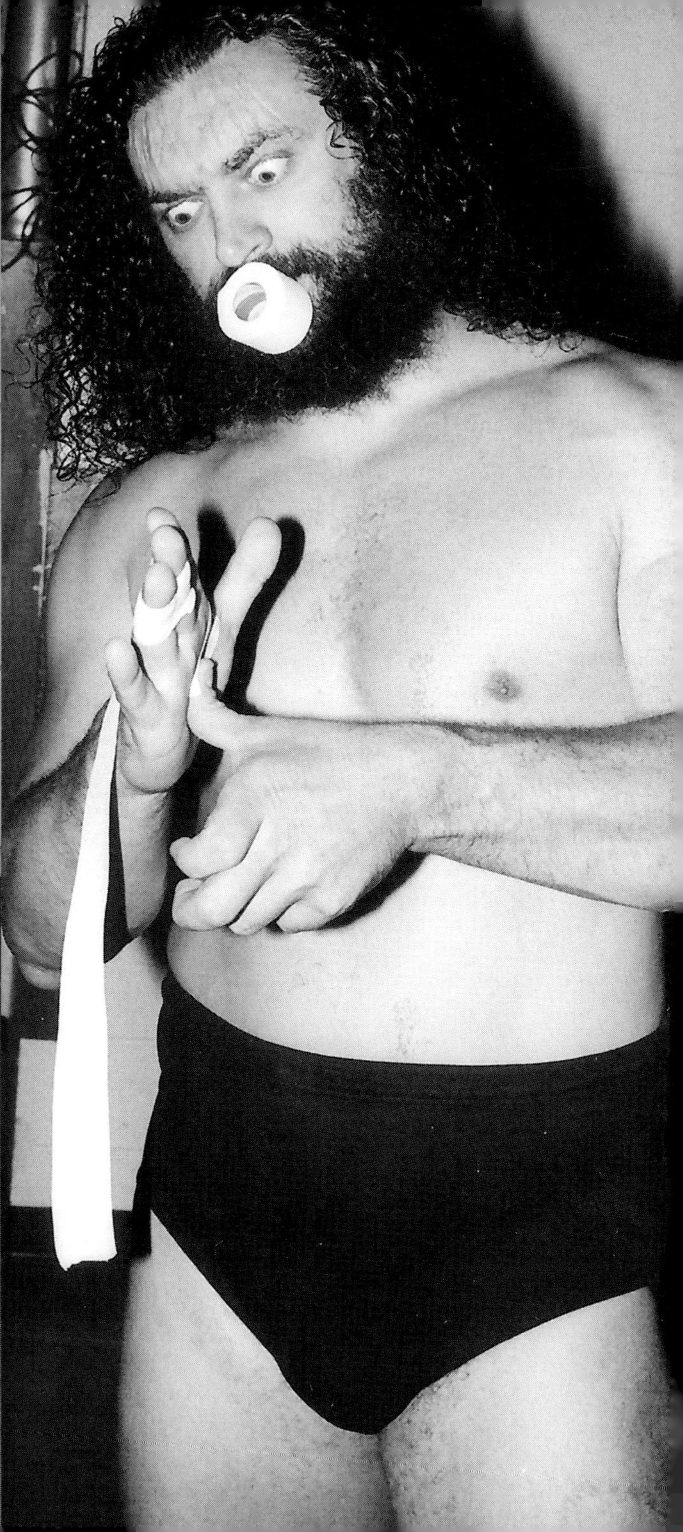

Index

CROWBAR PRESS

P.O. Box 2781 • Hendersonville TN 37077-2781 • (615) 824-3347
www.crowbarpress.com

Wrestlers Are Like Seagulls: From McMcMahon to McMahon

by James J. Dillon
with Scott Teal and Philip Varriale

ISBN: 0-9745545-2-9
6 x 9 Hardcover
360 pages, 208 B&W photographs

For over 40 years, James J. Dillon has been involved in the world of professional wrestling. Now he speaks candidly on all aspects of both his career and his personal life. J.J. offers a first-hand account and detailed history of one of the most influential wrestling promotions in wrestling history — the World Wrestling Federation. He also gives a insider's perspective on the ludicrous business decisions made by executives who took World Championship Wrestling down a path that led to the company's destruction and eventual demise. From the highs of making big money, winning championship titles, rubbing elbows with top celebrities, and appearing on television every week — to the lows of filing for bankruptcy, extramarital affairs, divorces, and drug use — J.J. leaves no stone unturned.

Inside Out: How Corporate America Destroyed Professional Wrestling

by Ole Anderson
with Scott Teal

ISBN: 0-9745545-0-2
6 x 9 Perfect Bound
384 pages, 130 B&W photographs

"If I had realized that you people would be so damned stupid as to give the world champion $750,000, I would have made myself the champion."
— Ole Anderson, to the executives at WCW and WTBS

The people who know him know that Ole is never hesitant to speak his mind — and this book is no exception. This is a straightforward look at the many phases of Ole's career in the wild, if somewhat seedy, world of professional wrestling. As a former wrestler, booker, promoter, owner, and executive producer, Ole goes deeper into the inner workings of professional wrestling than anyone ever has, tellings stories about the financial, legal, and drug problems that plagued the wrestling business. A "no-holds barred" book that you won't be able to put down.

Order by mail or directly from www.crowbarpress.com

Assassin: The Man Behind the Mask

by Joe Hamilton

with Scott Teal

ISBN: 0-9745545-3-7
6 x 9 Hardcover
304 pages, 278 B&W photographs

This autobiography takes the reader behind the scenes for a personal glimpse behind the mask of one of pro wrestling's hottest attractions: The Assassin!
When Joe Hamilton was just 19 years old, he and his brother, Larry, headlined a show at Madison Square Garden, drawing a record 20,335 people to see them wrestle Antonino Rocca and Miguel Perez. To this day, Joe remains the youngest wrestler to ever headline a main event in the Garden.
In 1961, Joe hooked up with veteran wrestler Tom Renesto to form a team called the Assassins, and for the next eleven years, they were considered to be one of wrestling's hottest attractions, drawing sellout crowds to arenas in California, Georgia, Florida, Oklahoma, North Carolina, South Carolina, Virginia, and Washington, in addition to foreign countries like Japan and Australia.

Joe takes readers on a journey as he tells about life both in and out of the wrestling ring—being attacked, stabbed, and shot at by angry wrestling fans; wrestling under a mask and trying to keep his identity a secret; legitimate fights and confrontations behind the scenes in the dressing rooms; a war between two wrestling promotions in Atlanta, Georgia; and never-before-told stories about legends like Ric Flair, Andre the Giant, Giant Baba, Toyonobori, Pedro Morales, Bill Goldberg, Ray Gunkel, and their biggest rivals, the Kentuckians.

"Is That Wrestling Fake?" The Bear Facts

by Ivan Koloff

with Scott Teal

ISBN: 978-0-9745545-4-9
6 x 9 Hardcover
208 pages, 205 B&W photographs

For decades, professional wrestling fans have asked the question — "Is that wrestling fake?" However, they wouldn't have dared ask that question directly to Ivan Koloff, whose work in the ring made believers out of the most cynical viewers.
Growing up on a farm in Ontario, Ivan learned the meaning of hard work and discipline. Unfortunately, he made wrong choices and wound up in prison for cattle rustling. Upon his release, he enrolled in a wrestling school and began a career in pro wrestling as Red McNulty, the Irish Rogue.
Five years later, on January 18, 1971, he appeared in Madison Square Garden under the name Ivan Koloff and did what had never been done before. He pinned Bruno Sammartino's shoulders to the mat and won the WWWF heavyweight title. When the referee called for the bell, you could have heard a pin drop as the more than 21,000 screaming fans were instantly moved to a stunned, disbelieving silence.
That accomplishment made Ivan Koloff one of wrestling's biggest superstars until his retirement from the ring in the mid-1990s. Competing in virtually every major promotion throughout the world, he feuded with every top name in the wrestling business, including Andre the Giant, Ric Flair, Dick the Bruiser, Bob Backlund, Billy Robinson, Dusty Rhodes, and Ivan Putski.
Here for the first time, Ivan tells the story of his life: the highs and the lows; his admission of alcohol and drug abuse; reflections of a life spent on the road, and the toll it took on his body and soul; the event in Kannapolis, North Carolina, that changed his life forever. This is a revealing memoir that will take you into the mind of the Russian Bear, both in and out of the ring.

Shooting with the Legends: Professional Wrestling Legends
Volume #1
by Scott Teal

ISBN: 0-9745545-1-0
6 x 9 Perfect Bound
384 pages, 130 B&W photographs

"Shooting with the Legends" takes over where "Whatever Happened to ...?" left off. Discover the drama of the fascinating world of professional wrestling — the inside stories, ribs, tales of the road — all written by those who were inside the wrestling business. For those whose recollections of professional wrestling are fading, happy memories, these books will rekindle past affections. Columnists include Frankie "The Great Mephisto" Cain, Killer Karl Kox, Ossie Timmins, Dean Silverstone, Bobby & Jerry Christy, Bob Roop, Ole Anderson, Tinker Todd, Dick Steinborn, Vic Orlandino and Harry White.

Volume #1 includes interviews with Tony Atlas, Bob "Superstar" Cook, and Danny O'Sullivan, plus part one of a special feature on George Bollas, the Zebra Kid.

Classic Clips

The "Classic Clips" series of books feature reproductions of hundreds of rare newspaper clippings. Most of them are not available anywhere else and have been found through persistent research on microfilm readers in public libraries. These feature article and promotional material reprints provide the reader with a rare glimpse of professional wrestling as it once was.

The following promotions have been featured in past issues:
New York (Madison Square Garden), Florida (Tampa, Jacksonville), North Carolina (Charlotte, Greensboro, Lexington), Alabama (Mobile), Ontario (London, Toronto), Tennessee (Nashville), plus a 1950s scrapbook.

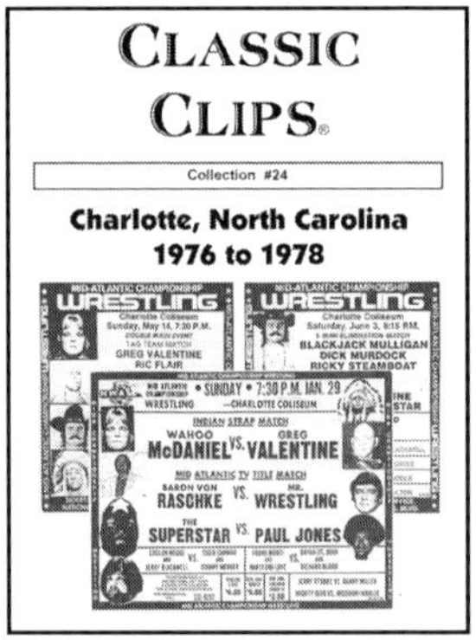

Many Faces of Paul Christy
by Paul Christerson

ISBN: 1-4184917-7-2
6 x 9 Perfect Bound
380 pages, B&W photographs

This book, written by wrestling legend Paul Christy, contains stories about cons, scams, and sex—all centered around Paul's career as a pro wrestler. Paul goes into detail about the people he hustled and explains how he did it, so that others won't fall for the cons. He has the ability to laugh at himself and will have you laughing right along with him as he tells about his most embarrassing situations. Hollywood has a reputation for being a wild and exciting place. According to Christy, when it comes to sex, Hollywood is tame compared to the wrestling business. Christy goes behind closed doors and exposes the life style of a professional wrestler. Warning: Contains graphic sexual themes and situations. This book is not a Crowbar Press publication, but it is available through our website.